Understanding Confusion in Africa:
The Politics of Multiculturalism and Nation-Building in Cameroon

Peter Ateh-Afac Fossungu

Langaa Research & Publishing CIG
Mankon, Bamenda

Publisher:
Langaa RPCIG
Langaa Research & Publishing Common Initiative Group
P.O. Box 902 Mankon
Bamenda
North West Region
Cameroon
Langaagrp@gmail.com
www.langaa-rpcig.net

Distributed in and outside N. America by African Books Collective
orders@africanbookscollective.com
www.africanbookcollective.com

ISBN: 9956-728-53-5

© Peter Ateh-Afac Fossungu 2013

DISCLAIMER
All views expressed in this publication are those of the author and do not necessarily reflect the views of Langaa RPCIG.

Table of Contents

Introduction..vii
  Cameroon and Africa.. vii
  Book's Driving Forces and Importance........................... viii
  Central Arguments...xi

Chapter 1: Advanced Multiculturalism and the February Story: The Politics of National (Dis) Unity in the Hinge of Africa.. 1
  Issues Experts Want Addressed..................................... 1
  Advanced Multiculturalism and the Palm Wine School.......... 8
  Defining Culture..13
  Is Culture without History Culture?............................. 16
  The February Story: Disuniting by Uniting?..................... 19
  The Intimacy of the 1972 and 1984 Name-Changes............. 22
  Disuniting by Uniting One History/Culture?.................... 28
  The 1984 Name or History Case...................................33
  The 1985/83 Education Case...................................... 42

Chapter 2: The Perfect Nation Is an Anathema to Multiculturalism... 57
  (The Usual) Democracy and Collective Participation............ 58
  Kontchoumeterized Participation and the Case of the Educational Systems... 61
  Minority Politics and Self-Determination in a Unitary Centralized State?... 62
  Minority Exchange...68
  The Territory and Population of the Minority................... 74
  The Educational Systems are Different but Not Different and at War?.. 84
  The Constitution and the Education Domain..................... 86
  The Philosophy of the Education Law............................89

Chapter 3: The One-Party System (Or 'Pluralistic Democracy') Is an Abomination to Multiculturalism.......................... **105**
  Monosity: A Prerequisite for 'Pluralistic Democracy'?............... 105
  Sexing Patriotism and Equality: The Illustrative Case of 1997 Legislative and Presidential Elections............................. 109
  The 1990 Multipartism Law and the Irreplaceable One-Party System.. 115
  On the Justification of the Single-Party State..................... 117
  Deconstructing the Multipartism Law..............................124

Chapter 4: Colonialism and the Leadership Mess in Africa: When History is Not Historical – From Cameroon to Njangawatar?... **135**
  On the Importance of History to Development....................136
  Theories Drawn from the Name-Changing Justifications......... 143
  From Cameroon to Njangawatar?.. 144
  "Intellectuals in Politics": Questioning the Discoverer Theory?... 146
  From Pidgin to Njangawatok?.. 155
  From Victoria to Limbe: Biculturalism in Cameroon?................. 160
  From Bilingualism/Bijuralism to Ngoa-lingualism/Unijuralism... 162
  Purpose and Objectives of Education plus *Epsi* As Preventing Biculturalism.. 168

Chapter 5: Leadership Non-Charisma and Non-Challenge of Historic Trivia: The Uniting of One History Is Why Cameroon Is not Championing in the Development Business in Africa   **187**
  Understanding the Political Economy of Cameroon   188
  Original Quality of Cameroon's Environment   192
  The Natural Qualities of the Cameroon People   194
  Health and Intelligence in Development in Cameroon   197
  Confusioncracy Passing for Balanced Development   199
  The Anglophone Factor and Absence of Known Rules   201

Turning the English-Speaking into the French..................... 203
Operating Without Local Governments and an Independent Umpire... 211
Stifling Industrialization... 217
Developing with Confusing and Incomplete Rules and Laws.... 220
The Role of Agriculture and Poverty............................ 224
Closing Observation.. 228

Conclusion... **233**

References... **239**

Introduction

Cameroon and Africa

Variously known as 'Africa in Miniature', 'Africa's Promised Land', 'Paradise in Africa', 'the hinge of Africa', 'the microcosm of Africa', etc., Johnson (1970: vii) thinks that a study of Cameroon, though an examination of a single case provides us with issues that are relevant to all of Africa, indeed, to most of the new states of the world. This is even the more so as Africa hinges on Cameroon in an assortment of ways that the country is "sometimes referred to as the hinge of Africa."[1] It is then the strong belief of several nation-building experts that Cameroon currently ought to be far ahead in terms of (1) development in all its ramifications and (2) materially and spiritually helping other Africans to advance. For example, Mbuy (1996) has interpreted the September 1995 papal visit to Yaounde to launch **Ecclesia In Africa** as "entrusting the spiritual leadership of the continent into the hands of Cameroon" because "[t]his is the first time in Church History that a document of such magnitude is signed outside the Vatican. Yet it happened in Yaounde, Cameroon." In addition, the numerous gestures of "continental leadership that Cameroon is receiving in a space of less than one year", according to Reverend Mbuy, only confirm "the future of Africa under our leadership." What is also more striking, the cleric concludes, is the fact that even the politicians of Africa did the same by conferring the defunct Organization of African Unity (OAU) Chairmanship in 1996 upon Cameroon's President Paul Biya.

Since 1996, Cameroonians, "convinced that the salvation of Africa lies in forging ever-growing bonds of solidarity among African People, affirm our desire to contribute to the advent of a united and

---

[1] CIA, *The World Factbook*, available at http://www.compufix.demon.co.uk/camweb (page 2) (last visited in August 2011).

free Africa."[2] On the formation of the Federal Republic of Cameroon (hereinafter FRC[3]) in Foumban in 1961, Benjamin (1972: 126) also cites the claim from former President Amadou Ahidjo in *L'Unité* N° 64 (6 octobre 1961) that the new Cameroon state was to be a real laboratory for an African Union, bringing together all the English-speaking and French-speaking countries of the continent and that in this noble task the imperative leadership role of Cameroon did not need to be overemphasized. The graphical question has then been: Is the Cameroon leadership up to the continental leadership task? In other words, how can Cameroon possibly unite and lead Africa when it cannot even correctly engage in nation-building itself?

Book's Driving Forces and Importance

Questions prompting this study are as numerous as the several subtle ways of 'intellectually' perpetrating the Foumban 'Historyless' Darkness in Cameroon – a strategy that can hardly help those who are now trying to understand what had actually happened to put them in the situation in which they find themselves today. They have to be told the truth for a number of sane reasons. First, I think the lay persons deserve to know from the intellectuals why their country is not working as others they find around them; and that intellectuals that cannot tell them the truth do not deserve to be intellectuals to begin with because I am made to know that the role of the intellectual (whatever the sex of this Janus[4]) is to shed light (and not

---

[2] *Loi N° 96-06 du 18 janvier 1996 portant révision de la Constitution du 02 juin 1972* (hereinafter 1996 Constitution), Preamble (2nd paragraph).

[3] See *Loi N° 61-24 du 1er septembre 1961 portant révision constitutionnelle et tendant à adapter la constitution actuelle aux nécessités du Cameroun réunifié* (hereinafter Federal Constitution).

[4] "I will consider to be an intellectual," Lantum (1991: 20) has very chauvinistically and in a conjuring manner told the questioning youths, "someone with a developed inquisitive and critical mind who applies his [a female can never be an intellectual then?] mind or intellect as rationally and objectively as possible, with full sense of responsibility to illuminate his milieu with the improvement of

to engender darkness) on the issues, controversial as they may be. This is not what generally holds in Cameroon, and the point might have been reached when/where this pitiful trend has to be contained, if not completely excluded.

Second and intimately tied to the foregoing, it is by properly comprehending what indeed went wrong (authentic history) that the youths can be properly educated to avoid repeating or committing the same errors, especially in the new political society that Cameroonians in particular and Africans generally are now clamouring for. It is in this vein that the present study has undertaken the task of throwing some light on the darkness created in this continent (that is often, wrongly or correctly, referred to as The Dark Continent) by the "intellectuals in politics". A critical and provocative review of the existing politics of history and of education is thus imperative in understanding Africa's multicultural nation-building or development – a conception about which there is much confusion engendered by the "intellectuals in politics", this vague phrase being also shown in this contribution as meant to further confuse the issues.

Third, Cameroon is unique on the African continent for countless reasons. One interesting area of this uniqueness concerns the remarkable historical influences that it has been subjected to, thus making the country a likely and captivating focus for studying federalism, multiculturalism and many other multi-isms. In other words, these characteristics should naturally make Cameroon the place *par excellence* where the federal structure would not only be dutifully instituted but, above all, also very religiously defended. But is that really it? This critical and provocative focus on the country's politics of history and of education as they impact on national unity would greatly aid in the search for answers. At this juncture, it can be safely stated that the politics of multiculturalism (seen through history and education) in Cameroon is simply that of assimilation and

---

the common good of humanity as his or her [where is *she* now from?] goal." More of such sexist exclusions would be found in Chapter 3.

not that of national integration or development; and this is seen in the (incomprehensible) denial of the history and educational system of the English-speaking people of Cameroon. It is then hard to see why this country (except for confusion) should be singing multiculturalism when the culture of some of its peoples is being excluded or effaced.

A book such as this is therefore important as it aids researchers in issues of multiculturalism (such as bilingualism, and bijuralism) to avoid both frustration and the wasting of considerable amounts of energy and scarce resources. For instance, Americans, tired of their Melting-Pot Experience (especially provoked by the massive influx from the southern part of their heavily patrolled border) and earnestly intending to comprehend how bijuralism (or trijuralism) and bilingualism do operate in polities claiming them, would simply have to drive across their northern (until *Ahmed Ressam*[5]) almost unguarded border: rather than fly for six or more hours over the wide Atlantic Ocean to what Anyangwe (1987: xiii) calls a "law and language laboratory" and/or what Bringer (1981: 1) labels "a unique recipe of comparative law" in the Hinge of Africa.

It has even been discovered that some Englishmen like Moorhouse (1977: 341), perhaps knowing exactly what they hurriedly left behind, had sternly warned against the Atlantic crossing to get to this fatally Advancing Ocean of confusing use of terminologies whose breadth "is much wider, say some who have made the crossing, than you ever can expect beforehand." Moorhouse captured

---

[5] "Ressam, an Algerian national who was denied refugee status in Canada on suspicion that he belonged to the Armed Islamic Group, was caught on Tuesday night in Washington State with 54 kilograms of explosive, when he arrived on a ferry from Victoria, B.C. The explosive, nitroglycerine, was enough to do considerable damage to a building and its occupants, officials said." Nicholas van Praet, "United States on Terrorist Alert: Bomb Squad Combs Van, Store – Intelligence Team Turns Up Links in Montreal with Man Arrested on Explosive Charge" *Montreal Gazette* (December 20, 1999), A3. See also M.J. Martinez, "Border Scare: Terror Suspect Denies Charges" *Montreal Gazette* (23 December 1999), A1 & A10; and Nicholas van Praet, "Search on Second Suspect: MUC Police Seeking Man Linked to U.S. Border Arrest" *Montreal Gazette* (19 December 1999), A1 & A2.

it so well but it seems the warning has hardly been heeded. Hopefully, this book could do the subject some justice and thus effectively bring about a change in direction: a change that is possible only if those concerned do properly understand Cameroon and its brand of federalism, of advanced democracy, of bicameralism, of self-determination; or its generalized confusion being called (advanced) multiculturalism.

The Central Arguments

While attempting responses to some of the numerous nation-building questions raised, the book argues essentially that competently furnishing the much needed African unity and leadership will all largely depend on the type of governance modality that Cameroon employs in specifically managing its own heterogeneous population generally, but more especially its two colonially-imposed cultural groups – English- and French-speaking. That success in this domain is exactly what successfully leading an erstwhile "multi-European" colonized Africa would principally entail. That uniformization or assimilation of any sort cannot be among the leader's governing strategies. Cameroon's success and/or failure continental-wise will thus depend on its handling of its national official bilingualism, biculturalism, etc. all of which must in turn (if success is the desired goal) be principally reflected in (1) the harmonious co-existence of its Systems of Education which must, of necessity, be linked to (2) effective federalization or decentralization of matters uniquely associated to those Systems. That all this cannot be workable until local government (the proper channel for the people telling their own story themselves) and the voter's decision would cease to be merely empty or non-existent rights.

Examining history as a component of culture, and therefore, of multiculturalism, the book demonstrates how nation-building is meaningless without the people's authentic history; arguing strenuously that Cameroon national culture cannot be a national culture without embodying the distinct culture of the English-speaking minority, the cautious inclusion of which necessitates effective federalism or decentralization; and that anything else is nothing but deliberate confusion of assimilation for multiculturalism, a confusion that is heavily tied to the country's camouflaged independence. It goes on to argue, in regard of education, that Cameroon's over-sung cultural or educational dualism is a charade; a sham that is now epitomized by the 1998 Education Law (*Law N° 98/004 of 14 April 1998 to Lay Down Guidelines for Education in Cameroon* – hereinafter Education Law) which, rather than reaffirm Cameroon's biculturalism as it avows, is really out to efface any semblance of cultural or educational dualism that may still be resisting assimilation. And that the continuous and persistent employment of terms such as cultural dualism, bilingualism, etc. in legal texts in Cameroon is only to confuse the international community especially from seeing exactly the kind of 'ethnic cleansing' which is taking place in the country.

Chapter 1

Advanced Multiculturalism and The February Story: The Politics Of National (Dis) Unity In The Hinge Of Africa

> I must admit that my own sympathies lie with Cameroonians who have courageously pursued the quest for freedom and identity in the face of pressures for conformity to some official version of the truth, whether proclaimed by colonial administrations or by the Cameroonian governments that succeeded them. If I condemn the repressive measures that have been imposed on the Cameroonian people, I do so in the belief that freedom of expression is a fundamental human right. [This book, like] *The African Quest for Freedom and Identity* is the history of one people's attempt to exercise that right [Bjornson, 1991: ix].

Issues Experts Want Addressed

Were anyone capable of exactly visualizing the African continent as a single unitary centralized State, they would have very accurately envisioned the Federal Republic of Cameroon (hereinafter FRC) or the Republic of Cameroon and thus also spelt an end to this modest book. The book must proceed however not only because the imagined continental African State is basically impossible but also because Cameroon essentially knows no impossibility in its dictionary of governance. I am here referring to just one of the famous doctrines (*impossibilité n'est pas Camerounaise*) that are persistently churned out of the presidency of Cameroon – the Unity Palace or Etoudi Palace. Some other popular ones are *Un seul mot: Continuer*, and that the truth comes only from the authorities, with anything else (such as this book) being mere rumour: *La vérité vient d'en haut et la rumeur vient d'en bas*. It is with an adequate grasp of this *là-haut* philosophy that readers can be able to comprehend, for instance, what is actually responsible for Cameroon being Cameroon (*Le Cameroun c'est le Cameroun*) and for the impossible not being impossible in Cameroon.

As the arguments of the President of the Republic (hereinafter shortened to POR) always go, since *impossibilité n'est pas Camerounaise, un seul mot: Continuer*! (As the impossible is never impossible in Cameroon, I can only say: Go on!) I will therefore just leave out all the obvious human rights questions that should normally be posed in their regard (such as just go on doing what or to where?) and simply continue, as commanded by Biya (1986: 10), to properly help "the poorly-informed foreign visitors [or readers] who quickly extend what [theory] they [read or] see on first encounter to the rest of the [other] countr[ies]." I would need to just obey the POR's command without questioning because, in addition, Wheeler also feels that it is time for someone to ably aid strangers (to Cameroon's advanced democracy) "to peer behind the curtain and see ... [Cameroon] as it really is... a far cry from what ... [its administrators] would have us believe."[1] One of such 'far-cry' theories is biculturalism that is being claimed in Cameroon. As biculturalism is multiculturalism, the task would be to find out what the real meaning of multiculturalism and its associates or components like federalism, history, education (and bilingualism) would indeed mean in this country and mini-continent.

The aim of this book is to aid in the construction of a new society in the Hinge of Africa that ensures respect for fundamental human rights and certain basic shared values that were dolefully mistreated by the Foumban arrangement and Federal Constitution – a constitution about whose 'name-changing' off-springs and successors there is much confusion. In clearing the discussion table

---

[1] Michael Wheeler, "Political Polling: The German Shepherd Factor" in Charles Peters and Nicholas Lemann (eds.), *Inside the System* 4th ed. (New York: Holt, Rinehart and Winston, 1979), 276 at 276-77.

of much of the confusion, I would be squarely confronting Cameroonians generally (and the leadership particularly) with a few graphical and elementary questions. For example, would the current nation-building malaise be resolved through putting all the facts (bitter and embarrassing as some of them are or may be) on the table for open, frank and seasoned discussion; or will it be through the ongoing farce of emasculation and refusal to recognize that serious national unity problems do exist? Shouldn't the guiding philosophy in every action in Cameroon be a very genuine *Quel Cameroun pour nos enfants* (What kind of Cameroon is to be passed on to our children)? The answer to these questions would have to be reflected in, or influenced by, certain other questions which are as many as they can go on and on. But they would all then (if Cameroonians are genuine to themselves as they should) boil down (according to Biya, 1986: 82), "in the final analysis, [to which] is the Cameroon we want to bequeath to our children?"

The importance of authentic history to a genuine response here can then not be minimized. Having dug a little bit into the history of Africa, it is my belief that Africans have to start standing upright and taking their own destinies into their own hands rather than waiting for others who might not even properly understand their situation and/or cultures to do things for them. Name-changing is not, by itself, a regressive exercise especially if it is done with progress in view and in a collective manner and to reflect national realities. This is clearly not the case with one-man Olympian decrees in this country; regarding one of which (presidential decree of 12 November 2008) has mandated that the ten long-time provinces of Cameroon should now be read as regions (even as that changes absolutely nothing in their status). Yet, the 1996 Constitution had indicated twelve years before this decree, in its article 61(1) that "The following provinces shall become Regions: Adamaoua; - Centre; - East; - Far North; - Littoral; - North; - North-West; - West; - South; - South-West." Are you wondering what then the value of the 2008 presidential decree is? I will tell you what and why right away (before you get to later read Part II.B.1 of Chapter 2). It is just a confusing way of saying that the constitution (which is still the POR's decree sort of, but requiring the rubberstamping of Ndi Chia's (1995) "rented jesters and political contractors" who approve in a place in Yaounde called the National Assembly) stands in an inferior position to the president's decree that does not need the whitewash of the National Assembly and the yet-to-be-created Senate.

I think it is also high time Africans stop referring to parts of their country through (colonial) "directional bearings" (like North-West, Far or Extreme North, South, East, etc.) when there are lots of indigenous natural features and endowments with which to meaningfully do so. For a start, I am therefore suggesting in Table 1 more meaningful names for the ten existing regions and a distinct federal capital.

Table 1: Proposed Cameroon State & Federal Capital Names

Proposed Name	Abbreviation	Capital	Former/Current Name
Adamawazone	ADZ	Ngaoundéré	Adamawa Region
Bamboutouszone	BBZ	Bafoussam	West Region
Benouezone	BNZ	Garoua	North Region
Debundschazone	DBZ	Buea	South West Region
Guinean-Savannazone	GSZ	Bertoua	East Region
Logonezone	LGZ	Maroua	Extreme North Region
Nyongzone	NYZ	Ebolowa	South Region
Sanagazone	SNZ	Akonolinga	Centre Region
Savannazone	SVZ	Bamenda	North West Region
Wourizone	WRZ	Douala	Littoral Region
Yaoundé City Zone	YCZ	Yaoundé	Yaoundé

I will henceforth try to use these names where appropriate so that readers can get acquainted to them; always being able to get back to Table 1, if and when necessary.

It is left to Cameroonians generally and the people of said states particularly to decide to adopt these proposed names or bring forth some other more appropriate ones; and not for anyone person, not even this writer, to have it imposed as has so far been the case.

In addition to other recommendations, I think what is needed in Cameroon as a federation would be a combination of what Etinge (1991) and the G.H. Adji of the Alliance for Democracy and Development – ADD (see Azeng, 1997) have proposed, namely, a ten-state bicultural federation with effectively elected officials (as fully discussed in Chapter 5 below). This means maintaining as states the former ten provinces/regions whose new momentous names I have suggested. This is an area where other multicultural federations, especially Canada, have to also come in to complement vital lessons from Germany's experiences after the Nazis – the institution and defending of constitutional democracy. The Canadian, Belgian, and Swiss experiences are always there for all to see and learn form. These are workable solutions worth emulating in Africa, if some of the Third World leaders (from the continent) are really as patriotic as we are being told they are. Patriotic and visionary leaders must surely draw positively on history in order to move the country forward.

History is, of course, graphical in genuinely answering the question concerning progeny's inheritance. The task in this book though is not to write Cameroon history but simply to provide historical outlines while analyzing and illustrating how denying a segment of the people's history is inconsistent with the pining of multiculturalism to the chest. The historical data provided here then can only be compressed, being justified, first, by space constraints and, second, by the well-known fact from Davidson that the writing of history would in any case become a hopeless venture if it involved explaining everything.[2] Furthermore, giving much of Cameroon history here is not the point and would even somewhat seem to be unnecessary because much of that history

---

[2] Basil Davidson, *Africa in History: Themes and Outlines* rev. & exp. ed. (New York: Macmillan, 1991) at 3-4.

is paradoxically even being denied. Denying a part of this country's history is thus not the proper way of responding to the issues.

The Belgians realized the folly of multiculturalism in a unitary state and made adjustments by adapting to federalism through their constitution that Shapiro (1995: 57) has characterized as "an example of the standard style of constitution which evolved during the nineteenth century" and has remained remarkably resilient, undergoing until more than 25 years ago only two uncontroversial amendments extending democratic freedoms and establishing a constitutional monarchy. In view of the Belgian experiences particularly, it would not be wrong to assert that multiculturalism is inseparable from federalism and political pluralism. Himmelfarb quotes Madison as saying "I go on this great republican principle, that the people will have virtue and intelligence to select men [and women] of virtue and wisdom [as their leaders].... To suppose that any form of government will secure liberty or happiness without any virtue in the people is a chimerical idea."[3] Anyone who supposes that such choosing can be possible in the absence of political pluralism (punctuated by a neutral arbiter) is, to say the least, crazy. The mirage of elections and multipartism in Cameroon (see Chapter 3) would thus clearly not be the case in a lively political community – a kind of community that is unthinkable in the absence of citizen awareness, which brings us again and again to authentic and purposeful education, which is also the focus of and springboard for liberalism.

Critically examining national unity or nation-building in Cameroon predicated on history and on education as they relate to multiculturalism, it is the position of this contribution that in countries with diverse historical and cultural backgrounds like Cameroon proper nation-building can be achieved mostly

---

[3] Gertrude Himmelfarb, "Democratic Remedies for Democratic Disorders" *The Public Interest* N° 131 (Spring 1998), 3-24 at 7.

through the federal devolution, a federalization that is also the best vehicle for development, multiculturalism, and independence. Although there is no single rigid standard definition or form for federalism (see Shapiro, 1996:; 4; and Stevenson, 1989: 7-9), it is believed that any discussion of the concepts tied to multiculturalism with regard to Cameroon must have to squarely address certain inevitable issues that have so far been overlooked, deliberately or otherwise. In attempting to comprehend important human rights questions tied to federalism and multiculturalism in Cameroon, there are obvious queries that some experts on the judiciary, poly-ethnicity, and bi-nationalism and bilingualism, would like to see addressed. The experts[4] would like to know what the effect is on national integration or fragmentation and on human rights generally, of such variables as the size of Cameroon and the territorial distribution of its constituent cultural groups. What is the feasibility of secession by one of the groups? What are the possible effects of the other societal cleavages with the bi-cultural, bijural and bilingual ones? What is the significance of the *perception* the various groups have regarding politics and governance generally?

They also want to know, for instance, what the specific arrangements are, if any, that have been made in Cameroon for adaptation to the realities, and demands, of biculturalism, bijuralism, and bilingualism in such areas as: government and politics; the national governmental bureaucracy and the public service; the judiciary; the armed forces; the educational system;

---

[4] See Yosef Israel Goell, *Bi-Nationalism and Bi-Lingualism in Three Modernized States: A Comparative Study of Canada, Belgium, and White South Africa* (Ph.D. Diss., Columbia University: University Microfilms International, Ann Arbor, Michigan, 1978) at 2-3; Frank N. Trager, "Introduction: On Federalism" in Thomas M. Franck (ed.), *Why Federations Fail: An Inquiry into the Requisites for Successful Federalism*, New York: New York University Press (1968), ix at ix-xv; Jerold L. Waltman, "Introduction" in Jerold L. Waltman and Kenneth M. Holland, eds., *The Political Role of Law Courts in Modern Democracies* (New York: St. Martin's Press, 1989), 6-30 at 4; and N. Tiruchelvam, "Introduction" in N. Tiruchelvam and R. Coomaraswamy, eds, *The Judiciary in Plural Societies* (New York: St. Martin's Press, 1987), vii at ix-xi

and the mass media. To what extent is the (apparent) continuance of legal pluralism in Cameroon conceived as a means of maintaining ethnic and cultural diversity? How has the country's judiciary been fashioned to respond to the demands and problems of ethnic/cultural pluralism? Some answers will be attempted in this book generally and in this Chapter as I discuss (1) advanced multiculturalism as seen by the Palm Wine School of Deconstruction, and (2) the February Story's capabilities of disuniting by uniting.

Advanced Multiculturalism and the Palm Wine School of Deconstruction

Multiculturalism, the experts will agree with my adaptation from Sally Engel Merry's much-cited definition of legal pluralism provided by Tamanaha (1993: 193), is a term that generally describes a situation where many cultures effectively coexist and operate in the same social field.[5] The specialists will also concur that multiculturalism and equality are two sides of the same coin; and that both are important aspects of human rights. Multiculturalism entails equality of the tendencies (such as the histories, languages, educational systems) of the cultures concerned. Were it otherwise, it is argued, some other appellation (such as assimilation) should be employed, not multiculturalism as is generally understood. To still go ahead and employ (advanced) multiculturalism as is the case in Cameroon is only to confuse; just as the country's confusing names.

According to political and constitutional historians like Le Vine (1971:1), Cameroon is unique among African countries in the remarkable variety of its historical experiences. Once a major portion of the West African slave trade coast, it became a

---

[5] *"Une définition du pluralisme juridique,"* according to Vanderlinden (1993 : 573), *"[c'est] l'existence, au sein d'une société determine, de mécanismes juridiques different s'appliquant à des situations identiques."*

German protectorate known as Kamerun; then divided, it was transformed into two League of Nations mandates under Britain and France. Thereafter by further colonial metamorphoses, it became two United Nations trust territories known as British Cameroons and French Cameroun. Finally, with the passing of the trusteeships, there was brief independence for one part (French Cameroun), and then unification of both in an independent federal republic. Because of its varied historical influences, Cameroon has also incidentally been blessed with what some critics now refer to as a name-confusion (Cameroon, Cameroun, the Cameroons, Kamerun). Comprehension of the arguments of this book will be enhanced by a brief survey of this inflation of or confusion in name.

A number of different spellings of "Cameroon" must be inevitable in most writings on this unique African country; especially since Le Vine (1971: xxii) says one is bound "to identify the components of the present [entities that constituted the defunct] federation at various stages of their political evolution. The [numerous and diverse] spellings are those employed during those periods." It is important to also register right away that some of these names persist notwithstanding the change in colonial powers over the country. For example, Kamerun refers to the German protectorate (1884-1916) but this appellation was still used by nationalists even after it was no longer under the 'protection' of the defeated Germans. Cameroun, the French spelling, was used in what used to be East Cameroon in the 1961 federation. That is, eight of the current ten proposed states, with the exception of the two 'Anglophone' states of Debundschazone and Savannazone. Cameroon or the Cameroons, the anglicized version, was used to refer to the Cameroons under United Kingdom mandate and later trusteeship. This appellation ("the Cameroons") is still used today – especially by the English-speaking inhabitants of what used to be West Cameroon in the federation – to refer to the entire country (see Le Vine, 1971: xxii-xxiii; and Anyangwe, 1987: chapter 2). Southern Cameroons was employed to describe the southern administrative half of the former Cameroons under British trusteeship, the section that became West Cameroon in the federation (1961-1972)

Southern Cameroonsian is employed in this book in connection with the people (and other things) of Southern Cameroons because this is the correct way of doing so rather than referring to them as Southern Cameroonians, as has too often been done in most writings and documents on the federalism and/or self-determination palaver in Cameroon. For example, in the *Champion Interview* [answering Question 2 which also uses the same appellation], Stephen Joseph stated (emphasis added): "The affinity of the rest of *Southern Cameroonians* to the people of Bakassi comes from the closeness that has developed over the years among all the ethnic communities of the Bakassi Peninsula….."[6] Southern Cameroons Frequently Asked Questions (hereinafter SCFAQ[7]) is also 'guilty' of this 'offence'; a 'crime' because, quite apart from the discussion of this nomenclature that follows later (in Part III.B.1), the explanation for the preferred employment is axiomatically simple. The underlying and subtle idea behind the 'Southern Cameroonians' (as well as the 'Anglophones') descriptions is to confusingly deny them the 'people' requirement that is capitally necessary for entitlement to the right to self-determination under international law.[8]

---

[6] *Champion* newspaper (Nigeria): interview with Stephen Joseph, Moderator of the IG's Southern Cameroons Peoples Forum. The interview was published in February of 2005 [hereinafter *Champion Interview*] found @ www.southerncameroonsig.org/2005/07/the_champion_ne.html (last visited 1 March 2011).

[7] See "Southern Cameroons Frequently Asked Questions", available @ http://www.southerncameroons.org/index3.htm (last visited in March 2011).

[8] For elaboration on the problematic nature of "peoples" in this theory, see, for example, El Obaid (1996: chapter 5); H.M. Kindred *et al*, *International Law chiefly as Interpreted and Applied in Canada* (Toronto: Emond Montgomery Publications Ltd., 1987) at 68-69; and B. Neuberger, *National Self-Determination in Postcolonial Africa* (Boulder, Colorado: Lynne Rienner Publishers, Inc., 1986) at 2.

The role of deliberately sown confusion is well known, especially to the Palm Wine School graduates. Comprehension of confusion is thus greatly assisted by the teachings of the Palm Wine School of Deconstruction. According to this school, the word 'confusion' can actually correctly replace 'advanced multiculturalism' because confusion is indeed what Cameroon's advanced multiculturalism is. On the face of it, advanced multiculturalism would look very attractive and, of course, attraction is what it is intended to command. But no one must go rushing to this alluring attractiveness until they have left the province of instinct and carried out what Mewett (1996: 386) and Okafor (2005: 182-89) have described as a rigorous analysis of relevance and purpose. Having performed that important exercise, readers must then confirm the commonplace saying that *All That Glitters Is Not Gold*. Readers at that point would be able to comprehend that advanced multiculturalism is advanced only in the sense that it is not advanced. This statement obviously seems to be confusing; but it could be only normal that confusion be confusing. Confusion has more than one connotation. Simpson and Weiner define it as (1) mixing up or mingling so that it becomes impossible or difficult to distinguish the elements; and/or (2) mixing up in the mind, failing to distinguish, erroneously regarding as identical, and mistaking one for another.[9]

It is in order to eschew unexpected expectations that a visit to the Palm Wine School of Deconstruction is essential to a correct understanding of what culture in the plural-Singular is in the Hinge of Africa. To the Palm Wine School graduates, the seemingly confusing statement above would merely signify that advanced multiculturalism is advanced only in the sense that one has not advanced before it. It is just to say that this multiculturalism is not advanced to those who can be in advance

---

[9] J.A. Simpson and E.S.C. Weiner, eds., *The Oxford Dictionary* Vol. XI, 2nd ed. (Oxford: Clarendon Press, 1989) at 720.

of it. Cameroon, it would seem, understands this *Advanced Logic* so well that it is now in advance of almost everything imaginable in the arena of good or responsible governance. Advanced Democracy is the mother terminology that readers have to be prepared to confront and similarly deconstruct like the "village Old Man" who

> could not but indicate in a playful but meaningful way over his cup of *mbu* or *moluh* that Advanced Democracy (like many other such masterful phrases in the Democracy) was very well chosen; and that it may only properly mean preparing in advance to *kill democracy before it lifts its ugly head in any form.* That is precisely then as far as Cameroonians have out-stepped North Americans [in the democracy business].[10]

Mbu and *moluh* are names from local or indigenous languages for the palm wine that has given the school its name. The 'advanced' employment of widely known terms is a very convenient device that this country uses to hide (to those outsiders who employ those terms otherwise) what Cameroon actually is; thus in a peculiar manner validating the authorities' *le Cameroun c'est le Cameroun*, etc.?

Is it perhaps this logic that makes Cameroon an interesting focus of study not so much because of what is generally known about it but for what is paradoxically not known? Why does Cameroon largely remain a mystery to the larger international community at whose central place it should normally have been since the First World War (1914-18)? "Cameroon is Cameroon" (*Le Cameroun c'est le Cameroun*) is the cloaked answer the authorities would quickly tender to the quiz; a confusing response that has also been largely deciphered by Eyoum'a Ntoh (1996) to mean that the outside world must be made to see Cameroon only

---

[10] Peter Ateh-Afac Fossungu, "Lesson in Advanced Government" *The Herald* N° 650 (21-23 August 1998d), 4 (emphasis as in original).

through its POR's eye (*"A part ça, le Cameroun est un grand pays habité par un grandissime président. C'est d'ailleurs à ce dernier que nous devons d'être autant 'respectés' et 'admirés' à l'extérieur!"*). This palm-wine scholar's thesis is particularly strengthened by, and seen in, the way the regime has been ordaining that its unique one-culture multiculturalism be known to the outside world.

To Biya (1986: 133), "In order to give a true picture of our country to the outside world, a more comprehensive mission should be assigned to the cultural advisers of our embassies, viz., to better propagate the image of our country and export Cameroonian culture." The promotion of "our" culture and country, according to the regime, can be done only through the diplomatic offices for obvious reasons. Here, presidentially appointed so-called cultural advisers (who will usually know nothing even about the culture of the specific ethnic groups they come from, let alone those of the entire country) must have done a lot of what Moorhouse (1977: 343) calls the fact-twisting or "what undiplomatic souls might crudely call brainwashing" that is their job. The brainwashing job might partly account for the fact that, apart from the country's exceptional performance at the World Cup in Italy in 1990 (soccer[11]), many people might not even be familiar with the name 'Cameroon', let alone know it for real: although this is one Third World country that should normally have been at the centre of world affairs generally and African relations in particular. Thus, as Wanaku (whose full contribution is discussed in Part III.B.1 below) has confirmed Moorhouse's thesis, "[d]o not be surprised at the number of people who will think aloud to you that, 'I thought Cameroon was French...?'. You can spill the beans from there if you have the time to listen." Can the working definition of multiculturalism

---

[11] For more on this sport that would now have become the best way to talk about Cameroon to most foreigners, see Arnold Pannenborg, *How to Win a Football Match in Cameroon: An Anthropological Study of Africa's Most Popular Sport* (Leiden: African Studies Centre, 2008).

given above then be divorced from culture in the plural without legitimately losing that term? Can one conveniently move on to the capital question of the culture(s) involved particularly for Cameroon without first defining culture? To appreciate the confusion, I will therefore be examining (1) what culture is for the purposes of (2) finding out if a one-culture state (the Perfect Nation) is compatible with multiculturalism.

Defining Culture

The (advanced) definition of culture can be better understood mostly within an appropriate grasp of the underlying principles of Cameroon's governmental system or advanced democracy which, according to Anyangwe (1987: xiii), are outlined in "his political blueprint, entitled *Communal Liberalism*, [by] Mr. Paul Biya, Cameroon's President." These principles have been summarized by Biya (1986: 123-35) as the "Thirty objectives for Cameroon"; being specifically partitioned as follows: 'national unity' which is the all-embracing cover-up known as 'The Perfect Nation' is given Objectives 1-3 since "I consider national integration, which is the ultimate step towards national unity, to be the cardinal, historic task of the highest priority which I have to carry out with all Cameroon people" (Biya, 1986: 28). Six of them (Objectives 4-9) are devoted to 'Democracy'; the 'Economy' has Objectives 10-18; Objectives 19-27 are occupied by 'social welfare and culture'; while Objectives 28-30 are the province of external relations. In all of these objectives there is culture; for example, political culture, democratic culture, historical culture, or cultural history, educational culture, etc. All these objectives are intertwined and each in its own way affects national development or unity which Biya (1986: 98) says is consolidated by culture; a culture which itself embodies language, education, history; all of which must therefore go straight into the basket of multiculturalism in order for national unity and democracy to be meaningful.

There is obviously a fundamental definitional problem of what culture is (see Toope, 1997: 180-81; and Vasek[12]). It has generally not been an easy task circumscribing what culture is. For instance, discussing 'What Culture?' in chapter 6 of his policy book, Biya (1986: 97) has come to the conclusion that "The one hundred and fifty definitions of culture given in philosophy textbooks are so many as they are divergent, to the extent that every definition seems to be a reduction of culture." The definitional diversity and divergence might all be because of Shestack's explanation that new insights from diverse cultural backgrounds have continued to be and will go on being added to the large and expanding field of human rights law.[13] All of these expansion and divergence would probably explain why Appiagyei-Atua (1996: 4-5) has strenuously argued for a cross-cultural, pluralistic approach to human rights discourse and praxis in Africa and contended that African societies have distinct notions of rights, concluding that recognizing the differences is the key to making rights exercise more relevant to the ordinary person.

These rights are meaningless except within a particular cultural context. The plain thesis from both Quashigah[14] and Enonchong (1967: 15) then is that rights are not concepts that are to be conceived *in vacuo* but must be studied with regard to the background of a particular community such as Cameroon. In this regard, Cameroon's administrators would appear to have paid particular attention since Biya (1986: 97) states:

---

[12] Karel Vasak, ed., *The International Dimensions of Human Rights* (Paris: UNESCO, 1982).

[13] Jerome J. Shestack, "The Philosophic Foundations of Human Rights" 20:2 *Human Rights Quarterly* (May 1998), 201 at 201 & 234.

[14] Kofi Quashigah, "The Philosophic Basis of Human Rights and its Relations to Africa: A Critique" 1:1 & 2 *Journal of Human Rights Law and Practice* (1992), 22 at 38.

Because of its geographical situation, Cameroon is a crossroads, a meeting point for Africa's cultural main streams. This peculiarity is strengthened by our country's history and ethnic configuration. Conscious of the fact that we are 'Africa in Miniature' geographically, historically and culturally, I think it [is] judicious, in our cultural policy, to move gradually from ethnic cultures to a national culture.

Bearing this necessity to be 'judicious in our cultural policy' in mind, the POR has then defined what he means by culture for Cameroon.

By culture, I mean all the original, positive and constant factors which have enabled Cameroon's ethnic groups to live in communities and guaranteed their survival in the course of history. These basic factors, herein referred to as cultural universals, are values that have to be recorded and fostered in the interest of the national community so that each Cameroonian should be at ease even in cultural activities which do not pertain to his ethnic group of origin. The identification and promotion of these cultural universals, therefore, uphold our people's cultural identity and national unity, for culture consolidates unity. It has several facets which range from moral, academic and aesthetic culture to civic and political culture.[15]

All this theorizing on culture from the Unity Palace is very interesting and apparently in keeping with what is generally accepted the world over. It is not so, however, since it is obvious

---

[15] Biya (1986: 98). For further discussion of 'culture', see USSR Academy of Science, *Problems of the Contemporary World (N° 110): Socialist Humanism, Culture, Personality* (1983) at 306-320; and Ikeda (1987: 16-35) ('A New Human Culture, of, for, and by the People').

that history is being denied, leading to the question of whether culture without history is worth calling culture at all.

Is Culture Without History Culture?

This question calls for an examination of the place of history in a people's culture. Culture and history are inseparable because, notwithstanding the fundamental definitional problem of culture just seen, Roy Preiswerk (as cited in Toope, 1997: 180) has defined it as "a totality of values, institutions and forms of behaviour transmitted within a society... [which] covers *Weltanschung* [or world view], ideologies and cognitive behavior." Culture and history thus travel together; but what culture/history is to matter in the Hinge of Africa? It is when one tries to answer this question that the presidency postulates on culture, do not tally in. That is, when one concretely confronts the authorities with the essential qualification that culture can only consolidate national unity in a country like Cameroon within the well-known rule of "unity in diversity" which necessitates federalism. Their theorizing on culture and national unity would hardly be in place especially when one gets into some of the "cultural universals" such as history, language and education. Nation-building or development is meaningless without the people's authentic history.

The denial of history in Cameroon raises a lot of questions since it is in direct conflict with basic human rights. It was in view of strongly rooted diversity in polities like Cameroon that federalism was brought in as a democratic means of uniting diverse communities in a single internationally recognized state, without destroying their individual or unique characteristics. The idea behind this is the avoidance of the uniformization or assimilation that is bound to follow in the unitary state because the experiences of Belgium quickly attest to the fact that the centralized unitary state is incompatible with multiculturalism. The experts do agree that any talk of multiculturalism and/or democracy is essentially one of respect for human rights in governance. These human rights have been shown by the members of the Bars of Cameroon and of Canada to be much more than jewelry displayed in a showcase; they are the very essence of the quality of human life.[16] Federalism (which is senseless in the absence of the familiar democracy) is strongly recommended as the device for protecting these rights as well as for a much more successful management of multiethnic and diverse polities as most African states.

As I show in subsequent sections of this Chapter and the Chapters following, even the choice of February 4, 1984 (birth of the 1984 Constitution) as the date of the denial of history in Cameroon is itself confusing. These confusion and denial of history would be elaborately studied and explicated in the Chapters following, all of which will be indicating the contents of multiculturalism in Africa (through Cameroon) as not including history; history which itself is part and parcel of culture. For now, the denial and confusion would be seen in this Chapter through briefly showing how a people's history, language, education constitute their culture and all of them must therefore go straight into the basket of multiculturalism in order for democracy and national unity to have real meanings. The history, education, and language of a society are intertwined and would all go into making its culture. I would afford to think that Cameroon national culture can simply not be Cameroon national culture without the distinct culture of the English-speaking people of this country therein included.

The working definition of multiculturalism that has been given earlier must lead us to concentrate on the cultures meant to be promoted, for instance, by the "Thirty objectives for Cameroon," by some recent constitutional provisions (notably

---

[16] *The Canadian Bar Association and the Cameroon Bar Council Committee Report: Model Human Rights Charter for Developing Countries 1989* (Ottawa: Canadian Bar Association, 1989) at 2.

the 1996 Constitution) and by other legal enactment such as the 1998 Education Law that keep talking about "our culture". This question is very important because, in addition, one is told by Ofege (1995a) that

> Mr. Biya's [1996] constitution is doomed to fail because (1) Anglophones reject it (2) the extra-parliamentary opposition [the SDF at the time] representing 40% of Cameroonians rejects it (3) the UNDP [*Union Nationale pour le Développement et le Progrès*] rejects it (4) the churches reject it (5) the Bameleke reject it especially the minority-indigene clause and finally a majority in Parliament reject it. Society can only exist and prosper because it owes allegiance to the interests, prejudices, cultures and histories of its components.

It is interesting that the bulk of Cameroonians rejected the constitution but it is still Cameroon's constitution. Is that the right way to *nationally integrate* the different peoples of Africa?

If the bulk of Cameroonians rejected that constitution, why (absent personal and absolute power) is it that since 18 January 1996 this document has been Cameroon's constitution? Again, where has President Biya's cherished 'majority rule' gone to now? Indeed some of these patriotic 'Third World Saints' can simply not be understood. It is really hard to believe that the current crisis in Cameroon is the handiwork of those Riemer (1985: 186) describes as "Current leaders of the Third World [who] remain staunch nationalists, determined to protect the vital interests of their people against outside domination, exploitation, dependence, and equally determined to help their peoples develop more fully." How are Cameroonians, for example, being helped to develop more fully here? And why is the problem on hand being tossed into the dustbin in preference of instead creating other more intricate difficulties? Whose/which culture(s) then would the 1996 Constitution be referring to, for example, in article 55(2)? Can the February Story give the correct response?

The February Story: Disuniting By Uniting?

Cameroon's Name-Changing Story can also be conveniently called 'The February Story'. Paul Biya, the principal protagonist in this story, was born in February 1933. Eighteen years later, the United Nations Plebiscites took place on 11 February 1961 and led to the formation of the Federal Republic of Cameroon (FRC) seven months later through the Federal Constitution. The FRC is said to have ended on 6th February 1972 with President Ahidjo's *Proclamation DF 72-270* that abrogated and replaced it with the United Republic of Cameroon (URC), being sanctioned by the 1972 Constitution (*2 June 1972 Constitution of the United Republic of Cameroon* [hereinafter 1972 Constitution]); with this URC itself being displaced (through *Loi N° 84-1 du 4 février 1984* [hereinafter 1984 Constitution]) on 4th February 1984 by the 'Republic of Cameroon' (*La République du Cameroun*), as epitomized by the 1984 and 1996 Constitutions. These name-changes, by themselves, are plainly denying history but even more intriguing are the justifications for, and theories drawn from, the changes. I will give you a bit of the tussle on the UN plebiscites and the denial of history before the justification.

Because of the incomprehensible and relentless attempt especially in Francophone Africa to deny people their authentic history, Cameroonian youths, for example, often remain completely lost on the issues, including those of Youth Day and of independence. As Bjornson (1991: 116) has put it, "From schoolbooks and the official propaganda, the younger generation imbibed a misleading picture of what had actually taken place during the colonial periods, [with the fabrication of] the villainy of the UPC." The UPC is *Union des Populations du Cameroun*, a political party that demanded outright independence for and unification of the two Cameroons and it was banned in 1955 before the farce of independence was staged in 1960, with French-appointed '*chef d'état*' put in the place of the patriots to camouflage independence. Sékou Touré's Guinea tells the story better. The French-appointed *chefs d'état* then needed to distort history in order to stay in power, knowing full well that as soon as the masses are aware of the truth, they would no longer be able to stay in power. Knowledge is power, it is said. It is thus scarcely surprising that Tchuiam has opined that 'these youths who are supposed to be leaders of tomorrow are completely lost because they do not even know what this Youth Day feasting is about.'[17]

Critics and youth-consciousness advocates have been ardently arguing that the better thing for the administration to do is to stop camouflaging to the African youths that they are 'the future of our country', and even charging that celebrating Youth Day on the day of the United Nations plebiscites in Cameroon is a plain denial of history.[18] 11 February 1961 is a very important date in Cameroon history since it is because of it that Cameroon, as we know it today, came about (after the 11 February 1961 UN plebiscites in British Cameroons). How come then it is now Youth Day, if not a distortion of history? It seems Moorhouse's thesis above on diplomats may not be lightly contradicted.

A diplomat at Cameroon's embassy in Moscow, Russian Federation, has a different message regarding Youth Day. In his 210-page book (*Youth and Nation-Building in Cameroon: A Study of National Youth Day Messages and Leadership Discourse (1949-2009)*), Churchill Ewumbue Monono, according to the publisher (Langaa Research Publishing Common Initiative Group in Bamenda, Cameroon), has linked the Youth Day to ongoing discussions in Africa about the role and place of youths as agents of development in Africa. Most significantly, he is said to have finally put Cameroon's controversial Youth Day in its appropriate historical context – not as a political device created by the

---

[17] Norbert Tchuiam, "Quelle jeunesse pour quelle fête? " *L'Effort Camerounais* N° 40 (1037) (10-23 février 1996), 13 (*"cette jeunesse qui devrait être sur les rangs demain...est perdue. Malheureusement, de cette fête [même] elle ne sait rien"*).

[18] Boniface Forbin, "Youth Day: A Denial of History" *The Herald* N° 419 (12-13 February 1997), 4.

Francophone politicians to distort Cameroonian history and erase 'plebiscite day' from the collective memory as Southern Cameroonsian nationalists claim, but as a British Cameroons colonial legacy, successfully sold to the Ahidjo regime (that preceded Biya's) as a day to be commemorated throughout the federation, by leaders of the federated state of West Cameroon.[19]

The debate or controversy over 'Youth Day' in the Hinge of Africa is unquestionably far from being over. But when teachers (that Cameroon's Education Law defines in section 32 as the "principal guarantor of the quality of education") are instructed not to impart knowledge of authentic history to Africa's youths who are supposed to be the leaders of tomorrow, why wouldn't the brutalized students remain completely lost on vital societal issues? What then would be the purpose of their education? These issues will be examined in later sections of this book; for now let us get one of the justifications for the name-changing story.

According to Biya (1986, 9), "The change of name from the Federal Republic of Cameroon to the United Republic of Cameroon [in 1972] and finally to the Republic of Cameroon [in 1984] indicates the desire of the Cameroonian State [and not the People] to solve a problem which was created by colonization and which has served as a springboard for political action during the past quarter of a century." This denial of history would lead inexorably to the thesis on moving from Cameroonians to *Njangawatarians* in Chapter 4. This justification (as well as the other one discussed in Chapter 2) of the February Story would be better understood in this Chapter through (1) a clarification of the resulting theses from that story on the part of the minority, and (2) the idea of disuniting by uniting one history or culture.

---

[19] *See* http://www.langaa-rpcig.net/Youth-and-Nation-Building-in.html (last visited on August 17, 2011).

The Intimacy of the 1972 and 1984 Name Changes

The 1984 name-change that revives the contested name (Republic of Cameroon) cannot be divorced from the even more controversial and anti-multiculturalism 1972 one. The first important question is that of why East Camerounians even had to participate in the 1972 referendum, if indeed this was a veritable federation. To bring out the significance of this query, the 1972 referendum (its secrecy and deception apart) can only be likened to 'the Rest of Canada' participating in a referendum on Quebec's sovereignty, with the Quebec Premier being the campaign manager for Ottawa. Is this what will happen in a federation proper or in Canada? But this is exactly what happened in Cameroon. The West Cameroon prime minister was the campaign manager for the 'glorious revolution'. N.N. Mbile of the ruling Cameroon People's Democratic Movement (CPDM) party is quoted as saying that during that "courtesy-fool" referendum it was even the then West Cameroon prime minister (and federal vice-president – what a federation!), Solomon T. Muna, who "served as campaign manager... and brought that 99.9 per cent 'yes' for the unitary system."[20] Why do the "intellectuals in politics" see black but keep telling us that it is white? Who is actually oppressing 'the minority' in Cameroon?

Talking of minority, it is necessary to throw some light on the confusing phrases 'minority/majority' themselves. I am employing majority/minority in this book simply for analytical convenience because it is not like in Cameroon all Francophones (the majority) are free from the repression and are oppressing all Anglophones (the minority). I am thus in accord with Konings and Nyamnjoh's (1997: 218-19) salient critiques of "this

---

[20] Njaru Philip, "Mbile Warns SCNC: Secession is Act of War – No Body Will Let Go Rich Anglophone Territory" *The Herald* (25-26 September 1996), 1. See also Konings and Nyamnjoh (1997: 210).

demagogic approach" of "The Buea Declaration" "which is commonplace in ethnic discourse, serve[ing] to emphasise the 'insurmountable' dichotomy that justifies the AAC call for autonomy.... and creat[ing] serious obstacles to any francophone sympathy for the Anglophone cause." It is such approach ("tend[ing] to blame the wicked francophones as a whole for the plight of the poor anglophones" – Konings and Nyamnjoh, 1997: 218) that makes a common front for change near the impossible; whereas everyone else is being oppressed by the Biya gang, including the gang members themselves.[21] It is just that Southern Cameroonsians feel the oppressive pinch much more deeply because of their different (but not different – see Chapter 2) cultural and political perspectives, worsened further by the fact that the Etoudi Palace gangsters know and understand well how to easily play what I would prefer to describe as the human rights 'Anglos War-Cry' with the 'majority' who, on being told that 'Anglos' are this and that, would not take a minute to think but simply join in the oppressive chorus.

This thesis largely explains a lot of things in Cameroon. It also explains, for example, why most of the English-speaking have come to make 'Francophone' and 'majority' synonyms. I well remember several occasions (especially in my student and lecturer days at the University of Yaoundé. Imagine being in a gathering of, say, fifteen – thirteen Anglophones and two Francophones – and finding almost all thirteen talking almost exclusively in 'bad' French. You then ask them why they cannot talk in the English language they are more comfortable in or with, and here is the response: "We want the majority to understand what is being said." You can see then that they are not here, as elsewhere, looking at 13/15 as the majority but themselves as

---

[21] See Appiagyei-Atua (1999: xi-xiv) ('A Prologue on Oppression'). Specifically, he states at page xii that sycophants like Kontchou and others that Biya surrounds himself with "are also oppressed because, by trying to avoid oppression by the oppressor, they betray the rest of the community and so live in constant fear of reprisal. Their conscience haunts them and this oppresses them."

Anglophones, the minority in Cameroon that can never count in any circumstance in the country; not even with a half Francophone in the midst of 800,000 of them. And do not think the attitude is limited only to being inside Cameroon because I have had to deal with this same Cameroon-Anglophone frame of mind even while studying/living in Montreal, Canada. Who is ever going to give you your language rights if you cannot stand tall and defend or impose them in glaring situations like these?

The 'war-cry' thesis also elucidates why the majority of the majority do not seem to see that federalism would benefit everyone, not only the minority. I would want to also think that, but for the human rights 'war cry', the majority of French-speaking Cameroonians would have opted for the stance that only the English-speaking had to vote in the 1972 referendum since they alone had voted in the United Nations plebiscites to reunite with French Cameroun. Of course, it is difficult to see how the result would have been any different, with West Cameroonians alone participating. "The eclipse of Foncha and the rise of Solomon T. Muna, who eventually became prime minister and vice-president," Bjornson (1991: 24) also indicates, "illustrate how Ahidjo marginalized people who cultivated their own constituencies at the same time that he rewarded those who offered him their unqualified support.... He [Muna] was the one who transformed West Cameroonian administrative structures in accordance with Ahidjo's desire for a unified system."

Yet, other sources have suggested that Southern Cameroonsians did not put up a great fight in 1972 largely because of the manner of effecting that year's change and of its implicit assumption of the continuous existence of two identities in "United'. Unlike his successor, it has been argued, President Ahmadou Ahidjo had the *courtesy* (in effecting his 1972 change of the federal to unitary appellation) to go through the controversial referendum that Mensah-Gbadago (1991: 4) castigates as the embodiment of the most significant of manipulations by which Cameroonians were made to opt for a unitary state and this has gone down in history as the most significant date in the political history of Cameroon. Taking roots from the secretive Federal Constitution, it is then not surprising that Anyangwe (1987: 133 n.18.) also states that the "1972 Cameroonian constitution [as well] was never publicly debated and discussed. Even its actual drafting was shrouded in secrecy and the people were called upon in a referendum to vote for a constitution whose contents they knew nothing about." Ondoa also indicates that the 1996 Constitution is no exception to the trend.[22]

Not everyone sees the 1972 change as a gross deception practised on the Cameroonian people though. There are other experts like Enonchong (1967: xii) who would instead describe its initiation in 1961 as "the Great Reunification Day", and Lantum (1991: 20) the 1972 event proper as a "great event [which] signalled the successful harmonisation of the political institutions during the ten years of the preceding period during which we all belonged to the *'Federal Republic of Cameroon'*" (emphasis as in original). The controversy over, or manipulation on, the issue is nowhere more accentuated as in the politics of minority protection and annexation by coup d'état, etc.

Cameroon's English-speaking people have, since the 1984 name-change, been arguing that changing the country's name from FRC to URC in 1972, at least, still indicated that there were two or more entities that had come together. Their history (or story), they have maintained, was thus still alive in the 'United' that replaced 'Federal'. (What is *actually* in those names anyway?[23]) They have thus preferred to see the controversial

---

[22] ‚Magloire Ondoa "Commentaire" 25 *Juridis Périodique* (*Revue de Droit et de Science Politique*) (1996), 11-14 at 11 & 14.

[23] Talking about the great expectations from the formation of the FRC, Konings and Nyamnjoh (1997: 207) have lamented that "Contrary to expectations, this did not provide for the equal partnership of both parties, let alone for the preservation of the cultural heritage and identity of each, but turned out to be merely a transitory phase to the total integration of the anglophone region into a strongly centralised, unitary state."

1972 transformation not in terms of what it actually is but in terms of its standing with the one in 1984. Thus, while this change in "1972 marked the overt beginning of [the] systematic subjugation, marginalization, assimilation and annexation of the Southern Cameroons", the argument of SCFAQ (Question 5) has proceeded, "There was however some recognition of the bi-cultural nature of the state in the structures of the United Republic of Cameroon." Was that enough for not standing up then? Rodino quotes Benjamin Franklin as saying that those who will give up essential liberty and constant vigilance, to purchase a little temporary safety, clearly deserve neither liberty nor safety.[24] Is this the lesson Mr. Biya believes Southern Cameroonsians have not comprehended? It looks very much like it despite arguments to the contrary.

The 1972 transformation picture, SCFAQ (Question 5) has pointed out, was very different from Biya's 1984 change that actually consummated the assimilation and annexation "with Decree N° 84-001 of February 4th 1984 [which had the effect of] reverting the country to La Republique du Cameroun, in an attempt to completely obliterate and annex the Southern Cameroons. [That is why] Many Southern Cameroon[s]ians intensified their vocal opposition to the [1984] annexation of their territory." According to Gorji-Dinka, the 1984 change from URC to the Republic of Cameroon was a forceful annexation and assimilation since 'Republic of Cameroon' is the name of French-speaking Cameroon before the 1961 reunification. For this charge, they easily invoke the Federal Constitution, by whose first paragraph of article 1, the FRC "is formed, as from 1st October 1961, of the territory of the Republic of Cameroon, henceforth called East Cameroon, and the territory of Southern Cameroons formerly under United Kingdom administration, henceforth called West Cameroon."

---

[24] Peter W. Rodino, "Living with the Preamble" 42 *Rutgers Law Review* (1990), 685 at 700.

They also invoke two interestingly confusing ('The New-Old Name Revival Equals Sublimation') theses. First, that *La République du Cameroun* (East Cameroon) has consequently seceded from the 1961 Union so that, second, they in Southern Cameroons – their own pre-federation name that they have since 1984 also revived – are no longer bound by *any* agreement to stay together.[25] Is this Southern Cameroonsian argument as forceful as that of the others, notably Eritrea's? Perhaps the argument could have been as forceful *only* in 1972, if there was indeed a federation in Cameroon? Was 1972 even the first time that the need for standing up for collective cultural rights and for the Federation presented itself? In short, why was there no massive protest in 1972, the seemingly and palpably right moment for the two-point Southern Cameroonsian argument? Put differently in the words of Stark (1976: 423), "Why was this [1972] change conceded so easily by West Cameroonians? Why was it trumpeted officially as a 'revolution'?"

Some analysts have tried to explain but their explications would only go to buttress the point I am making, namely, that there was no federation instituted in 1961 in Cameroon. As the SCFAQ (Question 5) has doggedly argued,

> Many Southern Cameroon[s]ians (then known as West Cameroonians) protested this treasonable annexationist act [of 1972], but had no means of fighting back since the federal institutions had seized [sic: it is ceased] to exist and those replacing them were not in their control. Even though they

---

[25] See F. Gorji-Dinka, "The Gorji-Dinka Concept of a New Social Order" *Le Messager* Special Political Issue (Thursday 6 June 1991), 5. Pomerance has similarly argued that the Eritrean secessionist movement erupted because of Ethiopia's violation, in 1962, of the 1952 federation agreement that had established Eritrea as an autonomous unit. M. Pomerance, *Self-Determination in Law and Practice* (The Hague: Martinus Nijhoff, 1982) at 115 n.382a. Moosnitec (1993: 60) has also held, for example, that the uniformists within the Hindu majority in India, in their drive to assimilate the Moslem minority, are breaching the two fundamental principles (of democracy and of secularity) of the Indian Constitution of 1950.

overwhelmingly rejected the centralized unitary United Republic of Cameroon that was replacing the Federation in the May 1972 referendum, their voices were drowned by those of their numerically superior francophone brothers.

This brotherhood thing always! Can the voices of Quebecers, for instance, be drowned by those of the rest of Canada in similar manner in the Canadian 'Confederation' or federation? The response is a no; the obvious reason being intimately tied to the invisible hand of Canadian federalism that is in no conceivable way comparable to the Cameroonian that is mired by the personification of public debates. In these circumstances (of the a priori personification of public issues), no *true federation* can be formed; and the proof is in the February Story itself that disunites by uniting?

Disuniting By Uniting One History/Culture?

4th February 1984 is considered as the spark plug that ignited the (until then) dormant February Story and the consequent new-old-name revival equals annexation theory. But that could not be exactly true because the denial of history seems to have begun even before Foumban amongst the English-speaking 'intellectuals in politics'. The *talk* of federating in Foumban in 1961 is only good for emasculating the fact that the then Southern Cameroons Government's own "difficulties of engineering the Union" (Franck, 1968: 169) began even before the United Nations 1961 plebiscites. That is, long before any need for union was involved. A formidable buttress to this thesis, inter alia, is John Ngu Foncha's 1960 declaration in Buea, some six months before the UN plebiscites and their results. Here is Foncha's speech in Southern Cameroons Press Release N° 909 of 18 July 1960, as cited by Stark (1976: 428, emphasis added):

Our people are eagerly listening to what we have to say about their future... All that we shall pronounce after our meeting will be an outline of what the setup of a United Cameroon government will look like. We know our place in the Federation of Nigeria. The place we hope to get in the unified Cameroon will not be the same. It will be like that of *divided brothers who have regained their liberty* and returned home to their fatherland.

This speech does not only expose the inverse reasoning of most Southern Cameroonian elites; it is also clearly indicative of the fact that federalism in Cameroon was not sought for the raison d'être that is its own; also explaining why the French Cameroun constitution was already governing Southern Cameroons even before Foumban: since Le Vine and Nye (1964: 31) refer to the controversial 1972 Constitution as Cameroon's third basic document since 1960. These experts could be thought as being wrong at first sight but they are in a way correct in saying that Southern Cameroons was in reality already assimilated by Southern Cameroonian 'intellectuals in politics' to that French-speaking colony long before the plebiscites and the Foumban Conference.

Dr. Fonlon (the Foumban translator and interpreter), we are told, had "translated and adapted the [East] Cameroon national anthem from French into English, before it was adopted by the West Cameroon House of Assembly and *later* at the Foumban Constitutional Talks, before being included in the Federal Constitution of October 1, 1961."[26] This fact also seems to

---

[26] Takwa Suifon, "Eleven Years After Bernard Fonlon: A Postscript" *The Herald* (26-28 September 1997a) 6 (emphasis added). At Foumban, Dr. Fonlon (who even had "prophetic foresight to start learning French since 1950, the thorough preparation in philosophy and theology at Okpuala-Owerinta and at Bigard Memorial Seminary Enugu respectively"), according to Lantum (1991: 21), became "an important bridge-man between the East and West" because "of the

specifically prove the celebrated thesis of Professor Bernard Fonlon himself on "Anglophones" in Cameroon. As Tangwa (1996) indicates, Professor Bernard Nsokika Fonlon had posited that "the greatest enemy of the Anglophone [in Cameroon] is the Anglophone." Tangwa's explanation is that, "As a minority with nothing to fall back on in times of crisis, the Anglophones devour each other." Yes, Tangwa, that is right; but the important question is not whether or not they have something to fall back on; it is more with why they do not have that something to fall back on; with the answer that is convincing being that they were manipulated out of their roots by their own intellectuals in politics. Professor Fonlon's thesis explains in a forceful way why the Federalism Question would end no longer being the one that has been given and sung as the rationale of the 1961 Foumban Enterprise. It would then only be the translator's own goal that had been set for *himself on 6th September 1954*; about seven years before anyone could dream of the Foumban Drama of July 1961.

That being the situation, according to Lantum (1991: 13), "the next question is to what extent did he [Dr. Fonlon] succeed as an intellectual cum politician?" In answering this question in the final sentence of his lengthy 'few paragraphs' exposé, Lantum has stated that "I believe that if Dr. FONLON was asked whether or not he had succeeded, he would simply say 'I did my best to follow my spiritual syllabus which *I set for myself on 6th September 1954*."^{27} Whatever happened to the 'syllabus' of his people's self-government, and the love of the youth's development, etc.? Is there anyone who is still in doubt that, in a

---

bilingual intellectual that he was" to properly understand the other language-party's constitutional text which was only in French (*ibid.* at 11).

^{27} Lantum (1991: 13) (emphasis added). "It was probably his [Dr. Fonlon's] faith, high spiritual attainment and moral integrity", according to Lantum, "that buttressed such formidable resistance to the enticement of the world, and it is precisely that which we need to discover and capture it [sic] for a lesson for *the formation and socialization of the youth and the elite of our time*" (*id.* at 13, emphasis added) because "Of special importance to him [Dr. Fonlon] was the intellectual development of the youth." *Id.* at 20.

scenario such as this, there is bound to be much facts twisting and the equation of personal for general interest? It is often when these narrow interests (egoism or self-centeredness) become the only and overriding concern in public affairs that something else is usually mistaken for politics. People thus have to invent facts to emasculate the case. But it is very hard to be consistent when one is desperately inventing facts to emasculate a situation that is so glaringly fatal. Most people in Africa simply do not realize the fatality principally because Africans have come to over believe in mirages called "intellectuals in politics".

Thus, assimilation or annexation began long ago (even before Foumban) and has since Foumban been the steady policy as even the squandering of the country's enviable continental historical geo-political-cultural position can plainly show. Geographically, Cameroon is situated along the Gulf of Guinea which Dzidzornu (1995: 441) describes as stretching from Mauritania in the north to Namibia in the south and making the sea a primary resource base for economic development for twenty-one African countries. Looking like a large triangle and with two foreign languages, Cameroon is wedged between three foreign languages: English-speaking (Nigeria to the west); French-speaking (Chad to the north, Central African Republic to the east; and Gabon, Congo), and Spanish-speaking (Equatorial Guinea) to the south. What a God-given advantage for uniting Africa! But why is there only national regression, with all these gifts? National regression is the inevitable thing since that is exactly what occurs when rather than unite two or more histories you 'unite' one history. This uniting of one history is even seen in the preference of what part of Africa Cameroon's unpatriotic administrators want it to belong to.

Preponderant evidence portrays Cameroon as properly fitting in both West and Central Africa but the leadership has always only preferred the Central African position. French (1997), a Canadian writer, has talked about the preferred location when he describes Cameroon as so profusely rich that it is considered to be central Africa's Promised Land. Another Canadian writer, in admiring Cameroon culture, also has this to say about Cameroon's West African geographical position: "He fingers the colourful embroidered loose robe and hat he must wear at ceremonial occasions in the country on Africa's *west* coast. Every stitch and pattern on the clothing is an ancient symbol of a culture going back hundreds of years."[28]

The preference of the central to the west description can also help to explain why Cameroon is a member of the 'mono-cultural' Central African Economic Union (UDEAC: the French acronym),[29] but not of "the beleaguered [bicultural] Economic Community of West African States (ECOWAS)."[30] And all this preference is pursued despite that it can and should belong to both; and in spite of the fact also that observers think that the UDEAC is worse off than the ECOWAS. As French (1997) has put it, because of political drift and economic disarray in France's former colonies in Central Africa, poor and landlocked Chad has recently expressed an interest in abandoning its membership in

---

[28] Jeff Holubitsky, "Out of Africa: Retired U of A Prof. Recalls Life as a Respected Elder Among the Nso People of Cameroon" *The Edmonton Journal* (March 9, 1998), C4 (emphasis added). See also Christraud M. Geary, *Images from Bamum: German Colonial Photography at the Court of King Njoya, Cameroon, West Africa, 1902-1915* (Washington, D.C.: Published for the National Museum of African Art by the Smithsonian Institute Press, 1988) (underlining added); and Daryll Forde, ed., *Ethnographical Survey of Africa - Western Africa Part X: Peoples of the Central Cameroons* (London: Hazell, Watson and Viney, Ltd., [no year]).

[29] See *Treaty for the Establishment of the Economic Community of Central African States*, 19 October 1983, 23 *International Legal Materials* (I.L.M.) 945. For more on this union (as well as the West African one of the next footnote), see Clément *et al* (1996).

[30] "France, US at War... Over West African Market" *The Messenger* (20 May 1996), 1. For its creation, see *Treaty of the Economic Community of West African States*, 28 May 1975: 14 I.L.M. 1200. For more on this union, see, e.g., U. Ezenwe, *ECOWAS and the Economic Integration of West Africa* (New York: St. Martin's Press, 1983); B. Zagaris, "The Economic Community of West African States (ECOWAS): An Analysis and Prospects" 10 *Case Western Reserve Journal of International Law* (1978), 93; and S.K.B. Asante, *The Political Economy of Regionalism in Africa: A Decade of the Economic Community of West African States (ECOWAS)* (New York: Praeger, 1986).

the region's foundering economic community, which includes a common currency. It has sought instead to join a neighbouring economic coalition of France's former West African colonies, which is doing better.

Cameroon simply cannot act like Chad mainly because, thanks to its Anglophobia, this country has traditionally avoided the English-speaking world, and particularly Nigeria; this perhaps also elucidating why it has been active in *La Francophonie* almost from inception but "bribing its way" into the Commonwealth only in 1995.[31] Ntonufor's charges would seem to be solidly founded, viewing the detailed and academic analysis of the issue by Konings and Nyamnjoh (1997:221-22). This awkward fact has obviously had a considerable negative impact on its otherwise enviable endowments – both physical and human – thanks to poor and ineffective and unpatriotic leadership that has colossally failed to make good use of the natural qualities of the Cameroon people as shown further in the Chapters following. Before those Chapters, I will need to catalogue here some of the consequences of the ignition on national integration. National integration has since the 1984 change changed to national disintegration because of not only the historical name change but also of some follow-up ill-conceived moves by the same President Biya on the educational system of the English-speaking. I will give a few examples of both instances of disuniting by uniting here, beginning with the 1984 name case.

---

[31] Talking about its admission into the Commonwealth in 1995, Ntonufor has concluded that "Mr. Biya, it would seem, had, true to type, bribed his way into an organization whose members are supposed to be gentlemen. Yes, he might have bribed his way through because even onto this day no possible reason exists for Cameroon's admission. Ngwa T.S. Ntonufor, "Open Letter to the British High Commisioner" *The Herald* N° 337 (16-17 April 1997), 4. These are quite serious allegations and, "If true, the accusations made…demonstrate how money has become ruinously pervasive in a movement that is supposed to be about higher ideals." Gazette Editorials, "Five-Ring Scandal" *Montreal Gazette* (15 December 1998), B2.

The 1984 Name or History Case

Since the 1984 name-change by President Biya, one can hardly sufficiently document the currying and bitterness that have been pouring out from Cameroon's English-speaking people. Publications like the April 1994 *Buea Peace Initiative*[32] and old editions of the *Cameroon Post* newspaper (from February 1984) have been very good at cataloguing their grievances; complaints that, according to the experts, if not properly addressed, augur badly for the integrity of Cameroon.[33] Awasom has stated:

> The threats of the disintegration of bilingual Cameroon are real, if we are to go by the activities of Anglophone pressure

---

[32] For further details of this initiative for peaceful resolution, see 'Southern Cameroons Landmark Documents'.
http://www.southerncameroons.org/index3.htm (last visited in November 2011). See also S.M. Buo, "Biya and the Anglophones" *West Africa* (August 12, 1985), 1639; J.K. Naweri, "Restless Anglophones" *West Africa* (January 30, 1984), 201; P.S. Engers, "Anglophone Cameroon: Drifting with the Rudderless Ship" *West Africa* (August 13, 1984), 1671; Jude Waindim, "Did Pope Address Southern Cameroons Issue at UN?" *Cameroon Post* N° 0274 (11-18 December 1995), 1; "Gov't, CRTV Management Mount Anti-Anglophone Campaign: Julius Wamey, Others Suspended" *Cameroon Post* (6-13 June 1991), 1; Asong Ndifor, "Foncha Alerts UN of Troop Deployment in NW and SW – Says Biya Regime Wants to Crack Down on Anglophones" *The Herald* N° 592 (3-5 April 1998), 1; "Will the International Community Forestall a 'Cameroonian' Rwanda Episode?" *The Herald* N° 319 (13-16 June 1996), 4; "Guerre et paix au Cameroun – L'Etat RDPC nous impose la guerre" *L'Expression* N° 190 (23 octobre 1997), 8-9; Alain Bengono and C. Yaho, "A quelques heures du verdict: le Cameroun au bord de l'implosion" *L'Expression* N° 130 (6 juin 1997), 1 & 4; Denis Nkwebo, "Temperature élévée: le Cameroun menacé d'explosion" *Le Quotidien* N° 288 (24 octobre 1997), 4; and Kum Set Ewi and Peterkins Manyong, "SDF Accuses Biya of Provoking War, Militants Urged to Regroup and Prepare to Defend Themselves" *The Herald* N° 473 (18-19 June 1997), 1 at 3 (indicating how during that party's rally "Voices were heard shouting that Kabila's approach [in Zaire] was the only way to oust the Biya regime")

[33] See Konings and Nyamnjoh (1997); Manasé Aboya Endong "La question anglophone au Cameroun: entre menaces secessionistes et revendications identitaires" 59:1 *Revue juridique et politique des états francophones* (2005), 115-134; and Piet Konings, *The Anglophone Struggle for Federalism in Cameroon* (Leiden: African Studies Centre, 2000).

groups in Cameroon, and the radicalism of the Anglophone Diaspora in the United States, who express their 'secessionist' views on the internet in the SCNC forum. But the situation can be reversed if a genuine decentralization of power, in the direction of federalism, is introduced, and Anglophones are constitutionally guaranteed equal status with Francophones in all spheres of national life.[34]

The earliest and clearest of the grave concerns about the future of Cameroon as a single political entity came in 1997 from Christopher Kiloh Fai Nsahlai, then Cameroon's ambassador to the Central African Republic. "The foundation of the Cameroon nation," Ndifor's report quotes the ambassador as stating in *his Looking Up to the Mountain Top: Beyond Party Politics*, "appears to be wobbling visibly on quicksand. It is now common knowledge that a considerable portion of the Anglophone public is speaking more and more the language of secession and independence than national unity." The ambassador, the report continues, had equally told his boss in a letter that "by far the greatest threat to national unity is the Anglophone problem."[35] Two years before the ambassador, Taku (1995: 3) had made the same point by indicating that "the most important problem that must be resolved and quickly too is the Southern Cameroons problem. No admission into the Commonwealth, no media campaign will

---

[34] Nicodemus Fru Awasom, "The Reunification Question in Cameroon History: Was the Bride an Enthusiastic or Reluctant One?" 47:2 *Africa Today* (2000), 91 at 113-14.

[35] Asong Ndifor, "Biya's Ambassador Expresses Concern about Future of Cameroon" *The Herald* N° 428 (5-6 March 1997), 1. See also Peterkins Manyong, "The Nsahlai Phenomenon in Cameroon Politics" *The Post* (3 September 2008); and Asong Ndifor and Michael Ndi, "Biya Bows to Progressives, Appoints Nsahlai to Head CPDM Reform Commission" *The Herald* (19 November 2003). Dr. Nsahlai suddenly died on 18 April 2008. See Kini Nsom, "Christopher Nsahlai Drops Dead in Yaounde" *The Post* (21 April 2008); and Peterkins Manyong and Willibroad Nformi, "My Father's Death Was Unnatural – Nsahlai's Son" *The Post* (12 May 2009).

side track this basic problem. It is the resolution of this problem that will guarantee durable peace in the sub region." As some other prominent opposition politicians did even warn in 1996, "It is in the best interest of France to understand the change of climate and to react accordingly. Or else, who knows, a worse scenario than Bangui [Central African Republic] will be in the offing in Cameroon tomorrow. God forbid that should happen."[36] The list is quite lengthy. But one Newspaper Editor appears to have summarized the puzzle when he affirmed in December 1997 that

> Anyone who knows of the friends of Paul Biya also knows that Anglophones are not among them. Since Biya was minister and prime minister, he has been known not to like Anglophones. After being president for fifteen years, Biya hasn't cured himself of his anti-Anglophone habit of thought.[37]

Because of the 'I-don't-care' attitude of the Biya regime toward them, some of these English-speaking Cameroonians, as far back as 1991, suggested the creation of an independent Anglophone state to be called Ambazonia.[38] Ambazonia comes from the two words *Ambas* (the coastal peoples of Southern Cameroons) and *zone*. The name was coined by some Southern Cameroonsians, according to SCFAQ (Question 21), to avoid confusion of Southern Cameroons with the South Province of La République du Cameroun. The Ambazonia 'Suggestion' has been hotly challenged not only by those who oppose secession (for the

---

[36] John Fru Ndi, "In the Interest of France: Trade Not Aid" *Cameroon Post* Special Edition (December 1996), 16.

[37] Boniface Forbin, "The Anglophone Problem Again (II)" *The Herald* N° 541 (1-2 December 1997), 4.

[38] See Sam-Nuvela Fonkem, "Suggestions for an Ambazonia Caucus" *Cameroon Post* (May 30-June 6, 1991), 7.

vagueness and escapism in its advocacy[39]) but also by those in favour of outright independence. One of the strongest arguments (of the pro-independence camp) against the name 'Ambazonia', the SCFAQ has again explained in Question 21, is that it recognizes the coastal *Ambas* ethnic groups from the south without mentioning the *Tikars* and others from the north. For this reason, it concludes, many independentists have proposed some 'Ambas-and-Tikars-recognizing' variants like AMBASTIKARIA and TIKARAMBA. Many other names have been floated around but the one that currently seems to stand (albeit confusing) is Southern Cameroons, whose independence and right to statehood is at the centre of the nation-building problems in the Hinge of Africa.

To further the independence of the Southern Cameroons, the Southern Cameroons National Council (SCNC) was created. There is controversy about the real aim of the SCNC though. In an August 1996 interview with *The Herald*, a Cambridge scholar (Dr. Simon Munzu), one of the architects of the SCNC, indicated how the Council's objective was simply "the restoration of the identity and autonomy of Southern Cameroons within a Federal Republic of Cameroon", but "[u]nfortunately, as a result of the intransigence of the Biya regime, the SCNC appears to have been driven to embrace an objective that was not originally its own, namely, the talk of [outright] independence."[40] Konings and Nyamnjoh (1997: 229) also agree that "It was only after the persistent refusal of the Biya Government to discuss this [return to federalism] scenario that secession, which used to be covertly

---

[39] See T. Dibussi, "Challenging the Ambazonia Fantasy" *Cameroon Post* (6-13 June 1991), 6; and Peter Ateh-Afac Fossungu, "Revisiting 'My Second Home'" *The Herald* N° 652 (26-27 August 1998), 10.

[40] See "SCNC Has Fallen Prey to Extremist Tendencies – Journey to New Zealand Was Pointless; Time-bound Independence Programme Was Crazy" *The Herald* N° 343 (14-15 August 1996), 6. See also Asong Ndifor, "SCNC Accused of Plan to Form Secessionist Gov't – Doubtful Evidence Presented" *The Herald* N° 447 (18-20 April 1997), 1.

discussed by a limited few, became an overt option with mounting popularity." Also explicating why the SCPC[41] has been preaching independence instead of its initial request for a return to the 1961 federal constitutional arrangement, SCFAQ (Question 12) has made it clear that

> From AAC to SCPC, the Southern Cameroons leadership has demanded dialogue with the leaders of La Republique du Cameroun, for a negotiated return to the 1961 federal arrangement. When it became evident after AAC II in 1994, that La Republique du Cameroun was not willing to sit down and talk with the Southern Cameroons, it confirmed the feeling among Southern Cameroon[s]ians that the francophone leadership did not care about their well-being. Southern Cameroon[s]ians therefore had no choice in the absence of a brother to negotiate with, but to assert their independence and part ways with La Republique du Cameroun. This is being done peacefully in line with the SCPC motto "The Force of Argument, Not the Argument of Force", and hopefully independence shall be achieved without any bloodshed if we can count on some civility from La Republique du Cameroun.

---

[41] As SCFAQ has explained them in Question 7, the acronyms AAC, SCPC, SCNC, and SCAC, respectively stand for the All Anglophone Conference (AAC), the Southern Cameroons People's Conference (SCPC), the Southern Cameroons National Council (SCNC) and the Southern Cameroons Advisory Council (SCAC). The first AAC was held in Buea in April 1993, and the second in Bamenda in April/March 1994. It was decided at Bamenda that the name "Anglophone" was too loose and limiting, portraying more of the colonial heritage and less representative of the territorial boundaries that defined a people with a right to self-determination. The AAC was then transformed into the SCPC: a name with a historical meaning and territorial significance. The Anglophone National Council (the elected governing body of the AAC) became the SCNC. The Anglophone Advisory Council (comprising non-elected elderly and retired statesmen, clergy, clerics, fons, chiefs, and Southern Cameroons political party chiefs) became the SCAC, which plays the role of advisor to the SCNC.

It is now clear to the Southern Cameroons independentists that there is no civility on the part of La République du Cameroun that any right-thinking person can count on.

It is not then surprising, from the way Konings and Nyamnjoh (1997: 219-20) have also exposed these issues, that, as they did approach the third millennium, it became obvious that Southern Cameroonsians were no longer interested in belonging to a society in which they have been incessantly treated as slaves bought with nothing, according to Justice Ebong Frederick Alobwede (Chairman of the High Command Council of the Southern Cameroons National Council (SCNC)) who read the Independence Proclamation.

> The year 2000 is fast approaching. Things are happening and people are coming up with ideas, some of the ideas are quite interesting, some are embarrassing and others loaded with very undesirable consequences. Among some of the bizarre ideas for the magic year, there is the one which shall remain indelible in the minds of the people of the world in general and the Southern Cameroons in particular. That is, *the Proclamation of the Restoration of the Sovereignty and Independence of the Southern Cameroons*. Hence we felt that there will be no other time appropriate to carry out this Proclamation other than the eve of the third millennium, as we are convinced that no well thinking Southern Cameroon[s]ian would want to enter the 3rd millennium as a slave in the regime of La Republique du Cameroun.[42]

The many happenings in Cameroon, including this Independence Proclamation, have not failed to further confuse

---

[42] See the Proclamation of the Restoration of the Sovereignty and Independence of the Southern Cameroons, Buea, Southern Cameroons, December 30, 1999, available at <http://www.southerncameroons.org/index3.htm> (last visited in July 2011) [hereinafter Independence Proclamation] (bold is original).

the name-confusion, leading some critics to wonder about "what we are called" or should be called.

Flowing from both their 'revival' arguments on the 1984 name-change and the 1999 Independence Proclamation therefore, some writers have tried to clarify, in connection with the nationality of the people and things of the Southern Cameroons in the SCNC Forum which was founded by Southern Cameroonsian nationalists in the Diaspora as a discussion and news group for Southern Cameroonsians and those interested in Southern Cameroons politics. In a contribution to this SCNC Forum in 2001, Fossungu wrote as follows:

> [R]ead[ing] a lot of materials concerning the independent Federal Republic of Southern Cameroons (FRSC)... I cannot help being amazed by the fact that the people promoting this country are at the same time plainly denying that they are a different and autonomous people and nationality from those of the Republic of Cameroon [*La République du Cameroun*]. This perceived denial is in the form of [them] always referring to people of the new country as 'Southern Cameroonians'. THIS IS WRONG.[43]

What are the reasons advanced for this position? Fossungu proceeded to lengthily explain his point by indicating that

> People of the Federal Republic of Southern Cameroons, since 30 December 1999 (if the Proclamation is actually what it is said to be), are SOUTHERN CAMEROONSIANS and NOT Southern Cameroonians. Why is this so? [It is] Very simple. People from Ghana (former Gold Coast) are known as Ghanaians, NOT Ghanians. The last letter ('a') in the name of the country has not been dropped to get to the people

---

[43] Peter A. Fossungu's Email "What Are We Called?" sent to scncforum@egroups.com on 15 January 2001 at 5.39 PM (capitals as in original).

who have the country's nationality. I don't understand why people from *Southern Cameroons* must do otherwise. Why should the letter-dropping be the case with Southern Cameroons? People of this territory are either Cameroonians or they are not. [If they have chosen not to be Cameroonians,] There must be no more confusion of important issues as all the people concerned have known as 'third-rate' citizens of the Cameroon Republic. One cannot therefore be of a different and independent country called FEDERAL REPUBLIC OF SOUTHERN CAMEROONS and still be (or always be mistaken to be) of the southern part of the Republic of Cameroon (*La République du Cameroun*). Is the high probability of this confusion not responsible for the late Professor Fonlon's invention of Ambazonia (as we have been told)? I am not an advocate for the change of the name FRSC to Ambazonia. The FRSC is not under question; what is under fire here is the calling of people from this country (FRSC) 'Southern Cameroonians'. If my suggestion above (that people of the FRSC are Southern Cameroonsians) is found to be inappropriate (and I doubt that it is) then here we go. Let us say they are FERESOCAMERIANS. What is this strange nationality? [It is s]imply an acronym that is logically derived from the FRSC. I think if people are serious about the country (FRSC), they will want to have nothing that confuses them and their things with those of *La Republique du Cameroun*. Therefore, I think these people are either SOUTHERN CAMEROONSIANS or/and FERESOCAMERIANS. What do you think?[44]

The next day (January 16, 2001), two people responded *at the same time* to Fossungu's question. The first contributor, Tayoba

---

[44] *Ibid*. Perhaps Fossungu was just using a lone case to make his point, but I must have to indicate here that people from Barbados, for instance, are Barbadians, and not Barbadosians.

Ngenge, "found this excellent. I too have called it Southern Cameroonians – adding the suffix to Cameroon instead of to Cameroons. It sounds terribly ugly when pronounced correctly. The better [thing though is] to emphasize the ugliness of the colonial name. And the better [thing again is helping] to remind us to baptize it natively ASAP."[45] At the same moment as Tayoba Ngenge, Edwin Ngang also wrote as follows:

> You have raised a very important issue --that of sovereign national identity— [that] anyone who claims to be involved in our 'restoration' or 'independence' struggle... should be concerned about. Thanks!
>
> In our experience with the 'international community', people are just plain CONFUSED with the appellation 'southern' CAMEROONS. This is why diplomats have never been able to accept the legitimacy of our case. They will logically, given the 'political environment' allowed by the confusion in the name 'southern cameroons', argue (and quite frankly have been lobbied by LRC [*La République du Cameroun*] agents) that there is no problem in the 'southern' Cameroons. The Ebolova region, of LRC ... [Southern] province has just had a delegate of its MPs declare their confidence in President Biya. Noting the potential for a public embarrassment if they support a 'Republic of Southern Cameroons' they will just play along with the politics. Diplomats have a career to maintain and cannot be in the position to be embarrassed when they speak of a 'southern cameroons' seeking to restore its independence when all the evidence [would] show otherwise!
>
> [O]nly in the academia would the true historic 'Southern Cameroons' be accurately identified after you have made your case, say by... research[ing and]... do[ing] archival research

---

[45] Tayoba Ngenge's E-mail "Re: What Are We Called?" sent to scncforum@egroups.com on 16 January 2001 at 2.29 PM.

[because] In the brutal world of politics, diplomats want to see resolve, and determination and the fighting spirit before they can place their careers on a cause. So far we, of what… [is now] called "Federal Republic of Southern Cameroons" have not done that… [We are] still labouring to recognize the value of a distinguishing national identity.⁴⁶

On 17 January 2001, Wanaku (whose response to this same "What Are We Called?" query was titled "Where Are You From? Your Answer in 30 Seconds") lengthily wrote:

> In Ibalikumato, when a child is born, every relative 'qualified' to give a name does so. They do so out of love and the more names you have shows how much love you are getting.
> At a regional level, we might be having the same problem. Our region is so loved that everyone wants to give it a name – in whole or in part – from Southern Cameroons, West Cameroon, Federal Republic of Southern Cameroons to Victoria-Limbe, Mamfe-Manyu, Bamenda-Tisong, Kumba-K-town etc … This probably is proving that there is a need for protocols to be written to establish naming conventions [including street naming – so the postman can know where you are] that future generations can work with. If we do not do it, someone will in the future. But please do not bring back names like NA [Native Authority]
> Meanwhile, if someone asks us where we come from, we simply say, "from *British Cameroon*". This *eliminates confusing Southern Cameroons with the southern province of Cameroun, this asserts the language of administration of the region [English], and places [albeit virtually] responsibility on the British for irresponsibly handing over 5.000.000 people to the GUILLOTINE.*

---

⁴⁶ Edwin Ngang's Email "Re: What Are we Called?" sent to scncforum@egroups.com on 16 January 2001 at 2.29 PM. (capitals as in original).

"From British Cameroon" works most of the time [at least in our case]. Do not be surprised at the number of people who will think aloud to you that, "I thought Cameroon was French...?". You can spill the beans from there if you [or they] have the time to listen. If not you have made your point in less than 30 seconds![47]

Whatever the case, in order to eschew some of the foregoing confusion, *Southern Cameroonians* is employed in this book to refer to the people of Southern Cameroons (or British Cameroons – for those who want to make their case in less than 30 seconds), especially since 4th February 1984 when assimilation is said to have taken on an accentuated phase in West-Central Africa with moves on and through education.

The 1985/83 Education Case

What biculturalism is actually there in the Education Law's use of educational biculturalism? The drive in Cameroon to assimilate the English-speaking minority is not auguring well with nation-building as the country seems to be heading instead for nation-destruction. "To some observers," Delancey (1989: 1) opens his illuminating book, "Cameroon is a glowing success in recent African history, a site of political stability and economic growth and development." This is exactly the image that the regime wants to portray through its *politique confusionnelle*. But, as the Cameroon authorities would still be smiling and felicitating themselves for having succeeded in deceiving this North American stranger, to their utter dismay, Delancey (*ibid*) would immediately bring out his "American stuff" by carrying on. "To others, Cameroon is a neo-colonial entity, existing under the

---

[47] See Wanaku's Email "Re: What Are we Called?" sent to scncforum@egroups.com on January 17, 2001 at 11.09 AM (bold & square brackets as in original).

influence of France, with no benefit of its independence accruing to the bulk of the population, and with revolution and division boiling close to the surface."

The 'war of dominance and destruction' between this country's two "sub-systems of education" is at the heart of these revolution and division that have especially come in only *as a consequence* of the seemingly endless sufferings of the Cameroonian people, particularly since 1984 when assimilation of the English-speaking minority took on an accentuated phase with what Fohtung (1995) describes as "Biya's rise to power [in November 1982 which] was one of those rare political miracles of modern times that almost always winds up in tragedy." This tragic rise to power was saluted by some ill-conceived moves on *education* in 1983 and 1985. Konings and Nyamnjoh (1997:213) have pointed out that in 1983 the Government promulgated an order modifying the anglophone General Certificate of Education (GCE) examination by making it rather similar to the *Baccalauréat*, and the ensuing demonstrations and boycott of classes were repressed by police brutality at the University of Yaoundé and in urban centres in anglophone Cameroon. It is principally the resistance being mounted by young Cameroonians to these incessant moves, especially since 1985, which may sooner or later thrust Cameroon unto the centre stage of "atrocities zones"; what some observers call 'another Rwanda-Episode'. This episode is going to happen most probably because, despite the string of academic degrees matching behind their names, poorly educated and unpatriotic administrators can scarcely learn anything at all regarding local government that Kneier (1939: preface) considers to be "the science of the second best."

Cameroon's administrators will not listen nor even understand the role and importance of this 'best political science' that Albert Einstein found to be more difficult than physics. Is it then the question of their not understanding politics because of its difficulty or simply that of deliberate confusion of powers? I would want to think it is the latter. I also like to believe that young English-speaking Cameroonians are not being fooled by the so-called National Education Board (NEB) that the 1998 Education Law purportedly creates in section 11(2) (for more of analysis of which, see Chapter 2). The English-speaking students did not fail in 1985 to see what could really be hiding behind the 'harmonization' or NEB. As they stated in their widely publicized Letter,

> The latest unscrupulous attempt we recall with unquenchable bitterness. By issuing confusing announcements on public examinations, MINEDUC was responsible for thwarting the efforts of many Anglophone youths to better their future and that of their families. The students did not sit in for the chemistry "A" and commerce "O" level papers of the just ended G.C.E. examinations. Though there is no doubt that irremediable damage has been done to some of the families concerned, nothing has been done or said to correct the situation. And, instead of calling for justice to fall on those involved in the scandal, the national assembly takes it as an opportunity to press for harmonization of educational systems (we might here ask what became of the G.C.E. Commission?). *Now the simple question we ask is what to expect from someone who condemns a system and is given the opportunity and liberty to select from it? No doubt, total rejection.*[48]

---

[48] See Students' Letter of 20th August 1985: "Letter From the English-speaking Students of the North West and South West Provinces to their Parents" (emphasis added). The entire 6-page letter is found at "Southern Cameroons Landmark Documents": http://www.southerncameroons.org/index3.htm (last accessed in August 2010). It has to be noted that their Letter, though addressed to their parents, was copied to a much wider audience. Copies of it were sent to "all party chiefs; all mayors; all D.O.s [district officers]; all lawyers and magistrates; all doctors and university lecturers; all Secretaries General and provincial chiefs of services; all directors and ministries; Hon. S.T. Muna; Dr. J.N. Foncha; Dr. E.M.L. Endeley; [and] Mr. E.T. Egbe." *Ibid.*

Of course, the preference of the NEB would only be for the French-speaking sub-system. These English-speaking students could not have been wrong then because a critic confirmed their views five years later, in March 1990, when he also explained that outright assimilation is what is involved.

> Over the years, a persistent assault has been maintained against the separate and unique cultural (linguistic) identity of this [Cameroonian] minority: suppression of the federal structure of the country, through which the minority maintained some autonomy in the running of its affairs; the non-appointment of members of this minority to top and sensitive positions in the military, administration, police, Cabinet, and state corporations, as well as in the diplomatic field. It is also being carried out through the economic impoverishment of their area (even though the resources from this area account for about ninety per cent of the country's foreign exchange) and by making sure that political leaders of this people (students) lose ability to communicate in nothing but the dominant language by the time they leave the vastly monolingual and mono-cultural university.[49]

So the idea really is not that of educational dualism. It is rather that of the destruction of the 'Anglophone' system and assimilating them into the French-speaking system; an educational system that cannot carry international reputation especially when the ministry can "fix" student results just as it

---

[49] Fonkeng (1990: 'Preface & Thanks', 3rd paragraph). For the Cameroon civil service and appointment situation, also see, e.g., Konings and Nyamnjoh (1997:213-214; & 225-229); David Tendong, "Civil Service Appointments: Musonge Says Anglophones Have 'Dirty Files', Can't Be Promoted" *The Herald* N°415 (3-4 February 1997), 1 & 3; Peter Ngea Beng, "Anglophones to Be Swept Out in Coming Shake-Up in Parastatals" *The Herald* N° 646 (14-16 August 1998), 1 & 3; and Boniface Forbin, "Parastatals: Why Are Anglophones an Endangered Species?" *The Herald* N° 646 (14-16 August 1998), 4.

likes. According to Johnson-Hanks (2006: 125), in May 1998 (the same year of the Education Law) the MINEDUC "declared an emergency, asserting that education levels were slipping dangerously. It responded by publicly inflating the scores of the *baccalauréat* to ensure that Cameroon's national pass rate would not decline vis-à-vis other Francophone African nations... This well-publicized grade inflation was almost uniformly condemned outside the ministry." As this French-speaking sub-system, with all its perceived shortcomings (more in Chapter 2 below), is the only one that the authorities are bent on promoting and imposing on everyone, Cameroon's integrity is then in question because, as it would now seem, the educational system is the one and only area left that has stood out, and probably will persist, as the point of Southern Cameroonsian solidarity in the country.[50]

The message that Southern Cameroonsians have been and are still sending out seems to be this: Caricaturize our "sub-system of education" as much as you will but don't you dare think of completely destroying it. Now that the authorities seem to have lost patience with piecemeal deformation and are now only bent on complete destruction, keen observers have every reason to wonder for just how long the 'Anglo-Saxon' institutions (G.C.E. Board, University of Buea, and University of Bamenda) would be and remain "places to be" in a *united* Cameroon. As Ndamukong (1996) has pondered:

> How can the Presidency, if it is interested in the unity of this country, sit and watch an individual [Mbella Mbappe, the then minister of 'National' Education] destroy part of the nation's culture? How can the Prime Minister [an Anglophone, it must be noted] not react when a Minister disregards his orders? How can Anglophone Parliamentarians, irrespective of their political leanings...[be] mute when a mere appointee in the

---

[50] See Francis Beng Nyamnjoh and R.F. Akum, *The Cameroon GCE Crisis: Test of Anglophone Solidarity* (Bamenda: Langaa RPCIP, 2008).

name of Minister is deliberately destroying the foundations of the culture and identity of the people they represent in Parliament? Does the government of this country not know that by allowing an individual Minister to mete out shabby treatment on one part of the country, seeds of hatred, conflict and eventual disintegration are being sown? How can parents, teachers and students sit down and see a wicked individual gradually annihilat[ing] the bedrock on which their educational system and identity rest?

The students have not been sitting down with folded arms. This fact would explain why many of the surviving student leaders are now abroad and highly wanted. According to Taku (1995), "Oppressive squads are being trained to terrorise and harass the citizenry, especially the voices of dissent. Several students, members of the student movement, *Parliament*, remain in exile having been banned from all universities in Cameroon and declared wanted." Another critic of the Yaoundé inhuman regime has catalogued, for example, the invasion of university student residential quarters by both the military and the private militias of Jean Messi – then *recteur* of Yaoundé University I – in the very early hours of 14 June 1996. By the next day (15 June), at least 800 arrests had been made, at least 100 student doors had been forcefully broken by the rector's militias with *"une violence redoubtable."*[51] If it were to depend, as usual, solely on Anglophone "politicians" or "leaders", it would all have been a different story today. That is why, for instance, the English-speaking students' first of "some pertinent questions" to their "Dear Parent[s]" is:

---

[51] Jean-François Channon, "Silence! On arrête, on moleste et on tue" *Le Messager* N° 516 (17 juin 1996), 8. See also "We Are Going to Return Home and Continue the Struggle for Students Rights – Exiled Cameroonian Student Leaders" *The Herald* N° 389 (29 November-1 December 1996), 6; and Ekinneh Agbaw-Ebai, "University Crisis: Soldiers Clash Again with Students" *The Herald* N° 313 (23-26 May 1996), 1.

> Tell us why for 25 years, the number of Francophone Cameroonians granted government scholarships yearly to study in France alone far exceeds the total number of scholarships awarded to English[-s]peaking Cameroonians to study abroad. We have the statistics – see Cameroon Tribune of 19th and 20th August 1985. This year [1985] 8 new scholarships have been awarded to Anglophones to study in Britain, 8 in Nigeria (one [of] whom is a francophone), 1 in Liberia and 1 in Sierra Leone, making a total of 18. Whereas there are 1,000 (one thousand) scholarships granted to Francophone students to study in France, Belgium, etc. The Francophones will tell you [that] most of your children will be given scholarships after the G.C.E. "A" Level results are published. Last year [1984], 50 were granted these scholarships and even if the figures were doubled (to be doubted) that would be nothing compared to the 1,000. [Students' Letter, 1985]

Having posed 17 questions in all, the students made it clear that there was "SO MUCH UNANSWERED AND YET SO MUCH UNASKED" before concluding that

> These are not things that can be left forever unnoticed. Even the blind man when he stumbles against an obstacle here and [there often] shouts, or warns, or pleads so that those with whom he lives can see that such obstacles do not reoccur. We gladly accept to be the heirs of your toil and sweat. You shall know, however, that the peace of the Cameroon we are set to inherit is quite unguaranteed [Students' Letter, 1985].

I think all what these students are asking for is genuineness in making them 'civilized'. Is there any justification for brutalizing these young people for wanting to be civilized?

Young English-speaking Cameroonian students have, since 1985, been adamantly bent – like the University Students

Association of East Africa (USAEA) – on "succeed[ing] where our politicians have so far failed [in becoming civilized]" (Southall, 1974: x n.6). As Bayles has also put it,

> Civilization or, to say the same thing, education is the taming or domestication of the soul's raw passions – not suppressing or excising them, which could deprive the soul of its energy – but forming and informing them as art. A man [or woman] whose noblest activities are accompanied by a music that expresses them while providing a pleasure extending from the lowest bodily to the highest spiritual, is whole, and there is no tension in him [or her] between the pleasant and the good.[52]

What this education and human rights expert is saying is simply the call for self-control in politics. To Frantzi also, the issue of human rights abuse and advocacy advances the imperative of educating children in a democratic way for humanistic growth. John Dewey based his philosophy of education on the belief that humans and their surroundings are living in unity, within a transactional process. Alienation and dehumanization appear when people cannot see this unity in their every thought and action, but set the dualisms of 'I-You', 'Us-Them'.[53]

The Cameroon leadership is not totally ignorant of the plain fact that self-control is a necessity for liberalism and democracy. "The history of mankind", they have pointed out in Biya's (1986: 113) political blueprint,

---

[52] Martha Bayles, "Body and Soul: The Musical Miseducation of Youth" 131 *The Public Interest* (1998), 36-49 at 39.

[53] Katerina K. Frantzi, "Human Rights Education: The United Nations Endeavour and the Importance of Childhood and Intelligent Sympathy" 5:1 *International Education Journal* (2004), 1-8 at 1.

reminds us of the close relations which have always existed between liberalism and democracy. We see liberalism in every attempt by people to regain their freedom restricted by the feudal [and/or dictatorial] system. Liberalism is thus a political and social philosophy whose main concern is Man, better still, the individuality of Man.

That is very well said. But all their declarations in this regard are meaningless or simply confusing because the same politicians making them do not only refuse to adhere to them but also starkly lack self-control. For further illustration, the Cameroonian students (especially the English-speaking ones) have been demanding nothing more than educational conditions that are "firmly rooted in their culture" (in the words of section 5(1) of the Education Law itself) through the creation and diversification or decentralization of universities; a process that, for linguistically raven societies like Belgium, Canada, Cameroon, and Switzerland, absolutely demands the federal structure. The Belgians, as portrayed by the specialists,[54] realized the idiocy of the unitary centralized state in their case and their leaders effected change accordingly.

In Africa, on the other hand, the administration's response to popular demands is, as usual, only to utilize *la politique du gros baton* (Big Stick Politics) and the politics of decreed peace. Because of this 'Big Stick' politics, on Cameroonian university campuses these days, Kameni posits, one would find 'everywhere police officers, both in uniform and in civilian attire, who are permanently stationed there'.[55] The presence, on university

---

[54] See Richard Cullen, "Adaptive Federalism in Belgium" 13 *University of New South Wales Law Journal* (1990): 346; A. Allen, *Treatise on Belgian Constitutional Law* (Denventer: Kluwer Law and Taxation Publishers, 1992); and J.H. Crabb, *The Constitution of Belgium and the Belgian Civil Code* (Littleton: Fred B. Rothman and Co, 1982).

[55] "*Partout, des policiers tant en tenue qu'en civils…qui y stationne en permanence.*" Tientcheu, Kameni, "Douala: chasse à l'étudiant sur le campus" *Le Messager* (6 juin

campuses, of heavily armed gendarmes[56] has led some critics to the pathetic yet convincing thesis that "[i]n Cameroon, the unique nation of advanced democracy, university students' fear of the gendarme is the beginning of wisdom. Each time there is slight disagreement between the acad[emic] authority and students, the impulse of the former is to rush to arms, to call the gendarmes with their smoking guns to *solve* problems which otherwise ought to be approached and solved in the civilized manner only academics can."[57]

The issues also being evoked here are tied, for instance, to the question of decreeing institutions as universities but not also taking the pains to have them recognized by other similar institutions in the international community – a recognition that is strictly bound to standards of excellence. No longer, it has been suggested, can any nation still be affording not to take the education of its youths seriously. As McMaster University president and vice-chancellor has stated,

> At the risk of offending some of my academic colleagues, I believe education *is* a business. Our 'business' is research, education and scholarship. Our 'product' is knowledge. And our 'customers' are the students, their parents, our graduates, business and government, Canada [or Cameroon] and the world. They demand and deserve outstanding scholars and teachers, innovative programs, relevant research, and a

---

1996), 8. See also David Acha, "Is UB Really Worth the Place to Be?" *The Herald* (12-13 February 1997), 4 (also condemning "the type of administrative machinery put in place there" as responsible for police presence on the 'Anglo-Saxon' University of Buea campus).

[56] Channon describes it as *"la présence des gendarmes armés jusqu'aux dents sur le campus."* Jean-François Channon, "Université de Yaoundé I: des affrontements en perspectives" *Le Messager* (17 juin 1996), 8.

[57] Cameroon Post Editorial, "Njeuma, Endeley, Please Eat Humble Pie" *Cameroon Post* (11-18 December 1996), 2 (emphasis is original).

commitment to excellence in everything we do.[58]

Each and every university, no matter where found, has to compete with the others on an equal footing. The scholarship and learning business, according to the Chancellor of Victoria University in British Columbia, Canada (Frye, 1985: 32), is one that knows no peripheries because the education market functions like all other aspects of the market since "Every university is fighting on the same front line, whatever its morale. A line of defence against Soviet missiles will be out of date long before it is built, but education's line of defence is never out of date, and it runs as directly through this community as it does through every community."

I wonder how Africa's universities hope to survive this market's pressures when their students' fear of the men and women in uniform has become the beginning of wisdom; and when there is a staggering lack of law reporting, of academic journals and well-stocked libraries.[59] Anyangwe (1987: 260) points out that "At the moment there is no consistent and efficient law reporting in Cameroon. There is no official policy concerning law reporting. There is no law reporting council. It is clear that in a situation like this each court remains in cloistered ignorance of decisions of the other court. In these circumstances even a loose system of judicial precedent cannot properly operate." It is simply amazing, as Mbuy (1996) regrets, that, while other nations have been taking their education very seriously, "here in Cameroon we play the drunkard in a sinking boat and go to shooting the best captains sometimes at the instigation of the very opponent we have to play our [education] match against.

---

[58] Peter George, "The Roots of a Great University" *Canadian Business* (December 1996), 78.

[59] See Peter Ateh-Afac Fossungu, "On the Lack of Academic Journals in Cameroon: Salute to *Juridis Périodique*" *The Herald* N° 612 (27-28 May 1998), 4.

What [a] folly!" This craziness is also seen in the sphere of decreeing peace.

As it often happens, where the smoking guns fall short of their targets most African regimes usually follow up with decreed peace, thus puzzling a lot of people as to whether peace can be decreed.[60] Fonkeng (1990: 'Preface and Thanks', paragraph 2) has even castigated this confusing

> 'peace', 'stability' and what have you, which are only too readily sold to and bought by the rest of the world. While internally, any vocal attempt to decry the process of elimination of the linguistic identity of the minority (who make up twenty-five per cent of the population) has been condemned as 'subversive', a charge almost synonymous to that levied against murderers.

Despite the 'smoking guns' and the 'decreeing of peace' solutions, the student *parlement* stood firm as a single force and consequently 'gave' Cameroon the six hurriedly decreed universities (see Chapter 4) largely because, as Dr. Mbangwana of the Department of English at the University of Douala has been cited by Bangsi (1997) as ably theorizing, "you cannot speak of peace when you have not created conditions necessary to bring about such peace." That is precisely the more reason why parents of the students have to provide acceptable answers to their '17 pertinent questions'. These students cannot comprehend why they cannot be given satisfactory answers and would seem to have already made up their decision as to what to do.

It is for these reasons that we say that the peace of the Cameroon we are set to inherit is quite unguaranteed. For, if there is no permanent solution to the sectoral injustice and

---

[60] See Augustin Kiteh, "Can Internal Peace Be Decreed?" *The Herald* N° 452 (30 April-1 May 1997), 4.

economic deprivation that we witness today, if there is no end to the assimilation destined towards us in guise of integration, we, your children, assure you that sooner or later we shall smear the homes, streets, and gardens of this nation with blood. We won't accept to be eternally stigmatized as second class citizens, nor shall we want to be deprived of the cultural heritage which is ours and which we recognize is of greater significance around the globe. So we shall fight for the justice we cannot otherwise have [Students' Letter, 1985].

That is how the regime throws into the dustbin the true solution which is federalism within which each national group would be able to develop and foster its own unique characteristics to the fullest; preferring to disunite by forcefully uniting. All this occurs largely because of the historyless political science that was exhibited in 1961 in Foumban where federalism was grossly distorted. Yet it is being claimed in the various secession theses that a solid rights-respecting federation was created there. The preventable camouflage in Foumban largely explains the existing gross human rights abuses that are characteristic of Africa's leader, Cameroon – a human rights record that has kept worsening until it now "stinks like a garbage wagon... [with] psychopaths like Oben Ashu as governor... [and] the security forces [who] can shoot citizens for breakfast, lunch and supper, and go scot free."[61] To emphasize the point, all this

---

[61] Charly Ndi Chia, "Francis Nkwain: The Fall of a Lyrical Warrior" *The Post* N° 0040 (23 December 1997), 7. See also "Country Report on Human Rights Practices for 1997 – Cameroon January 30, 1998" *The Herald* N° 569 (9-10 February 1998), 6; Jean-François Channon, "Grève à l'Université de Yaoundé I: Mgr. Zoa prend position" *Le Messager* N° 508 (23 mai 1996), 9; Alain Bengono, "Assassinat de Betsogo Faustin: Mgr. Jean Zoa se déchaine contre la barbarie du régime de Yaoundé" *L'Expression* N°.93 (21 fevrier 1997), 10; Kum Set Ewi, "Cardinal Tumi Warns Politicians Against Violation of Human Rights" *The Herald* N°.553 (31 December-4 January 1998), 2; Asong Ndifor, "U.S. Nails Cameroon in Newly Issued Human Rights Report" *The Herald* N° 569 (9-10 February 1998), 1; Boniface Forbin, "Human Rights Abuse: Can We Set an Example?" *The Herald* N° 369 (14-

would happen because federalism in Cameroon was not sought for its proper raison d'être: special protection of human rights. Yet, some scholars have taken up as profession the presentation

---

15 October, 1996), 4; The Post Editorial, "Time to Check the Brutality of Security Forces" *The Post* (24 October 1997), 4; Pegue Manga and Midiatress Musi, "The Menace of Security Forces in Our Streets" *The Post* (24 October 1997), 9; Nyenty Egbeachang, "Limbe: Taxi Drivers Stand Up to Police Extortion" *The Post* N° 0067 (8 May 1998), 6; Hamadian Hamza, "Ngaoundéré Security Forces Warned to Stop Arbitrary Arrests" *The Herald* N° 421 (17-18 February 1997), 3; Suleiman Mohammed, "The Police Force and the Public" *The Herald* N° 326 (5-7 July 1996), 4; and Christel Ebenson, "The Public Increasingly Scorns Our Police Force" *L'Effort Camerounais* N° 82 (15-22 octobre 1997), 6.

Cameroon's poor human rights record simply knows no bounds and can also be seen in the countless open letters from concerned individual foreigners to its administration (President Biya, his ministers of justice, of internal security, and of territorial administration) on human rights violation. See, e.g., T. Andrew Hicks [U.S], "Open Letter to Luc Loé on Torture and Repression in the North West" *The Herald* N° 478 (June 30-1 July 1997), 4; Brian Brewer [Hong Kong], "Letter to President Biya" *The Herald* N° 472 (16-17 June 1997), 4; Daniel T. Quilty [U.S.], "Letter to Luc Loé" *The Herald* N° 470 (11-12 June 1997), 4; Sir Roger Young [U.K.], "Message to Biya From the U.K." *The Herald* N° 563 (26-27 January 1998), 4; Barbro Gabrielsson [Sweden], "Political Victimisation in Cameroon Again!" *The Herald* N° 551 (24-28 December 1997), 4; J.G. Robinson [Great Britain], "Letter to Biya on Human Rights Abuse" *The Herald* N° 526 (27-28 October 1997), 4; Mirjam Pressler [Germany], "Open Letter to Luc Loé" *The Herald* N° 468 (6-8 June 1997), 4, & "Letter to Andzé Tsoungui on Torture of Detainees" *The Herald* N° 515 (26-28 September 1997), 4; M. Otter [England], "Letter to Biya on the Awful Treatment of Detainees" *The Herald* N° 513 (22-23 September 1997), 4; Nagaiko Ando [Japan], "Biya and Detention Without Trial" *The Herald* N° 572 (16-17 February 1998), 4; Amnesty International Group Italy 5, "Letter to Biya on Continuous Detention of Citizens" *The Herald* N° 510 (15-16 September 1997), 4; Louise Jameson [England], "Free Njawé – Britain Joins the Chorus" *The Herald* N° 572 (16-17 February 1998), 4; Dr. K. Schmidt [Germany], "Laurent Esso, Justice Delayed is Justice Denied" *The Herald* N° 557 (12-13 January 1998), 4; Dr. A.R. Moore [Great Britain], "Letter to President Biya on Ill-Treatment of Detainees" *The Herald* N° 474 (20-22 June 1997), 4; Anja Niederhauser [Switzerland], "...And to President Biya" *The Herald* N° 466 (2-3 June 1997), 4; Dan Tsai [Taiwan], "Letter to President Biya" *The Herald* N° 465 (30 May-1 June 1997), 4; Gabriella Saibene [U.K.], "Letter to President Biya" *The Herald* N° 469 (9-10 June 1997), 4; Levina Vuyk [The Netherlands], "Are Cameroonian Authorities Shame-Proof?" *The Herald* N° 624 (24-25 June 1998), 4; and Peggiy Duthie [USA], "For the Sake of Cameroon's Image Abroad" *The Herald* N° 624 (24-25 June 1998), 4. The list can never be completed but I think these few letters from abroad can begin to tell the Cameroon human rights story well enough.

of the contrary, namely, that the Foumban constitutional arrangement instituted lots of human rights guarantees and special protection of the minority in a 'perfect nation'.

Chapter 2

The Perfect Nation is an Anathema to Multiculturalism

> Despite our country's immense economic potentials, material comfort is still the prerogative of a privileged minority, while poverty is the lot of the majority of Cameroonians.... such injustice existed and is still widespread in our society, leading to a great deal of frustration and eventual resignation [Biya, 1986: 10-11].

The President cannot be seriously regretting the existence of these forms of injustice in the Cameroonian society when he is tenaciously clinging to the root cause of the same – the perfect nation. On 6 November 1982 Biya, who since 1975 was President Ahidjo's Prime Minister, became the president of Cameroon by virtue of a constitutional amendment of 29 May 1979. As constitutional historians like Delancey (1989, 70) would put it, after having swiftly abolished the prime minister post through which he became president, "Biya also changed the name of the country to the Republic of Cameroon, claiming that this symbolized greater unity than the previous United Republic of Cameroon. There was, he said, only one Cameroon people, so there was nothing left to be united." The first and most important consequence to be drawn from this theory is that the president at that date had his long-sought perfect nation. Biya's (1986: 27-30) 'Perfect Nation' is clearly against multiculturalism since it is specifically defined by the POR at page 29 as "The nation... [which] is characterized by a partial or total combination of certain specific material and spiritual elements which reinforce its homogeneity and its members' awareness of unity. It is a union of communities with one race, language, territory, economic life and history." This is a type of nation that, for a diverse society like Cameroon, obviously excludes (1) the normal democracy and collective participation, ushering in (2) Kontchoumeterized participation, and (3) a new kind of 'pluralistic democracy' (discussed in Chapter 3).

(The Usual) Democracy and Collective Participation

The two are intertwined but for convenience I will first briefly survey democracy before seeing if there is collective participation in Cameroon, as claimed. Democracy has been found by both de Jorge (1993: 304, 301-302, & 306) and Biya (1986: 36) to have some universal characteristics. Based on the realization of this universality, the various forms of democracy have been briefly surveyed by the *Encyclopedia Britannica* and other writers like Archer and Reay[62] who have advanced and described these four variants: direct democracy, representative democracy, economic democracy, and liberal or constitutional democracy. It is the last kind that is currently in vogue and fits into the question at hand. Liberal or constitutional democracy is a form of government, usually a representative democracy, in which the powers of the majority are exercised within a framework of constitutional restraints designed to guarantee all citizens individual and collective rights (such as equality, freedom of speech and of religion).

As Riemer (1983:121) further explains, while some of the ideals of liberal democracy may change in both theory and practice, certain fundamentals will remain the same (the universal features). Its persistent democratic ingredients include (i) popular rule, (ii) freedom, and (iii) equality; while the persistent liberal ones include (a) constitutionalism, (b) protection of basic rights,

---

[62] See *The New Encyclopaedia Britannica* Volume 4, 15th ed. (Chicago: Encyclopaedia Britannica Inc, 2002) at 5; and Peter Archer and Lord Reay, *Freedom at Stake* (London: The Bodley Head, 1966) at 163-64.

and (c) political and economic competition and free choice both at the ballot box and in the marketplace. Riemer (*ibid*) adds that f actor (c) here has changed from a laissez-faire position to one that favours government intervention in the interest of the public welfare, social justice, and fair play. These requirements could partly explain why most genuine democracies of today do have some form of Bill of Rights (like the USA's) and Charter of Rights and Freedoms like Canada's *The 1982 Canadian Charter of Rights and Freedoms*, Part I of the *Constitution Act, 1982*, being Schedule B to the *Canada Act 1982* (U.K.), 1982, C.11; and *The Charter of Paris for a New Europe*.

It was to take care of the problems of (cultural and ethnic) minorities, for example, that liberal or constitutional democracy has come to prevent the tyranny of the majority by requiring that the powers of the majority be exercised within a framework of constitutional restraints designed to guarantee all citizens individual and collective rights. Politicians and scholars from this type of democracy have hardly spared the minute in reminding themselves of this plain fact. In his 1985 address to scholars at the University of Toronto, Canada, Chicago historian, William McNeil (cited in Driedger, 1989: 3), clearly stated that poly-ethnicity is normal in civilized societies, whereas the ideal of one ethnically unitary state was exceptional in theory and rarely approached in practice. Marginality and pluralism were and are the norms of civilized existence. Canada's Prime Minister Trudeau, cited in Driedger (1989: 192), could not also pass by without warning that a nationalistic government is by nature intolerant, discriminatory, and, when all is said and done, totalitarian. A truly democratic government, to him, cannot be nationalist, because it must pursue the good of all its citizens, without prejudice to ethnic origin.

This means that the "perfect nation" seekers must have to be constantly told in Day's strong terms that if the State is held to be an absolute entity, and the repository and first source of all authority, power, right and privilege (as is currently in

Cameroon), its acts will be deemed to be above judgment; its final purpose will be posited as its own selfish interest – as race was for German Nazism, as Nation was for Italian Fascism, and as Economic Community was for Russian Communism.[63] In constantly telling them all this is to say that they must adopt a different state-governing strategy that protects human rights and is inclusive, not exclusive. One time Quebec Premier, Lucien Bouchard, is also known to have told 1,800 Péquistes (members of the *Parti Québécois*) in a 45-minute speech opening the party's biennial policy convention how "We must illustrate in policies and in our programs a plan for a country that is inclusive and tolerant [because] We are the government of all Quebecers and we will not turn our backs on a single citizen."[64] Not turning "our backs on a single citizen" would mean that every citizen counts.

Every citizen can only properly count in a multicultural society if we strictly follow Trudeau's advice that every region and national group be assured a wide range of authority and fields to enable it develop its national characteristics to the fullest. The true solution then is federalism, the best state form through which Prime Minister Pierre-Elliott Trudeau (as cited in Driedger, 1989: 192) thinks

> We must [necessarily] separate once and for all the concepts of State and of Nations, and make Ca[meroon] a truly pluralistic and polyethnic society. Now in order to do so, the different regions within the country must be assured a wide range of local autonomy, such that each national group... may be able to develop the body of laws and institutions essential to the fullest expression and development of its national

---

[63] F.D. Day, *Criminal Law and Society* (Springfield, Illinois: C.C. Thomas, 1964) at 32.

[64] Philip Authier, "Bouchard Calls for Tolerance: Economy First" *Montreal Gazette* (23 November 1996), A1 at A11.

characteristics.

That is the proper diagnosis to the problem because a country after all, Trudeau has declared in closing up his sane and persuasive stand, is not something you build as the pharaohs built the pyramids, and then leave standing there to defy eternity. A country is something that is built every day out of certain basic shared values. And so it is in the hands of every Cameroonian to determine how well and wisely they shall build the country of the future.[65] But would the Cameroon regime that is plagued with lots of *Kontchoumeters* learn anything from Canada?

Kontchoumeterized Collective Participation and the Case of The Educational Systems

The perfect nation has always been found hiding under the cover of national unity in Africa. For instance, Enonchong (1967: xiv), in his "Preface" directs his "immense" appreciation to Dr. Foncha (who, with Ahidjo, fabricated the FRC)

> for writing the laudable foreword for this first edition of the work. Both for his keen interest in the unity of the nation and preservation of its democratic institutions and his constant plea for justice as the rock-foundation of peace, coupled with his progressive views on what educated citizens should be, cannot be overemphasized.

It thus appears not to be by accident or inadvertence that Enonchong's (1967: i) book, which is dedicated "To the Cause of Cameroon Unity and Democratic Federalism," does employ *National Federal Assembly* (NFA) throughout: despite the fact that the Federal Constitution itself talks of the *Federal National*

---

[65] Pierre-Elliott Trudeau, *Memoirs* (Toronto: McClelland and Stewart Inc., 1993) at 366.

Assembly (FNA), for instance, in articles 15, 16, 19, 20, etc.; and *The Federal Legislature* in its Title IV (articles 16-22).

I do believe that genuine federalists will always put the federation (that is, what it is adopted to promote: unity in diversity) before all else, including the uniformization being euphemistically called 'national unity' (diversity in unity, otherwise known as the 'New Ethnic Group' – see Chapter 3). This would explain why such federalists would always refer to an institution as the one in question simply as the Federal Parliament. Or, if they must employ the word 'national', they would prefer to talk of Federal National Assembly (FNA) and not National Federal Assembly (NFA). The preferred appellation of FNA is not only because there are other effective non-federal 'parliaments' (legislatures or legislative assemblies) in the Union. By FNA, federalists are putting the emphasis on the federation. National unity thus passes through the federation, and not vice versa. NFA stands for just the reverse: 'federation' passing through national unity; thus, in a peculiar fashion, "justifying" the anti-human rights and undemocratic Cameroon Unitary 'democratic federal' arrangements under question. A democratic federalism punctuated in article 15 by open-ended emergency powers in the hands of the President of 'Federal' Republic of Cameroon, who sees only the assimilation of the English-speaking citizens as national unity. Yet, they would be talking of (1) self-determination and (2) educational biculturalism.

Minority Politics and Self-Determination in a Unitary Centralized State?

To the Ahidjo-Biya administrations, federalism, designed for self-determination within the state, according to Biya (1986: 30) is "the most effective vector of political destabilisation" used against ethnically diverse states like Cameroon and, therefore, is unacceptable since it is another name for secession – a threat to national unity. Biya (1986: 18) has further argued that there is even no need for federalism (the vehicle or channel for self-determination) since the Cameroon people are already having more than enough "opportunities to exercise their right to self-determination" in Biya's (1986: 46, emphasis added) 'modern Cameroon' that is

> *a serene and disciplined community*, solidly based on the dual principles of *respect for majority decisions* in the freely established hierarchy between the organs and the members, and the protection of the minority which, although momentarily in disagreement with the majority, still continues to enjoy the same rights and obligations.

Majority rule is not absolute in a liberal or constitutional democracy, which usually takes the federal form for diverse societies. It is not clear (absent confusion) why anyone should be talking of the respect of minority rights in the first place when the "majority" *must always* prevail. This is the zenith of the *Political Master Plan of Assimilation* (that has been shown to have been clearly known to 'inner circle' Anglophones before and in Foumban, part and parcel of which also includes Premier Amadou Ahidjo's (Biya's predecessor) philosophy of the Francophone majority 'dealing' with the Anglophone minority on a "footing of equality".

Talking about the suspected conspiracy for the annexation of the Southern Cameroons at the 4th Committee of the 13th Session of the United Nations General Assembly in February 1959 (this February again!), Amadou Ahidjo of *La République du Cameroun* is quoted by the Independence Proclamation (1999) as having declared that "we do not wish to bring the weight of our population on the Anglophones. We are not annexationists, in other words, if our brothers of the British zone wish to unite with an independent Cameroon, we are ready to discuss the matter with them, but we will discuss on a footing of equality." Brotherhood has always been the magic word with the Foumban actors only and until their ulterior goals are attained. Isn't this speech very purposefully philosophical? And isn't it just as vague as the phrase 'an intellectual in politics'? I pose all these questions because it can be, and has been, strenuously argued that '*bringing the weight of our population on the Anglophones*' is exactly what the Francophone leaders have done in order to opt out of the federation (if a true federation it was indeed) and into the unitary assimilationist state: by having East Cameroonian participation in the 1972 referendum on the basis of one-person-one-vote and thereby 'drowning the voices of West Cameroonians' who were against the change. This would not be the case in a true federation as I have already stressed.

But could this one-person-one-vote application in the 1972 referendum not be part and parcel of Mr. Ahidjo's 'footing of equality' that he gave to the unwary Anglophones through the UN General Assembly in February 1959? Ahidjo's arguments could now run like this: "You want equality and you get unqualified equality (or equality in vague terms) which you happily accept and embrace. Then when unqualified equality starts being applied, you start to complain: what is actually wrong with you Anglo-Fools?" The Anglo-Fools can then only retort: Only France's fools (or those who "under the French did not really free themselves from France"[66] because of their sheepish

---

[66] Enoh Meyomesse, cited in Larry Eyong, "Enoh Meyomesse: Jailed for Truth or Theft?" [On File with Author, received through email on Wednesday, December 28, 2011]. As some critics also put it, "[a] certain infantile attachment between La République du Cameroun and France persists which is completely disgusting to Southern Cameroonians and which is responsible in part for the rift between Southern Cameroons and La République du Cameroun. Former British colonies are not perfect and many of them such as Nigeria, Ghana, Uganda, etc. have had major goofs since independence but they are still ahead of the French neocolonies because those goofs were their own and they have learned from the experience. As things stand, we do not know when the French neocolonies will crawl, talk le[ft alone] walk." SCFAQ (Question 37).

belief in the doctrine of "Join me, and you're like me"[67]) would think that self-determination is a possibility in a unitary centralized State with a Supreme-Majority.

Furthermore, could it not also be argued that the 1972 referendum was what Hogg (1996: 125-27) would see as 'secession by amendment' on the part of both East Cameroun and West Cameroon? In view of the fact that the Foumban 'intellectuals in politics' did not create a "true federation" that would have impeded secession (as theorized by Stevenson, 1989: 8-9), this secession-by-amendment argument would seem to be quite plausible in Cameroon: except that both entities never became two separate countries thereafter. Otherwise, why is West Cameroon still trying to 'secede' from East Cameroon today if the latter is said to have seceded 'by unilateral act' from the FRC in 1984? Secession by amendment is thus out of the equation; leaving us with change by means provided by the constitution itself. And did the Federal Constitution's means of change protect the minority as claimed? It did not at all, especially in view of its article 15 I have just mentioned above (open-ended emergency powers to the president). I am working on a separate contribution that elaborately examines this claim of the minority's protection under the Foumban Constitution in the context of Federalism, separation of powers, and constitutionalism in Africa.

Nevertheless, some of these people in power in Africa have to be specifically directed to study treatises such as Commager's (1958) as well as de Smith's (1964).[68] By the way, if the Biya administration is so interested in the *respect for majority decisions*, why is Mr. Biya still the President of the Republic of Cameroon

---

[67] Le Vine (1986: 163). Most of the French-speaking "intellectuals in politics" are even fascinated by the argument of Cameroon's one-time external Affairs minister that "The dog of the King is the king of dogs." Ferdinand Oyono, *Houseboy* [translated from French by John Read] (London: Heinemann, 1966) at 24.

[68] See Stanley A. de Smith, "Federalism, Human Rights, and the Protection of Minorities" in David P. Currie (ed.), *Federalism and the New Nations of Africa*, University of Chicago Press (1964) 279-341.

when the overwhelming majority of Cameroonians have on several occasions voted him out, as shown by French (1997), Konings and Nyamnjoh (1997: 214-216), and others[69]? And yet they would be talking of democracy? There is just no point in bragging about majority rule *only* in situations where it would mean oppression. But that is precisely what "advanced democracy" is all about – advancing before democracy in order to preclude the latter's birth and growth. It does explain why since 1982 Biya has been in power whereas during that same period the United States of America has had five presidents, with most of them having been re-elected for a second four-year term; France (itself that is propping them up and forcing all these dictators on Africans) has had four presidents; and Ghana in Africa has seen four presidents. So just tell me how Ghanaians are ever going to give even an iota of one ear to Cameroon's talk of African unity when the 'advanced' President Biya talking to them is equal to four plus of their presidents? And when, moreover, they can see the very shabby way Biya treats the English-speaking in Miniature Africa?

The best (and most enjoyable) way to learn, according to an expert on comparative government (Magstadt, 1991: 4), is to engage in lively, informal discussions with peers. That's just what educated citizens in ancient Greece and colonial America did, with results that left an indelible imprint on world history. Has the Cameroon leadership engaged (or would they even countenance engaging) in such dialogue with their 'across-the-Atlantic' peers? They have not and would not, most probably because they cannot have anything to talk about in the first place

---

[69] "They have disenfranchised us by not registering us. They have manipulated the electoral register, refused to issue cards to the few they registered, and finally refused proclaiming the results as they were. Mr. Chairman you said during the last rally in Bamenda that you will set the pace for new democracy in Africa and Mr. Biya too is setting the pace for his own sterile democracy. What was the need for this election when they can't accept the verdict of the ballot box?" Cosmas K. Keba, "Fru Ndi, What Next?" *The Herald* N° 471 (13-15 June 1997), 4.

since their governmental variant is not at all listed in the recognized books of democracy. The Yaounde regime (with its unlisted 'advanced democracy' instead has something else to say in response to Canada's governors; namely, that there is collective and noble participation in the nation-building task on their own side of the wide Atlantic separating the democracies. Is that really it?

The Cameroon administration is littered with lots of lies-fabricating machines or *Kontchoumeter*s. As Tegha has proceeded to explain this italicized advanced democracy term, "[w]ords ending in 'meter', for example, thermometer, barometer, hydrometer, voltammeter, are scientific devices or instruments used for measuring various things passing through those various instruments. *Kontchoumeter* is also a scientific device or instrument used for measuring the magnitude or the number of lies that is coming from government through its presumptuous spokesman, Augustin Kontchou."[70] This *Kontchoumetered* regime is obviously out of touch for thinking that the will of the Cameroon people is important in the building of Cameroon's confusing 'serene-and-disciplined' national unity. They do think these citizens do matter a lot, the more reason why Cameroon, according to them, is legally and practically a bicultural society (as indicated in 1996 Constitution, article 1(3)), being the work of each and every Cameroonian. According to Biya (1986: 111-112), "Indeed, national unity constitutes the mainstay of this [administration's] action which, to me, ought to be a collective venture because it

---

[70] Epo Joseph Tegha, "Kontchoumeter Spawns Lies Again" *The Herald* N° 470 (11-12 June 1997), 4 Almost everyone seems to know this minister-*porte parole* as the best liar in the entire country (*"meilleur menteur de la République"*). Antoine Marie Zanga Zanga, "La nouvelle carte du gouvernement post-électoral se dessine" *Le Quotidien* (27 octobre 1997), 2-3 at 2. Others like Nouwou have described him as 'the devil's advocate' (*'l'avocat des mauvaises causes'*) who never 'spares the chance to abuse the intelligence of those listening to him or his audience' (*'manquer de choquer l'intelligence de ceux qui le regardaient et qui l'écoutaient, en le subissant'*). David Nouwou, "Conférence de presse du Mincom: Kontchou nargue les Camerounais comme toujours" *L'Expression* N° 175 (22 septembre 1997), 9.

can be nothing but collective. The concern for concerted and noble action to be conducted with due respect for the originality and dignity of each and every one is one of the aspects of communal liberalism." It is not clear if this is confusion or straightforward talk; but some experts like Appiagyei-Atua (1999: 97-104) have already offered an elaborate critique of Political Participation among 'Civil Society' in (Neo)Colonial Africa, a conspicuous portion of which Cameroon is.

The Biya administration would still be disputing with the experts by claiming that simply because they have been very vaguely invited "To build a modern Cameroon [which] is a lofty and noble task" (Biya, 1986: 12), Cameroonians, without distinction, are *all* fully participating in the nation-building task. As Biya (1986: 139) thus claims, "I do not think and how could I ever think that there are two categories of Cameroonians: ....There is no doubt that the recent past of our country has left the regrettable impression that some Cameroonians were excluded from any real participation in the political life of the country, while a certain class was considered more suitable." This is precisely what Konings and Nyamnjoh (1997:224) would be condemning when they state that "Attempts have often been made to minimalise the Anglophone-francophone divide by emphasising that this did not exist during the German colonial era. At present, Cameroon is officially a bilingual and multi-cultural nation, which many regard as a safe guarantee for the preservation of its differential linguistic and cultural heritage" It is, moreover, hard for one not to doubt how exactly the "regrettable impression" has now changed; and how the Cameroon people are actually having "greater opportunities" of self-determining when the biting 'Anglophone Problem' must be sidestepped at all cost and some funny concept of 'minority protection' invented for the purpose in article 57(3) the 1996 Constitution. For better comprehension of the confusion, it is important then that I discuss (1) the minority exchange, and (2) minority territory and population.

The Minority Exchange

The numerous misleading theses in Cameroon on the concepts tied to multiculturalism are nothing but part of the generalized confusion in the country; a confusion that is also responsible for hiding itself to many of the people who have attempted to diagnose its engendered problems, as can be deduced especially from the postulation now radiating out from the English-speaking minority that wants to secede (or has already seceded but not seceded?) from the oppressive French-speaking majority. What the minority for the purposes of this discussion that is demanding cultural protection is, is a question that would seem to be superfluous; but it is in order in Cameroon because Konings and Nyamnjoh (1997: 208) have ably theorized that

> The Government has not surprisingly devised various strategies to safeguard the unitary [mono-cultural] state, including attempts to minimalise or even deny the existence of an `anglophone problem', to create divisions among the English-speaking elite, to remunerate some allies with prestigious positions in the state apparatus previously reserved for francophones only, and to repress all actions designed to change the status of the Southern Cameroons.

True to its devilish efforts of minimalisation and denial of the mounting concerns and demands of the real minority (Southern Cameroonsians), the concept of the country's minority has had to be largely deformed in article 57(3) of the 1996 Constitution; creating even more intractable problems by ushering in the notions of *allogènes et autochtones* ('settlers' and 'indigenes') which, to the authoritarian regime, is geared toward protecting the minority.

The putting of those concepts into the constitution is in reality only a means of killing two birds (the Anglophone demands for protection and the hardworking Bamileke) with one potent stone. The Bamileke are very central to the Federalism Question in Cameroon, most of them also being 'Anglophones' or the disenfranchised so-called Eleventh-Province People (EPP). These people have been cleanly disenfranchised or stripped of citizenship because Cameroon has only ten provinces (which are now called regions by article 61 of the 1996 Constitution). As they do not belong to any known or existing Cameroonian province, are these EPPs then Cameroonian citizens? All this could be the price to pay for their love of federalism? Most French-speaking Cameroonians (especially those in power) were not at all interested in reunification and have never been fascinated with federalism mostly because of these "citizenship-less" citizens. As Johnson (1970: 49) narrates,

> The Bamileke are important to an[y] analysis of the Cameroon Federation because: (a) many Cameroonians have considered the reunification issue as essentially a Bamileke issue, (b) many Cameroonians also considered certain features of Bamileke society disagreeable, and consequently were less favourable to the idea of reunification, (c) relations between Bamileke and other groups are among the most hostile in the country, (d) much of the violence and terrorism associated with the *Union des Populations du Cameroun* (UPC) rebellion has occurred in Bamileke country.

Tixier (1974: 16) has also stated: "The most revolutionary [of the political parties] was the Cameroon Union headed by Reuben Um Nyobé of Marxist inspiration. This party, which had a well-defined structure, claimed independence and reunification of the two Cameroons. Following the bloody events of 1955, the [colonial] Government dissolved the Cameroons Union and its leaders went underground." *Upecistes* are thus members of the UPC.[71]

The "settlers" concept, as shown by Johnson (1970: 56-59), had in earlier years (even before 'independence') been used in an open attempt to boot the Bamileke out of the major cities and especially Douala (Cameroon's economic capital) where they have dominated in almost all fields. But the 'Settlers Concept' was never, until 1996, put in the constitution; the putting of which now has been categorized as lack of self-control. As critics like Eyinga (1996: 7) have then affirmed, by institutionalizing some of these things now, Mr. Biya has indeed awakened the soundly sleeping Ethnic Demon. (*"Aujourd'hui, Biya, en mettant ces choses [allogènes et autochtones] dans la constitution, franchit vraiment le Ribicon."*)

From Biya (1986: back cover), we learn that, born in February 1933 and married, with children, President Paul Biya comes from southern Cameroon where he was brought up in the Christian faith. A brilliant student, he won a scholarship to study in Paris where he obtained a Bachelor's degree, a postgraduate diploma in public law and a diploma in political science. As soon as he completed his graduate studies, he was employed at the Presidency of the Republic, first as Director of Cabinet and then as Secretary General. Appointed prime minister in 1975, he, in accordance with the Cameroon Constitution, succeeded President Amadou Ahidjo when he resigned on 6 November 1982. The stark lack of self-control in the attitude of Cameroon's administrators has not failed to drag in some very critical comments and doubts about their education. Commenting on the 'settlers' concept in article 57(3) of the 1996 Constitution that now converts some Cameroonians into 'settlers' in their own country, some critics have declared that "My conclusion from his

---

[71] A more extensive discussion of this party and its programme can be found in Richard A. Joseph, *Radical Nationalism in Cameroun: Social Origins of the U.P.C. Rebellion* (Oxford: The Clarendon Press, 1977); and Wang Sonne, "U.P.C.: 1955-1996: 41 ans de musellement et de divisions" *Le Messager* N° 542 (12 septembre 1996), 6-7.

[POR's] haughty and senseless behaviour was that spending long years in formal education systems and earning a string of academic qualifications does not necessarily make one educated, let alone gain wisdom."[72]

These critics may not be over stretching their conclusions since the worst is still to come especially as these concepts of *allogènes* and *autochtones* (like most other constitutional and legal creations in Cameroon, including educational dualism) are yet to be defined. At the moment of writing then, only the POR of Cameroon, of course, would know (as always) the actual content of "th[is] dynamic concept which I yet have to define and which embodies my image of Cameroon" (Biya, 1986: 112). The POR's real 'image of Cameroon' that is capped by undefined concepts in laws and unknown laws that are announced as coming later, as the critics have discovered, is one of creating confusion and thereby abusing human rights without raising the international dust within (sponsoring) international economic/financial circles. When there is revolution and/or division (orchestrated by disagreement over the undefined concepts) or even their semblance, good cause under the cover of national unity arises for an all-out wiping of what has so far not been systematically effaced in Cameroon.

The idea of protecting the minority from the ultimate dictatorship of the majority is quite laudable. As I have already shown above, this task is performed with the introduction of liberal or constitutional democracy. But because here in Cameroon this is not the desired goal, the regime can only be pretending to be realizing this noble goal through the sowing of wild seeds that will rather destroy the existing harmony and cooperation among Cameroonians. By and large, Ndi Chia (1995)

---

[72] Simon J.A. Mope, "So-called Settlers: The New 'Cancer' in Cameroonian Political Discourse" *The Herald* N° 447 (16-17 April 1997), 4. See also Peter Ateh-Afac Fossungu, "When Will Cameroonians Ever Grow Up?" *The Herald* N° 635 (20-21 July 1998), 19.

has posited, the protection of citizens (majority or minority) cannot be worked out by constitutions only because, without lubrication by reason, compromise, sagacity, magnanimity and the greater good, no constitution could even be worth the paper on which it is printed. Fombad (2003) says the same thing in discussing the constitutional protection of values in Africa. The Editor of *L'Effort Camerounais* also could not have put it any better.[73] The Editor of *The Herald* has then asserted that it is Mr. Biya's "government [that] must be accused of encouraging ethnic violence... Why does the government... generate unrest among its different people who have learnt to live together in harmony and self-respect? Observe how everywhere in the country different ethni[c groups] live together happily until [no-good] politicians come in with divisive ideas to create conflict."[74]

These newly introduced concepts of *allogènes* and of *autochtones*, according to Yondo Black, are indeed notions that subsequent Cameroonian governments must banish forever from the country's political discourse since ethnicity should not provide any cover behind which some officials have to hide their

---

[73] The Editor of the Catholic weekly has actually thrown more light on this "*notion d'autochtone (art.57-3) qui, certes, reste à définir, mais dont on peut déjà se demander si elle permettra à l'Etat de remplir la mission que le préambule lui assigne: 'L'Etat assure la protection des minorités et préserve les droits des populations autochtones conformément à la loi.' Bien sûr, il est louable de vouloir protéger les minorités d'une éventuelle 'dictature de la majorité', mais faut-il pour autant créer des situations acquises qui peuvent devenir des blocages à l'évolution inéluctable d'une société? La solution ne réside-t-elle pas plutôt dans l'exercice raisonné et raisonnable du pouvoir, dans la capacité des responsables à associer toutes les compétences disponibles quelles soient leurs origines? Il est vrai que cela ne se décide ni par un décret ni par une loi; il faut que chaque responsable le veuille.*" L'Effort Camerounais Editorial, "Associer toutes les compétences" *L'Effort Camerounais* N° 40 (1037) (10-23 février 1996), 1. For a further critique of the "autochtones-allogènes" ideology embedded in article 57(3), see the very instructive 'dossier' titled "Minorités, Autochtones, allogènes et démocratie" *La Nouvelle Expression* (23 mai1996). These are 28 pages of 'Dossiers & Documents' contributed by top-notch experts on the issues involved.

[74] Boniface Forbin, "North West Terrorism: Gov't Provokes Anti-Anglophone Violence" *The Herald* (18-20 April 1997), 4.

personal failures or inadequacies.[75] What is to be done to banish this regressive attitude from the Cameroons? Federalism is the way to go, according to Garga Harman Adji (president of the ADD). Azeng (1997) narrates how the ADD boss declared that "There is no way we can succeed in Cameroon if we don't go federal," adding that

> ADD's option is federalism because what we are suffering from today is tribalism and segregation. We have an initial proposal for a ten-state federation but with a possibility of merging states which share boundaries. The number of states does not necessarily have to be four, five or six as some parties are proposing. I don't know who gave them the power to determine the number. We are already used to our 10-provinces. We can maintain these provinces as states and allow them to merge if they so desire.

That is very well said and the implicating question on the power to determine the number of states would be directed particularly to the Social Democratic Front (SDF) described by Konings and Nyamnjoh (1997:216) as "the party [which] is losing its initial appeal for English-speaking Cameroonians, because of its half-hearted stand as regards the `anglophone problem'." I would go ahead and also add that it is as well because its proposed four-state federation is geared toward preventing multiculturalism,[76] refusing to recognise the more important cultural and political ties between Debundschazone and

---

[75] *"Les prochains gouvernements doivent expurger[ces concepts] de notre Constitution"* because *"La tribu ne doit pas être une 'planche de secours' pour ceux qui ont échoué dans leur démarche personnelle"* See "Un peuple qui ne renouvelle pas ses cadres est un peuple sans avenir" [- Yondo Mandengue Black], *Le Messager* (23 mai 1996), 6-7 at 6 & 7.

[76] The federation submerges the two English-speaking regions (Debundschazone and Savannazone) into two different French-speaking regions of Wourizone and Bamboutouszone, respectively. See Solomon Endali, "Is Ekindi Suffering from Political Confusion?" *The Herald* N° 327 (8-9 July 1996), 4.

Savannazone "(obviously with the South West/North West divide in mind)," to borrow from Konings and Nyamnjoh (1997:219).

One would naturally think that the biting 'Anglophone Problem' should have dominated in the 1996 Constitution. But *absolutely nothing about the issue* according to (Ofege, 1995b, original emphasis) is said in "this anti-Anglophone heathen document [that even] *forgets* to dedicate Cameroon to God." This 1996 Constitution, true to its description, has not only reaffirmed and consolidated the contested 1984 name-change in its article 1(1): "The United Republic of Cameroon shall, with effect from the entry into force of this law, be known as Republic of Cameroon (Law N° 84-1 of 4 February 1984)." This constitution has also apparently gone ahead to confuse and side-step the issue by rewarding laziness at the expense of hard work (contrary to what the 1998 Education Law, coming two years after it, would be saying in section 5(6), namely, that one of the objectives of education in Cameroon is to "cultivate the love of effort and work well done, the quest for excellence and team spirit"). According to the critics,

> Nothing in the preamble and the rest of the text even shows a remote awareness of it [i.e., the Anglophone Problem]. It has grotesquely distorted reference to the protection of minorities which instead aims at rewarding lazy land-selling natives at the expense of hard working immigrants in industrial and urban centres. Could it be that Mr. Biya is unaware of the Cameroonian situation?[77]

Ofege (1995b) has then concluded (assuming that it is ignorance

---

[77] Fohtung (1995), citing *Cameroon Post* N° 178 at 12. See also Rogers Tabe Egbe Orock, "The Indigene-Settler Divide, Modernisation and the Land Question: Indications for Social (Dis)order in Cameroon" 14:1 *Nordic Journal of African Studies* (2005), 68-78.

on his part) that "Mr. Biya ought to be told that the one minority recognized by international law as being in Cameroon is the Anglophone minority and it is not very hard for the state to protect the Anglophone minority." Knowing now what this real minority is, the next issue concerns studying its territory and population.

The Territory and Population of the Minority

If there is much confusion of what minority means in Cameroon there is even a good deal of bewilderment regarding the size or population of that minority. I will first talk about its territory before the population.

Territory

With a total size of 183,500 square miles, according to Nelson *et al* (1974: vii), Cameroon has a north-south length of 700 miles and east-west 450 miles. In its update in March 1999, *The Political Reference Almanac* (PoliSci.Com) put the land area at 183,568 square miles.[78] Some researchers like Tixier (1974: 16-17) have estimated the land area in square kilometres to be 476.000 while Peaslee (1974: 83) says it is 475,442. Southern Cameroonsian territory – current regions of North West (Savannazone) and of South West (Debundschazone) since May 1972 – would represent one-tenth of the total land area of Cameroon. With a total land area of 43,000 square kilometres, the Southern Cameroons is situated between Longitudes 8° and 12° East and between Latitudes 5° and 10° North. Southern Cameroons is located in West Africa, sharing boundaries to the west and north with the Federal Republic of Nigeria; to the east with La République du Cameroun (East Cameroun in the 1961 Federation), while the Atlantic Ocean marks its southern limits.

---

[78] *See* http://www.polisci.com/almanac/world/nation/CM.htm.

The Mungo River serves as the eastern boundary between the Southern Cameroons and La République du Cameroun.[79]

In responding to a question of Nigeria's *The Champion* newspaper seeking to know who the people of Southern Cameroons are, Stephen Joseph stated in 2005 that

> Geographically, the people of the Southern Cameroons are the people native to the southern part of the former United Nations Trust Territory of the Cameroons under United Kingdom Administration. Known internationally and internally as The Southern Cameroons, this territory is bounded on the west and north by Nigeria along the boundary alignment described in the Anglo-German boundary treaty of 1913; and on the east by the French-speaking State of *La République du Cameroun* along the line defined by various boundary treaties between Britain and France, in particular the Anglo-French boundary treaty of 1931.[80]

Addressing the concerns of some critics who see the size and geographic location of the territory as a deterrent to independence, advocates of Southern Cameroons independence like SCFAQ (Question 25) have pointed out that these factors are no impediments. The Southern Cameroons, according to them, is a lot larger in land area than Equatorial Guinea, Djibouti, Guinea-Bissau, Rwanda, Burundi, etc., to name just a few countries in mainland Africa. Its geographic location, they have concluded, is not worse than that of Togo, Benin, Malawi or Eritrea, but

---

[79] *See* 'Location' at <http://www.southerncameroons.org/index3.htm> (last visited on 14 September 2011).

[80] *Champion* newspaper (Nigeria): interview with Stephen Joseph, Moderator of the IG's Southern Cameroons Peoples Forum. The interview was published in February of 2005, found @ www.southerncameroonsig.org/2005/07/the_champion_ne.html (last visited 1 March 2011).

definitely better than that of Lesotho, Swaziland or The Gambia, yet all of these are independent countries. What is the population of the people who inhabit the territory in question?

Population

At 'federation' the population was given in article 60 of the Federal Constitution as 800,000 for West Cameroon and 3,200,000 for East Cameroon. But it is simply hard to take official figures in Cameroon without some considerable amount of scepticism: especially knowing the "secretive manner" (see Johnson, 1970:184; Konings and Nyamnjoh, 1997: 209-210 n.9: and Anyangwe, 1987: 129) through which the Federal Constitution (as all the others following it) came into being. By 1970, the population of Southern Cameroonians was estimated to constitute 20% of the entire population of close to 6 million (Tixier, 1974: 16-18; Johnson, 1970: ix). Peaslee (1974: 85) estimated the entire population to be 5,736,000 in 1969. In 1990 some researchers such as Fonkeng (1990: Preface & Thanks) would be talking of "the [anglophone] minority (who make up twenty-five per cent of the population)." SCFAQ (Question 16) posits that Southern Cameroonians "make up more than 30% of the Cameroonian population, but their participation in government has never been more than 15%." The next questions that arise have to do with (1) what we are talking of twenty-five or thirty per cent of and (2) what the Anglophone/Francophone categorization do mean in Cameroon. Take the total population first.

Because of confusion, a conflicting answer is given here despite that the experts studying the problem had up to six and more years to dig it out. In 1996, one of these painstaking findings (Eyoum'a Ntoh, 1996) said that the entire population was 13 million rascals. But another expert on Cameroon politics (Eyinga, 1996: 7) declared it in the same year to be twelve million.[81] Yet some other sources put the population at 14.31 million.[82] Even the CIA (Central Intelligence Agency) that is noted for being very accurate in and sure of its findings could only *estimate* the population of Cameroon in July 2000. Thus, in explicitly taking into account the effects of excessive mortality due to AIDS, the CIA estimated it to be 15,421,937.[83] This is not exactly the same as *PoliSci.com*'s 15,029,433. Cameroon's population as of 1st January 2010 is said to stand at 19,406,100, a figure revealed on 15 April 2010 at the Yaoundé Hilton Hotel by Yaouba Abdoulaye (Minister Delegate at the Ministry of the Economy, Planning and Regional Development).[84] Where does one actually stand with these somewhat conflicting figures? Rubin (1971: 9) appears to have summarized and settled the controversy on the country's population and size when he tersely noted that Cameroon presents unrivalled ethnic and cultural patterns "much of which is still shrouded in uncertainty."

This uncertainty is compounded, of course, by the administration's tendency to twist the facts. This facts-twisting politics is responsible, as a critical document has put it, for the mystery that surrounds the actual population of Southern Cameroonsians. As SCFAQ puts it in Question 24,

> Our population is far greater than that of many countries in Africa and the world. There are more Southern Cameroon[s]ians than Gabonese, Equato-Guineans, Central

---

[81] "*Biya ne veut pas donner l'impression qu'il céde à quoi que ce soit même si ce sont les 12 millions de Camerounais qui lui demandent. Pour lui, le pouvoir est quelque chose qui n'obéit pas aux gens. C'est quelque chose qui obéit au ciel, à la religion.*"

[82] See http://www.newafrica.com/profiles/profiles.asp?countryID (last visited in March 2010).

[83] CIA, *The World Fact Book* pp. 2-3@ <http://www.compufix.demon.co.uk/camweb>.

[84] See *Cameroon's Population Hits 19.4 million*, posted by: "achanyi abila" achristus2002@ yahoo.com. I will henceforth use the population data revealed here without further references to this email source as such.

Africans, Congolese, Gambians, Eritreans, Lesothans, Liberians, etc., to name just a few. The real population of the Southern Cameroons has always been a mystery. The numbers have been dramatically played down by the leadership of La Republique du Cameroun, to make the Southern Cameroons an insignificant minority in the union. In 1961, the Ahidjo government without explanation slashed the Southern Cameroon[s]ian population from about 1.1 million to 800,000 inhabitants. Since then population growth figures have been down-played to the extent that the Eastern and South Provinces in La Republique du Cameroun with less inhabitants than Bui division in the North West Province in the Southern Cameroons for example, each has about triple the number of Parliamentary representatives of Bui division. If we go by United Nations approved population growth rates for our region over the past 35 years, the current population of the Southern Cameroons should be between 4.3 million and 5.0 million inhabitants. This is more than the population of a host of OAU and United Nations member countries.

The twisting of facts obviously has not left out the equally important concepts of *Anglophone* and *Francophone*.

The aggravated confusion in Cameroon makes a concise census of "Anglophones", for instance, very difficult, if not impossible. In Cameroon, the 'Anglophone/Francophone' categorization has been politicized and/or deformed to the extent that, for most issues, it has nothing to do with cultural connections but with the province of origin of the ethnic group of the person concerned. By Cameroon's categorization, most Albertans and Manitobans in Canada, for instance, will be regarded today as Ontarians even as they might only have been hearing of that name (Ontario) in the air: since most of the people of those Canadian provinces are descendants of people who "migrated" from Ontario.[85] This type of categorization in Cameroon, according to Fossungu's critical report, has been greatly promoted by the French-instituted human rights violation machinery called *carte d'identité nationale* and other similar '*pièces*' in which *province d'origine* is now taken not to mean where one was born or has decided to reside in but only where the ethnic group one belongs to is territorially situated in the country. This unfortunate classification, the report concludes, has inevitably created a lot of "citizenless" citizens or what is commonly called the 'Eleventh Province People'.[86]

The Cameroonian categorization of people based on the ethnic-region of origin is one "which makes being `anglophone' more of a geographic and administrative reality than a cultural one" (Konings and Nyamnjoh, 1997: 218); and could explain the attitude of EPP politicians such as the Tiko parliamentarian who declared to a journalist that "blood is thicker than water". This man (of the Bassa ethnic group in East Cameroon) was in parliament, having been "elected" by the people of the Tiko municipality (in West Cameroon) but he spent too much of his time there only fighting for the creation of a so-called Bassa Region or Province. He gave that response when the journalist wondered if he should not rather be there fighting for the interest of those who elected him to parliament, that is, fighting for the "Anglophone Problem". So, are people like this man to be characterized as Anglophones or Francophones? Could their "belonging" to two provinces or regions (one blood, the other

---

[85] For more on this Canadian migration, *see* Bruce Hutchison, *The Unknown Country: Canada and Her People* (Toronto: Longman, Green & Co., 1943) chapter 7.

[86] Peter Ateh-Afac Fossungu, "So-Called 'Eleventh-Province People and/or Settlers'" *The Herald* (29-30 June 1998), 10. For more on this EPP (whose other recently constitutionalized name is 'Settlers') in Cameroon politics, see also Beltus Bejanga, "Position-seekers Should Be Stopped from Calling Other Cameroonians 'Settlers'" *The Herald* N° 446 (April 16-17, 1997), 6; Bonny Kfua, "Of 'Minorities' and 'Settlers'" *The Herald* (27-29 May 1996), 4; and "We Are Creating a System of Apartheid in Cameroon – Ambassador Nsahlai [an interview]" *The Herald* (16-17 June 1997), 6.

for its advantages) be the real reason for their being called the EPPs?

The 'Eleventh Province People' (EPP), SCFAQ has explained in Question 3, "are people whose parents and grandparents fled oppression in French Cameroons and settled in Southern Cameroons. The loyalty of these people [as Southern Cameroonsians] should not be called into question, but must be nurtured because Southern Cameroons has always practised acceptance of people. It was like that then and it must always be like that in the future. Witch hunts and loyalty tests are not our way." This deplorable classification and its fallout, it seems, are going to have no place in the independent Federal Republic of Southern Cameroons (FRSC) because a Southern Cameroonsian has been defined by SCFAQ (Question 2) as

> Anyone born in the Southern Cameroons or of Southern Cameroons parent(s)....Citizenship of the Southern Cameroons can also be acquired by naturalization. Immigrant residents of the Southern Cameroons who meet civil and other residency requirements can be granted Southern Cameroons citizenship. The conditions for citizenship and duties and immunities that come with it are currently being enshrined in the constitution and laws of the Southern Cameroons. Southern Cameroons citizenship is not based on language (foreign or domestic), ethnic affiliations, ethnic or national origin, race, religion, or any discriminatory factor.

Thus, anyone born in the territory will be a Southern Cameroonsian, whether or not the parents are originally from, for example, La République du Cameroon or Nigeria because SCFAQ (Question 30) posits that "Even the French could be conferred Southern Cameroons citizenship if they meet residency and other requirements." As previously said, the eleventh province people have been disenfranchised because Cameroon has only ten provinces/regions and there is no known plan for the creation of the Eleventh Province. Are the people of the non-existent Eleventh Province Cameroonians or not?

By the Cameroonian categorization, for instance, every French-speaking Canadian must be a Quebecer and all English-speaking Quebecers will similarly be non-Quebecers. Brought back to Cameroon, would the 'revealed' 1,384,286 as the population of oil-rich Debundschazone (South West), for example, be referring just to people of Debundschazonian origin or to all who are resident in Debundschazone? Revealing this population during a solemn ceremony presided by Amadou Ali (Vice Prime Minister, Minister of Justice and Keeper of the Seals), Yaouba Abdoulaye made known that "the [19.4 million given as Cameroon's] population is distributed in the ten regions [of article 61(1)] as follows": Adamawazone, 1,015,622; Bamboutouszone (West), 1,785,285; Benouezone (North), 2,050,229; Debundschazone (South West), 1,384,286; Guinean-Savannazone (East), 801,968; Logonezone (Far North), 3,480,414; Nyongzone (South), 692,142; Sanagazone (Centre), 3,525,664; Savannazone (North West), 1,804,695; and Wourizone (Littoral), 2,865,795. Once more, would the total population of both Debundschazone and Savannazone here be taken as representing people of Southern Cameroonsian origin or everyone that has taken up residence there? Reverse the argument and the question would still not have been answered. What a messy confusion that has been brought about by the facts twisting.

Whatever the facts-twisting, Cameroon's English-speaking minority (whether or not it is the twisted official 25% of the total population) still constitutes a very sizable proportion: compared to other similar recognized cultural minorities, especially those of India and Switzerland. While the influential Muslim minority in India is 11% of the population (Moosnitec, 1993: 60), in Switzerland, even the 4% Italian-speaking minority is also recognized and respected just like the other more populous German-speaking and French-speaking ones (Liebich, 1996: 11).

French Canadians (who include a sizable proportion of non-Quebecers) are only a third of the total population of Canada. As Norman Ward has indicated in the *Preface to Fourth Edition* of a renowned treatise on the Canadian government (Dawson, 1970: vii-viii),

> Almost the whole of the earlier text could have been read without giving the reader an adequate appreciation of the third of the country that is French-speaking, and the impact of that fundamental fact of Canadian politics on the country as a whole; the book was, in short, an English-Canadian version of Canadian government, and while I cannot pretend to have made it any less so, I have where possible amended the text to include references to the rest of us.

Hodgins *et al* in 1989 estimated Canada's French-speaking minority to be 33% of the population.[87] The population of powerful Quebec (including Anglophone Quebecers) out of this figure cannot be very far from the 25% that is now officially the case of Southern Cameroonians or "Anglophones" in Cameroon. Why is this sizable group (Southern Cameroonians) the most marginalized and forgotten around the world?

It is important to also quickly note and stress here that Canada has not always been what it is today – having, according to Newman (1975: 386) been almost like Cameroon in the management of its ethnic minority problems "until 1965 that the power structure of this country was examined in detail. That was the year when John Porter, the Carleton University sociologist, published his monumental *Vertical Mosaic* and banished forever from the Canadian psyche the comfortable notion that this is a

---

[87] Bruce W. Hodgins, John J Eddy, Shelagh D. Grant and James Struthers, eds., *Federalism in Canada and Australia: Historical Perspectives, 1920-1988* (Peterborough, Ontario: Frost Centre for Canadian Heritage and Development Studies, 1989) at 507.

classless (or at any rate an entirely middle-class) country." As Newman has concluded at page 390, "the Waterloo – or Vietnam – of the Canadian Establishment consisted in its failure to comprehend what had then been happening in Quebec, where a popular rage has been mistaken for a 'quiet revolution'." Yes, Canadians (English- and French-speaking) realized their errors and speedily moved toward correcting them since they have always been ready to learn.

Konings and Nyamnjoh (1997: 229) have therefore cautioned that the Government's continued denial of any `anglophone problem' in Cameroon, and its determination to defend the unitary state by all available means, including repression, could lead to an escalation of anglophone demands past a point of no return. One of the indelible imprints of learning in ancient Greece and colonial America is American federalism that has been largely regarded as an important solution to the chronic problems of secession; with David Wippman arguing that even "the international community supports as the preferred approach to resolving a number of international conflicts the adoption of federal or confederal structures that effectively confer limited independence on subnational groups."[88] As Ofege (1995b) also put it in 1995, redressing the present imbroglio in Cameroon requires an effective "Re-creat[ion of] the Anglophone State... within the Cameroon polity if Anglophones are still interested in belonging." Are Southern Cameroonsians and the Cameroon State ready to sit down and candidly talk and negotiate in the interest of the larger internationally recognized nation, bilingual and bijural Cameroon? It appears that they cannot do so in view of the regime's unending love for absolute power, as embodied in the 1996 Constitution that specialists like Mback (2007: 63-68) have simply castigated as "The Dashed Hopes of 1996." These dashed hopes could also be seen in the 1998 Education Law that

---

[88] Cited in Fédérick Charette, *Les driots collectifs – de quel droit?* (Thèse de Doctorat, Université de Montréal, 1996) at 204 n.30.

incessantly preaches biculturalism in a serene and disciplined unitary state, claiming at the same time that the country's two inherited educational systems are different only to the extent of requiring two separate sections but not different enough to require federalism or effective decentralization.

The Educational Systems Are Different But Not Different and At War?

I can, with fair accuracy, evaluate the two "sub-systems of education" in Cameroon not just because of what I have read in books and other writings. Most importantly, my knowledge on these matters also comes from my experience as a teacher who has taught for a long time in both sub-systems at both pre-university and university levels. Differences and diversity, if properly managed, are supposed to be Africa's strength. The channel for properly managing them is federalism. But, rather than give the differences and diversity their proper channel that is called federalism, the Cameroon administration, for instance, only imposes the unitary state and then continually promote what Bringer (1981: 4) describes as the official fanning of the "internal friction within the...bench and tensions between East Cameroon and West Cameroon judges due to different patterns and levels of education and qualifications." The government's confusing policy is that of fanning the differences (for divide and rule purposes) but at the same time refusing that the two educational "sub-systems" responsible for these differences are different. This is simply being stupid since the differences are so deep-rooted and will not just go away simply because someone is trying to behave as if nothing was different. To better demonstrate this, the two systems will later be briefly compared and contrasted as I examine the effect on national unity of one wanting to assimilate the other, rather than co-existing with it as the Education Law confuses people in section 15(2): "The above-mentioned educational systems shall co-exist, each preserving its specific method of evaluation and award of certificates.

Confusion is so deeply embedded in the Education Law that would be superficially preaching educational dualism that it is solely out to prevent or efface. By educational dualism, I am merely referring to the existence and effective 'near-independent' operation of two educational systems in the same social field or country; a description that draws largely from section 15 of Cameroon's Education Law. As previously noted in Chapter 1, the real purpose of this law is not the one that is stated; it is the destruction of any remaining traces of cultural dualism in Cameroon — a strategy that does not augur well with what Mbuy (1996) sees as Cameroon's 'entrusted and confirmed' spiritual and legendary continental direction. To concretize this thesis, Parts II and III of said law (portions that deal with organization, management and financing of education) will be carefully studied; matters that would require a digging into the issue of whether education is a national or regional domain in bicultural societies.

The query is apt because of the endless talk of the guarantee of quality education to children in Cameroon. The Cameroon state, according to section 2(2) and (3), has guaranteed quality education to Cameroon's children by actually providing it to them with the assistance of private sector partners. The critical issue to resolve relates to who should be at the forefront and with whom as assistant in the guarantee and provision of this essential cultural service, especially in a bicultural state. For instance, while education was generally a private-sector affair in English-speaking West Cameroon, it was the reverse in French-speaking East Cameroon. Now, how does one properly integrate two opposite or divergent views like these? Canada's Pierre-Elliott Trudeau, as Driedger (1989: 192) indicates, would think it cannot be done in any other way except through genuine federalism, a device which permits each national group to fully develop its unique national characteristics within the larger state. There is even research that reveals a worrisome fiscal crisis in state-supported education in

Cameroon. This fact, Boyle (1996: 617) has indicated, has now meant "greater parental involvement in the finance and management of most schools, and the near sudden appearance of private education. If such changes are not surprising, their existence suggests that education in Cameroon has entered a new phase that merits further examination." This important further inspection must also entail delineating the appropriate domain to which education should belong in a multicultural society; a job that will be done here through examining (1) the constitution and the education domain, an inquiry that enormously aids the comprehension of (2) the philosophy or design of the Education Law.

The Constitution and the Education Domain

The content and quality of education provided in any society are largely, if not entirely, coloured by the country's education politics. Cameroon's would seem to see no necessity for federalization and/or decentralization of educational matters. In a federal or decentralized state that is characterized by linguistic differences, according to Shapiro (1995: 67 n.255), "education, inexorably linked with the survival of language and hence culture, assumes great significance. Among Canadian experiences, we could recall the history of the Manitoba School Question or the more recent controversy over educational language restriction in Quebec." As Green has stressed, in Canada (as in most proper federations or effectively decentralized multicultural polities) "education is subject to provincial jurisdiction." This has been so in Canada since the 1867 *British North America Act* whose section 93, Green again emphasizes, permits provincial legislatures to exclusively make Laws in relation to education, including the language of instruction.[89] This Canadian arrangement is just another version of the Swiss geographic language principle which Liebich (1996: 11) explains to mean that there if you cannot or do not want to speak or use the language of a canton the only option is for you to move on. Yes, National unity is not turning diversity into *monosity* or what is generally known as assimilation.

Let us now find out what the education-domain situation is like in "The Republic of Cameroon [that] shall be a decentralized unitary State. It shall be one and indivisible, secular, democratic and dedicated to social service" (1996 Constitution, article 1(2)). From this constitutional provision one would naturally expect to see a lot of powers and responsibilities (especially those revolving around cultural issues like education) devolved to the regions or provinces. That is the usual thing to expect, the more so with the firm approval of Mback (2007: 74): "Indeed, like democratization, decentralization is a process involving the sharing of powers; therefore it involves a civilized management of the socio-political contradictions within the state." But that is only dashed hope or expectation because the same 'decentralizing' constitution has exhaustively listed matters reserved for the national/central parliament in article 26(2) to most significantly include "The system of education"; being just the re-written version of federal article 24.[90]

---

[89] William Green, "Schools, Signs, and Separation: Quebec Anglophones, Canadian Constitutional Politics, and International Language Rights" 27 *Denver Journal of International Law and Policy* (1999) 449 at 453 & 454.

[90] According to article 24 of the Federal Constitution, "The following matters shall be within the sphere of Federal Law, within the framework of the powers specified in Articles 5 and 6

(1) The fundamental guarantees and obligations of the citizen: protection of the freedom of the individual; public liberties; labour and trade-union legislation; the duties and obligations of the citizen in respect of national defence.

(2) The law of persons and property; nationality and personal status; the law of personal property and real property; the law of civil and commercial obligations.

(3) Political, administrative and judicial organisation with respect to: the electoral system of the Federal Assembly; the general rules relating to the

To reiterate the point, the system of education apart, most of the matters captured by article 26(2) are obviously not to be central government matters. A quick visit to Canada, Belgium and Switzerland would furnish confirmation that the federal or national parliament is usually clothed only with residual legislative domain or "*le pouvoir législative résiduaire.*"[91] What is even more interesting and which must be highlighted for the plain case of assimilation is the fact that nowhere in that federal document is there any convincing talk of state domains, a position that stands unaltered till date. From the 1996 Constitution's article-26 list (a mere rewritten version of the Federal Constitution's article 24), it is doubtful that there is anything at all left for the regional authorities. The 1996 list of the domains of the national parliament is all-embracing and very catastrophic for any effective decentralization and local government – the viable vehicles for multiculturalism. Mback (2007: 64-66) has already extensively exposed 'The Ambiguities of the Constitutional Principles of Free Administration of Local Government'; I will then solely talk about the domain-listing provisions.

Articles 23 and 47 of the Federal Constitution made legislation-making to belong equally to the President of the Federal Republic and the Deputies of the Federal National Assembly. Replacing the federal, the 1972 (Unitary) Constitution, in "allocating" legislation-making domains, listed the legislature's domains in article 20 and matters reserved for executive decrees

---

organisation of national defence; the definitions of crimes and offences and the establishment of penalties of any kind, criminal procedure, means of enforcement, amnesty, and the creation of new orders of jurisdiction.

(4) The following questions of finance and property: the currency issue system; the Federal Budget; the institution, assessment and rates of federal taxes and dues of any kind; legislation relating to State lands.

(5) The aims of economic and social action within the framework of the laws, relating to economic and social policy.

(6) The Educational system."

[91] Bernard Bissonnette, *Essai sur la constitution du Canada* (Montréal: Les Éditions du Jour, 1963) at xiii.

in article 22. Its article 21 (being successor to Federal articles 23 and 47) then says "the National Assembly may empower the President of the Republic to legislate by way of ordinance for a limited period and for given purposes" on the article-20 matters usually when the National Assembly is not in session. Anyangwe (1987: 207-211) has more extensively discussed these three Unitary Articles (20-22). That 'limited period' and 'for given purposes' authorization has since become the usual method of law-making in Cameroon because National Assembly sessions were shortly thereafter made more infrequent by the President of the Republic (POR) through one of such article-21 *laws*.

The same strategy applies to date; hence, the alluded disaster to the 1996 Constitution's local government. The long list of matters reserved to the central "legislature" in article 26(2) is not all that makes the disaster. It is most especially capped by the fact that the matters (if any at all) that are not enumerated in the article-26 list become the exclusive prerogative of the POR (1996 Constitution, article 27), and not of the regional and local authorities. In addition, the POR does also legislate on the article-26 matters and, when he does so, his legislation on these article-26 subjects "shall enter into force on the date of their publication" whether or not the National Assembly and [the yet-to-be-created] Senate have ratified them (1996 Constitution, article 28(2) & (3)). The 1998 Education Law is an apt example of the president's laws that 'enter into force on the date of their publication' whether or not ratified by the two chambers of the one-chamber parliament. This knowledge gleaned from the constitutions is very helpful in comprehending the philosophy of the Education Law.

The Philosophy of the Education Law

The Education Law is composed of 42 sections that fall under five parts. Part I gives the General Provisions (sections 1-10) while Part II deals with the Formation and Implementation of Education Policy and Financing of Education (sections 11-13). Part III has two chapters (section 14-31). The first chapter, running through sections 14-29, governs Organization of the Educational System, while the other chapter, of two brief sections, talks about Evaluation of the Educational System and Research in Education. Part IV is devoted to the Educational Community and has three Chapters (sections 32-39). Chapter I (sections 32-33) defines The Concept of Educational Community; chapter II (sections 34-36) outlines Students' Rights and Obligations while chapter III (sections 37-39) enumerates the Rights of Teachers. The final Part concerns Miscellaneous and Final Provisions (sections 40-42).

Being an apt example of the lack of self-control in this country, it is not very surprising then that one finds, for instance, that it is the central state (and not the regions) that will "formulate and implement educational policy with the assistance of regional and local authorities, families as well as public and private institutions" (Education Law, section 11). I am inclined to think that in a situation of genuine biculturalism and decentralization the arrangement has to be the other way round. That is, the regional governments, including public and private institutions, should be those to formulate and implement their respective educational policies (within a national constitutional context) with the national or central government instead being the *assistant*. If it is otherwise, one cleanly has to stop talking of decentralization and educational dualism.

As Wallace and Athamesara have theorized in support, while it is possible to develop multicultural education programs by adding modules about various ethnic and minority groups to existing curricula, or even finding texts that include multiple points of view, "we have found that having communities and schools write their own texts and pull together their own curricula create processes of participation that have far more potential to encourage and help develop the cultural and emotional imaginations of teachers, students and community members."⁹² Perhaps partly explaining the desperation of its teachers is the fact that not an iota of these things would happen in Cameroon, with or without the Education Law: since it is even well known from Mback (2007: 74) that the Cameroon "government, hesitant to undertake any true democratization, [would not] subscribe to a significant decentralization." That being the case, what then is the Education Law generally and its section 11 particularly really after?

The goal could be the subtle destruction of Anglo-Saxon institutions that have so far not been demolished. In this enterprise the power of subvention has played and is still to continue playing a very vital role. The purse-pulling strategy of the ultra-centralized government in Yaoundé is being constantly enhanced; with the General Certificate of Examination (G.C.E.) Board and the two 'Anglo-Saxon' Universities of Buea (UNIBU) and of Bamenda (UNIBA) being obvious targets of the strategy. The falling status of Anglo-Saxon institutions in Cameroon has, inter alia, been largely attributed to drastically reduced or no government subvention. As Ndamukong (1996) would put it, "[t]he meagre amount of 160 million francs in the first year of the [G.C.E.] Board's creation and 40 million francs in the second year and nothing in the third year is nothing compared to the 3.5 billion francs which were spent on the same [G.C.E.] examinations yearly when they were conducted by the Ministry of Education." As a result of these deep cuts, there have been very serious problems, especially with honouring engagements with the teachers who mark the examinations.⁹³ Researchers like

---

⁹² Merle Wallace and Raynou Athamesara, "The Thai Community Curriculum as a Model for Multicultural Education" 5:1 *International Education Journal* (2004), 50-64 at 51. As Fohtung (1996) has explained, Cameroon school children are being grudgingly taught by teachers whose "visible pain, desperation, estrangement and their hypocrisy reminds a regular church-goer about Bible stories of the Israelites in the wilderness separating them from the distant and receding promised land."

⁹³ See Kum Set Ewi, "1998 G.C.E.: Marking Begins as Teachers Receive Half Claims for Last Year" *The Herald* N° 632 (13-14 July 1998), 2.

Boyle (1996: 618) have found out that the beginning of the same kinds of delays in the payment of salaries for teachers since 1993 "demonstrates the extent to which public and state-supported denominational schools faced a virtually identical set of problems created by the penury of public resources (despite their allocation on paper), and exacerbated by the rapid expansion of the [school] population."

There is a general and heightened lack of transparency in the way things are done in Cameroon. For instance, Azebaze has discussed and condemned the education minister's unpublished inter-ministerial orders that imposed school fees in public schools, together with some other illegal provisions that would be geared towards benefitting the partisan clan.[94] What else would anyone be expecting from the education minister whose boss, the POR, can get out of bed any morning and, for no stated or clear reason, just sign one of those his decrees or laws imposing fees on students of state-run universities? In view of this generalized absence of transparency, it might be hard not to believe the charges against the Yaoundé regime regarding subvention to the G.C.E. Board.

But the same transparency logic must keep one on guard. In other words, one should embrace some of these charges from Buea against Yaoundé with some scepticism. For instance, there is the somewhat contrary account of a former Chairman of the G.C.E. Board (that is based in Buea). Dioh has indicated that the G.C.E. Board management in Buea should not shift the blame to the wrong quarters but rather "Accept full responsibility for the fate that has befallen you and your Board." According to Dioh, this Board is failing because the Chief Executive of the Board has personified everything (in the same way as the POR); turning the

---

[94] The National Education minister's *"arrêté interministeriel non publié généralisant les frais de scolarité dans les établissement publics"* and several *"des actes illégaux" "au service de la clientèle partisane."* Alex Gustave Azebaze, "Gestion financière des établissements scolaires publics: Mbella Mbappe dupe parents d'élèves, communes et... le MINFI" *Le Messager* N° 543 (16 septembre 1996) 11.

Board into his private property, and by-passing its regulations, etc. Dioh documents his claims so well with rules and regulations and instances of this and that: it is simply hard not to believe him. Above all, he points out how the Board's personified executive has been feeding the gullible private press with wrong information about the true state of affairs because the Ministry of Education (MINEDUC) had been sending in the subvention money as usual: until the MINEDUC discovered what was actually happening to the money.[95] But could it just be the allocation of subvention money on paper only, as earlier seen above?

Whatever the actual position of subvention could be, it is certain that one will remain in the dark as long as the current centralized and personified system persists. The persistence of the system easily finds a comfortable haven in the politics of the purse or what Edokat *et al* would want to describe as 'The Economics of Education'.[96] This purse-politics would now seem to be overwhelmingly decisive in the assimilation strategy of the law under review. The politics of this law aims at largely and doubly confusing so as to easily reign and assimilate unchallenged. For instance, it purports to be "lay[ing] down the general legal framework of education in Cameroon" in section 1(1), but curiously (at the same time) does not apply to university education; only "apply[ing] to nursery, primary, secondary grammar and technical education, as well as to teacher-training" in section 1(2).[97] Or, are universities sufficiently covered by 'technical education' and 'teacher training'? So, where does one

---

[95] Sylvester N. Dioh, "G.C.E. Board: Anglophones are not Responsible for the Mess, But the Management" *The Herald* N° 471 (13-15 June 1997), 4.

[96] See Tafah Edokat, J.U. Umo and R.E. Ubogu, "The Economics of Education: Evaluation of the Determinants of Primary School Performance in Cameroon" 2-2 *Zimbabwe Journal of Educational Research* (1990), 93-110.

[97] The French text seems to exclude the points following when it states: *Elle s'applique aux enseignements maternel, primaire, secondaire général et technique, ainsi qu'à l'enseignement normal.* Does "*enseignement normal*" mean 'university education'?

actually stand at this point as far as university education is concerned? No one can correctly divine that until some 13 kilo-sections away, a distance after which most scrutinizers' enthusiasm and critical eyes would have waned or tired out. At that time and point, section 14 makes clear that "The organisation and control of education at all levels shall be the bounden duty of the [central] state." Is the limitation in section 1(2) then necessary?

The answer will principally depend on what 'necessary' is taken to mean to the 'intention'; but, according to the law that this much faraway now applies to all levels of education (including university), while the responsibilities of the regional and local authorities in the implementation and financing of the education policy shall be defined by a separate law from the POR (section 13), the financing of education shall be by: budgetary allocations from the state; contributions from education partners; budgetary appropriations from regional and local authorities; donations and legacies; all other contributions provided for by the [POR's] law (section 12). What then has indeed been decentralized in Cameroon since 1996 (or 1961)? To cloth the assimilation points being made, the entire section 11 ought to be scrutinized. "To that end" (of the regions *assisting* the central state rather than the other way round), it pursues, the Cameroon State shall:

- set the objectives and general guidelines for national teaching and training syllabuses in conjunction with all the sectors of national life in order to make education more professional;
- ensure the constant adaptation of the educational system to national economic and socio-cultural realities, and also to the international environment, especially through the promotion of bilingualism and the teaching of national languages;
- lay down the conditions for the creation, opening and running of government and private educational establishments

and control them;

- define standards for the construction and equipment of public and private educational establishments and control them; [and]

- draw and update the school location map.

(2) The state shall realise the above objectives with the assistance of an advisory body, the National Education Board whose organisation, duties and functioning shall be laid down by decree of the President of the Republic.

There is much that can be said about this entire section 11. For example, it is not clear whether the authorities in Cameroon do in fact comprehend what "Guidelines" (in the title of the law) would actually signify. That meaning-confusion alone could furnish enough material for a book of its own from linguistic experts. I am not venturing there though. To buttress the doubt being cast on Cameroon's educational dualism, I will here simply comment on section 11(2). This important comment turns on (1) the question of whether Cameroonians really need a National Education Board (NEB) and (2) the consequences on the existing G.C.E. Board.

The National Education Board and/or the PROBAC Board?

My reasoning is that Cameroon does not need a NEB which is obviously superfluous: assuming that this country is in point of fact and law bicultural. If multiculturalism or cultural dualism is the rule in Cameroon, as the authorities do claim, then this is a suggestion of what they can do, since they seem to be so urgently in need of something to create. They should rather decree only a *Probatoire/Baccalauréat* (PROBAC) Board to cater for Cameroon's "French-speaking sub-system" of education because there is already a G.C.E. Board that handles this country's "English-speaking sub-system". This suggestion or interpretation is quite sane, being crushingly supported by a number of factors.

To begin with, I would like to indicate that I have had to simply talk of the Ministry of Education (MINEDUC) in this book in order not to further complicate a lengthily incomprehensible duplication matter. There is in fact no ministry of education in Cameroon (as one speaks), but about seven ministries that deal with education: ministry of basic education, ministry of primary education, ministry of secondary education, ministry of higher education, ministry of scientific research and innovation, ministry of sports and physical education, and ministry of employment and professional and technical training. Perhaps this unnecessary multiplicity or duplication of education ministries could be this government's unique way of selling the idea that it is making education "a top priority of the Cameroon State" as per section 2(1) of the Education Law. Is this a sellable idea?

I do not think that claim could easily sell. Education can simply not be a top priority of the Cameroon State when, according to data published in *Cameroon Tribune* of 13 March 1991 and cited by Boyle (1996: 610 n.3), up to 40% of Cameroonians over the age of 11 are illiterate; the situation being aggravated by what Boyle (1996: 616 n33) castigates as a significant drop in funds allocated to education by the centralized administration from earlier levels of 20-30% to just 12% in the 1986-90 period. Education can indeed not therefore be a top priority of the Cameroon State when it is also well known from Johnson-Hanks (2006: 125) that "Not only the economy, but also Cameroon's instructional system is in [serious] crisis." It basically cannot be its main goal when there is the well-known distressing story of some teachers from "the dubious 'Ecoles Normales'" (as Fohtung (1996) would put it) who must always abandon school children for weeks and months in order to make the usual 'pilgrimage' to the 'supermarket ministry of finance' in Yaoundé in view of "bribing and 'screwing' their way to integration in Yaounde's civil service or towards their meagre salaries."

Ex hypothesis, there is no other convincing reason, absent

assimilation, why this administration would be willing to create those many ministries to carter for education but would not entertain the idea of having two (through now forming only the PROBAC) boards to, respectively, handle this country's two educational sub-systems under the auspices of an Education Ministry. Or, why not even create two ministries such as (a) Ministry of Anglophone Education and (b) Ministry of Francophone Education? That would appear to be the logical thing to do since creating ministries would seem to be easier than creating examinations boards in Cameroon. Two education ministerial departments like these would still be in order, if educational dualism is in fact the rule.

Furthermore, the education law itself (if it is not confusion but anything to actually go by) talks of Cameroon's educational system as being "organised into two sub-systems: the English-speaking sub-system and the French-speaking sub-system, thereby reaffirming our national option for biculturalism" (section 15(1)). In addition, it further stresses in section 15(2) that "The above-mentioned educational sub-systems shall co-exist, each preserving its specific method of evaluation and award of certificates." That being the case indeed, then the third point follows, namely, that creating a NEB now would not only needlessly duplicate the MINEDUC but, above all else, would be very loudly denying the avowed biculturalism by re-assimilating the G.C.E. Board that was not easy in bringing into existence in the first place.

The Obliteration of the G.C.E. Board?

The answer is yes. The creation of the G.C.E. Board to cater for the English-speaking "sub-system" of education, according to Abanda, was itself the result of the determination of various groups which galvanized and channelled public opinion to "resist cultural assimilation." At the launching of a book on the G.C.E. Board (*The Cameroon GCE Crisis: Test of Anglophone Solidarity*), Archbishop Verdzekov of Bamenda is reported by Abanda to have decried "An unwritten policy of absorption and assimilation" existing in Cameroon where "one could have to be Frenchified in order to be accepted." Referring to the leakage in the 1996 G.C.E., Abanda reports, the archbishop declared that "Recent events seem to indicate that the forces of evil and of darkness have not been disarmed. They are deploying their lethal arms to destroy the credibility which the G.C.E. Board has established through great sacrifice."[98] Similarly, Afoni reports that Reverend Dr. Betene (the National Catholic Education Secretary) also talked of there being "a massive attempt this year [1996] ... to make the good work of the G.C.E. Board fail."[99] Both clergymen were accurate in their predictions/suspicions because two years later the 1998 law was there to spell the end of the G.C.E. system, not just its failure.

Quite apart from the negative official attitude toward the G.C.E. and its Board that has already been largely catalogued in the literature already cited in this book, the fact that assimilation is its real goal is very evident even in two sections of Part III of the Education Law that deal with the organization and evaluation of each 'sub-system'. According to section 16 that purportedly organizes the English-speaking 'sub-system',

(1) The English-speaking sub-system shall be organised into cycles and fields of study as follows: nursery education with a duration of two years; primary education with a duration of six years; secondary education with a duration of seven years; post-primary education with a duration of two years; teacher training with a duration of two or three years.

(2) Secondary education shall comprise: a first cycle of five years having an observation sub-cycle of two years with a

---

[98] Abeng Abanda, "At Book Launch: Archbishop Verdzekov Decries Assimilation of Anglophones" *The Herald* N° 327 (8-9 July 1996), 1 & 2.

[99] Julius Afoni, "Forces of Darkness Blamed for G.C.E. Board Crisis" *Cameroon Post* N° 0028 (8-14 October 1996), 3.

common-core syllabus and an orientation sub-cycle of three years of general or technical education; a second cycle of two years of general or technical education.

(3) In addition to general education, practical training shall be provided to students in vocational colleges and high schools, on the basis of the courses they choose.

By section 17 that is meant to deal with the French-speaking 'sub-system',

(1) The French-speaking sub-system shall be organised into cycles and fields of study as follows: nursery education with a duration of two years; primary education with duration of six years; secondary education with a duration of seven years; post-primary education with a duration of two years; teacher training with a duration of two or three years.

(2) Secondary education shall comprise: a first cycle of five years having an observation sub-cycle of two years with a common-core syllabus and an orientation sub-cycle of three years of general or technical education; a second cycle of two years of general or technical education.

(3) In addition to general education, practical training shall be provided to students in vocational colleges and high schools, on the basis of the courses they choose.

Tell me here what the difference actually is to the government's 1983 order modifying the G.C.E. examination (see Konings and Nyamnjoh, 1997: 213) that I have discussed in Chapter 1. Only in their degree of force, this 1998 one being a law while the other in 1983 was just an order. From a simple reading and re-reading of the two sections of the law here, the only difference between these two different 'sub-systems' would be just the two hyphenated terms

"English-speaking" and "French-speaking".[100] Hence, to the regime, they are different (only to the extent of meriting separate sections) but not at all different. Nothing can be as far from the truth.

An expert on Cameroon constitutional law (Enonchong, 1967: 24-25) has poignantly indicated that the "differences between the French-trained lawyer and the English-trained lawyer in what is and what is not constitutional law are not trivial. They range from the form to content of the entire spectrum of constitutional law." This sharp contrast in perspectives would thus turn the issue of 'What Cameroon Constitutional Law is' (Enonchong, 1967: 19-43) into one which "is certainly a difficult question to answer because it bristles with a multiplicity of complex problems which are of historical origin" (Enonchong, 1967: 19). Justice Nyo'Wakai's recent 2008 book (*Under the Broken Scale of Justice: The Law and My Times*) also neatly demonstrates how the conflict of judicial concepts, procedures and usages have led to the Francophone judicial system trying to impose itself on the Anglophone judicial system in Cameroon. Often reduced to toothless bulldogs by new constitutional dispensations informed largely by the French colonial legacy and Francophone realities, according to the justice, Anglophones have bemoaned the independence of the Judiciary identified with their Anglo-Saxon heritage.[101]

A complicated historical question or not, the well-couched strategy of fanning the differences (while refusing their existence rather than trying to bridge them) would take the form of unfettered appointments of the less qualified to positions where they boss over the more qualified, punitive transfers, unjustified promotions/demotions, etc. The G.C.E. Examination (representing

---

[100] There is already a detailed review by Anyangwe (1989: 198-200) of some of the differences in cycles and other disparities (before this law) that are rooted in the pre-university academic programs in both educational "sub-systems". Kanyongo (2005) provides more information on the issue, with regard to Anglophone Africa generally.

[101] See http://www.langaa-rpcig.net/Under-The-Broken-Scale-of-Justice.html (last visited in February 2011).

the "English-speaking sub-system") would principally provide the root/explanation of the differences in those lawyers' education. There is little doubt that the lawyers and judges being talked about above would all have generally earned a university law degree – the *licence en droit* or LL.B. But on the whole, looking at their pre-university education, there is research showing that Anglophone students are better well-prepared to embark on the study of law than most of their Francophone counterparts (Anyangwe, 1989: chapter 11). The G.C.E. model which is responsible for this better preparation is envied enormously by Francophone students for a host of reasons (including the absence of the failure-instigating *moyen general* and the capricious *tirage* system) thus explaining why this G.C.E. system is being targeted by the regime.

For a private law student at the UNIYAO, for example, there are courses such as equity, *droit du travail, régimes fonciérs Camerounais, sociologie générale, histoire des institutions,* and *initiation à l'économie,* that are simply called *matières de tirage au sort.* There are usually three of these *tirage* courses per year of study. As the name can indicate, students are required to study all of these three subjects but they are tested on only the one that is picked at random from the pack on the day of the examination. The remaining two *tirage* subjects are then met at the disreputable oral examination by those who can make the general minimum score (*moyen général*) in the overall written part.[102] To several education critics like Anyangwe (1989: 206), the *tirage* system, "of course, is examination by ambush [and] No one has been able to explain convincing[ly] the rationale of a system as capricious as this one." These *tirage* subjects and *moyen général* are concepts that most

---

[102] The oral examination is described as notorious because "Given the fact that the teacher always has so many students to interview within a short time, most candidates are hardly ever interviewed for more than five minutes. Furthermore, given the fact that the teacher conducts the interview alone, it is extremely doubtful that these interviews are completely objective and that all the marks given adequately reflect the performance of the candidates. Indeed, there have been cries not altogether unfounded, of favouritism and victimization by the teachers during oral examinations." Anyangwe (1989: 207).

English-speaking students would meet for the first time only at the then 'one and only' UNIYOA. The University of Yaoundé II at Soa (former UNIYAO's Faculty of Laws and Economics) and all the other 'East Cameroon' universities (Douala, Dschang, Ngaoundéré, Yaoundé I) are, of course, still continuing with the same practices. This strange educational arrangement is one of the numerous factors accounting for the fact that, by 1990, according to Boyle (1996: 616), Cameroon's educational "system was plagued by high costs and drop-out rates, as well as by its ambiguous value for economic development." The decried "capricious *tirage* system" is one of the several hurdles that, until the advent of the UNIBU in 1992, have stiffly stood in the way of English-speaking students at the UNIYAO, since they are accustomed to the G.C.E. model that gives no room for examination by ambush or the *moyen général*.

Yet, this is the faulty system that must be imposed on everyone while brandishing biculturalism to the rest of the world. Again, one cannot help but wonder what the difference in the two 'sub-systems' is to the authorities: except the two hyphenated words of "English-speaking" and "French-speaking". Contrary to the biculturalism postulates of the education law, this could be precisely what has too often been described by Benjamin (1972: 126) as 'Being Bilingual in French' and/or by Fossungu (1998a) as living in a 'common Civil-Law Country'. Furthermore, what exactly do the specific things that are to be preserved by each sub-system (in section 15(2)) consist of? There would appear to be absolutely nothing of the sort especially as the same law commands a little afterwards in section 18(3) that the certificates issued by each sub-system of the educational system shall be determined by decree of the POR. Assimilation! Assimilation! Assimilation! That is what is written all over this law. All this happens largely because the Foumban gathering did not occupy itself at all with guaranteeing the rights and institutions of Cameroonians generally and the English-speaking in particular.

The biggest problem and irony though would concern some of the English-speaking "intellectuals in politics" who, when given the golden chance to do so, would not even make an attempt to correct things. For example, Fossungu has reported that the then minister of higher education (incidentally an Anglophone) visited Canada in 1996 and met with the Cameroonian community at the Université de Montréal. During that Montreal meeting, the minister was all through only talking in 'French' and only about the French-speaking sub-system of education (*Baccalauréat* and *Probatoire*). When asked specifically by a participant (in English) whether he was higher education minister for both brands of educational settings in the country or only for the Francophone one, the minister (who studied in the USA) responded in 'French' that "There was nothing like Anglo-Saxon education in Cameroon."[103] This is not coming from just any person; it is coming from Biya's minister of higher education.

Yet we are being told in its section 6 that the Education Law has guaranteed the right of every child, without distinction, to education (in accordance especially with articles 2(1) and 28(1) of the United Nations Convention on the Rights of the Child). The higher education minister has told us the only kind of education that is available, with the same education law itself telling us in section 37 that the teacher is the "principal guarantor of the quality of education." It is then not hard to know the kind and quality of education that children are guaranteed in Cameroon because it is perfectly reflected in the quality of Cameroon's teacher-training institutions and the trained teachers. That is exactly how the Cameroon state has (according to section 2(2) and (3) of the Education Law) guaranteed low quality mono-cultural education to Cameroon's bicultural children by actually providing it to them with the assistance of private sector partners, as evidently reinforced by section 18(3) and others.

In view of section 18(3) of the Education Law (president's decree determining the certificates to be issued by the educational system) one wonders what to make of the much-sung administrative autonomy of the regional authorities in article 55 of the 1996

---

[103] Peter Ateh-Afac Fossungu, "Paradoxes of Cameroon's Intellectuals" *The Herald* N° 559 (16-18 January 1998), 4.

Constitution. The 1998 Education Law is a sure part of the new subtle strategy in Cameroon of obliterating anything Anglo-Saxon there but still camouflaging biculturalism. The unmistakable targets are the so-called 'Anglo-Saxon' universities and the G.C.E. System and Board. The continued existence of these institutions in a united Cameroon is then greatly in question, thanks to improper management. For proper governance of radically diverse polities like Cameroon, federalism is the most cogent form or structure. Belgium would easily testify here, having successfully moved from the unitary form to the federal. If it worked for Belgium, there is no reason why it would not work for others, absent confusion and manipulation that are rooted in the absence of patriotic leadership.

Once more, how does the section 18(3) provision also tally in with section 15(2) that is talking of each sub-system preserving its specific characteristics? Furthermore, how does section 14 that organizes and controls education at all levels also tie in with a law that conspicuously opens by being limited to only nursery, primary and secondary education in section 1(2)? All this is surely what critics have chastised as "half a step forward and one hundred steps backward"; and in this instance, some of them like Mensah-Gbadago (1991) have asked, how far has one actually moved? Of course, in Cameroon one would still have 'advanced' a lot because in this country's advanced democracy regression (or upside-down rolling-back[104]) is happily and positively measured since the democracy gets its essence from the absence of self-control and of positive development, as can also be seen in the perfect nation's 'pluralistic democracy'.

---

[104] See Peter Ateh-Afac Fossungu, "Our Up-Side-Down Pride in Diversity" *The Herald* N° 615 (3-4 June 1998), 10; and O.T. Mbuagbo and R.M. Akoko, "Roll-Back: Democratization and Social Fragmentation in Cameroon" 13:1 *Nordic Journal of African Studies* (2004), 1-12.

Chapter 3

The One-Party System (Or 'Pluralistic Democracy') Is an Abomination to Multiculturalism

Paul Biya, according to Fohtung (1995) and Ahidjo (1996), had spent so many 'patriotic' years of his shadowy life in some of the highest offices of Cameroon, pretending to be something else so as to get to this almighty POR position in which, with the mere stroke of his pen, he can secure the hanging of his predecessor as well as decree his beloved Perfect Nation. The perfect nation is then a fait accompli in 1984 and nothing, absolutely nothing, on earth can therefore take this darling outmoded 'perfect nation' away from the POR. That can only happen over his dead body, or, to be precise, the death of Cameroon. That thesis from the critics can well explain why, despite all the bitter challenges directed at the 1984 name-change and the grave dangers it poses to national unity, it was again reaffirmed and confirmed by the 1996 Constitution. This 1996 reaffirmation logically leads to the questioning of what had happened to the 'only one Cameroon people' attained in 1984 (as justifying the name-change). Elusive national unity, always appearing and disappearing! Does that not *happen* simply in order to justify perpetuity in power?

Monosity: Prerequisite for 'Pluralistic Democracy'?

Third World leaders, Riemer's (1983: 187) argument thus runs, have often been pushed to instead tread their preferred road to Limbo (which is some sort of shortcut to Heaven) because of:

(1) lack of an historical sense of belonging and working together; (2) the absence, often, of common language, religion, history, and custom; (3) the reality of widespread poverty and

illiteracy; (4) the divisive influence of caste and tribe... and (5) the lack of instrumentalities that function to keep a nation together, such as effective national leadership, political organization, civil servants, national economic ties, and national education [the numbering has been added].

These so-called obstacles, according to Riemer (1983: 187-88) of Drew University, "help to explain why many of the new states have often moved away from liberal or even democratic socialist ideas and toward rule by a strong charismatic leader, a single party, a disciplined military junta, and even (often reluctantly) toward authoritarian methods in order to foster primary national values." Does this roundabout bullshit give enough cover to the African leadership? I do not think so because it is the absence of the first example of the fifth factor that is largely responsible for the existence or absence of all the others.

With the type of patriotic and charismatic people Riemer describes as being in leadership positions in the Third World, the so-called democracy 'inhibiting factors' can clearly not provide any excuse for regression. I will take you later to Indonesia during the elaborate lessons in patriotism and charismatic leadership but, for now, it is even untenable to employ those factors to justify the absence of the same thing (democracy) one is claiming to have. As Fossungu has argued,

> Democracy must be nurtured and developed through channelling or curtailing those so-called 'inhibiting' factors as illiteracy, poverty, tribalism, etc. Using them to instead justify the non-institution of good and responsible governance would be clear evidence of non-charisma and absence of patriotism; not to forget that it is also philosophically untenable, especially when, at the same time, the same Cameroonians would be claiming the very democracy whose absence they appear to be justifying. *Demoncrazy* appears to be precisely what is in place in Cameroon.

Illiteracy and poverty can only justify that.[105]

Further illustration of the points can be found in Konings and Nyamnjoh (1997: 224 & 210); all pointing to the persistent stance from the Unity Palace that looks at federalism not as a means of channelling, but as the actual cause of, the country's multifarious diversity – cultural, ethnic, linguistic, and religious in particular. This diversity, according to the authorities, has been standing in the way of democracy and must first be eliminated for the purposes of national unity: only after the doing of which can pluralistic democracy (if that is not tautological) come.[106] The oneness of the Cameroonian People (perfect nation) of 1984 was the prelude to this "pluralistic" democracy, it was claimed. But why has this tautological type of democracy not be instituted since 1984 with the existence of only one Cameroon people? The surprising answer is that the national unity situation of Cameroon is now different from those of other countries (including even France from where Cameroon dishonestly and largely copies without acknowledgment – see Chapter 4) since Cameroonians do not yet have the "Perfect Nationhood" which they even had in 1984. What happened? The Perfect Nation of 1984 mysteriously disappeared overnight. That is, just two years later. The higher reappearance of this vanished 'Perfect Nation' in the form of a New Ethnic Group (NEG) is imperative. According to Biya (1986: 44, emphasis added), "Having to date ensured the peaceful co-existence of the rich diversity of Cameroonian ethnic groups, it [the Biya administration] can credibly embark on the *higher* phase of its task – that of uniting the ethnic groups into one New Ethnic Group"

Until this is done, as the authorities have then been claiming

---

[105] Peter Ateh-Afac Fossungu, "Responsible Governance" *The Herald* N° 694 (2-3 December 1998), 10.

[106] It is tautological to talk of "pluralistic democracy" because democracy must necessarily be pluralistic to be democracy. Pearson and Rochester (1984: 593, emphasis added) have defined it in the simplest terms as "An open, *pluralistic* governmental system, allowing for the free expression and flow of ideas and for rival political groupings."

through Biya (1986: 28), "the realization of this dream [called 'pluralistic' democracy]" simply cannot come to reality principally because it "encounters a major obstacle, that is, the absence of a real nation due to persisting ethnic, religious and linguistic particularisms." As the Logic of Advanced Democracy goes, it is now the irreplaceable mandate of the authorities in place in Cameroon[107] to transform the country's pluralism into one (through the irreversible creation of the NEG) "which is the pre-requisite for the institution of pluralistic democracy" in "*An entirely democratized single party.*"[108] This is quite amazing or confusing? The authorities that would never want to realize that times have changed are still disputing with the experts who say neither democracy nor federalism can be feasible without some sort of effective separation of powers and multiplicity; stiffly disputing any change to their One-Party System which, according to them, has a "Solid Foundation", spanning over four decades because, as far back as 1966 – just five years after 'federating' – "the political parties were [voluntarily] dissolved and a single new party the *Union National Camerounien* (UNC) was formed, the President believing this necessary to create national unity out of the diversity of the tribes and for reasons of development."[109]

---

[107] The ruling party, "[t]he CPDM, therefore, remains an irreplaceable instrument in the medium term for national unity" (Biya, 1986: 43) because "The CPDM whose responsibility it is *to determine the destiny of Cameroonians* has made a commitment to promote" the NEG (Biya, 1986: 126, emphasis added).

[108] Biya (1986: 45, emphasis as in original). "The present phase of the history of Cameroon does not permit the institution of a multiparty system. Our Party is, therefore, responsible for the reduction of the existing ethno-cultural divisions in order to promote national integration which is the pre-requisite for the institution of a pluralistic democracy." *Id.* at 127.

[109] Peaslee, (1974: 83). The italicized portion of this quotation (which should normally be *Union Nationale Camerounaise* – CNU in English, see Konings and Nyamnjoh, 1997: 210) is exactly as in the original and can be perfectly understood in the context of the new language or confusion called *Francanglais* that is now in the offing in Cameroon. See Fossungu (1998b); and Ntemfac Ofege, "Government Should Stop Corrupting the English Language (Culture)" *The Herald* N° 590 (30-31 March 1998), 4.

It has long been decided therefore, according to Biya (1986: 45), that "the [unique CPDM] Party will become an important vehicle for spreading the spirit and practice of democracy in our society. The Party must also above all become a real party of sovereign militants. This objective calls for the fulfilment of certain conditions. For instance, no obstacle, no manoeuvre, whatever its nature...." This 'advanced democratic' stance, according to Biya (1986: 43, my emphasis), is because, "for the sense of patriotism of every Cameroonian really interested in the future of *his* country," the ruling party, "[t]he CPDM, therefore, remains an irreplaceable instrument in the medium term for national unity." Two essential theories stand out here, namely, (1) the patriotism/equality of females and (2) the irreplaceable party in power.

Sexing Patriotism and Equality: The Illustrative Case of the 1997 Legislative and Presidential Elections

Several researchers have studied the important but not well-articulated role that women have played in the liberation movements in Africa generally, but especially in British Southern Cameroons; largely regretting the visible neglect women have had to know in 'post-independence' participation in public life.[110] And this neglect could be seen in the Foumban Conference of July 1961[111] which was plainly a male affair despite attempts from some writers to emasculate the facts. For example, Enonchong (1967: 83-84, emphasis added) talks of the 'Foumban Constitution Assembly' "delegates to which included chiefs, representatives of all political parties, of religious and trade union movements and *members of the Cameroon Bar Association*. It was a broad based conference with the

---

[110] See Adams (2006); and Henry Kam Kah, "Women's Resistance in Cameroon's Western Grassfields: The Power of Symbols, Organization, and Leadership, 1957–1961" 12:3 *African Studies Quarterly* (Summer 2011), 67-91.

[111] See *Record of the Conference on the Constitutional Future of the Southern Cameroons, Held at Foumban 17th to 21st July 1961* (Buea, 1961).

object of encompassing views from *all sections of Cameroon national life.*" All this, it must be indicated, is untrue and can only go to further the confusion and manipulation in regard of the Foumban Enterprise. To even leave the female issue out, one can simply want to know what 'the Cameroon Bar Association' here consisted of. Was it that of East Cameroon or that of a "federal" Cameroon that they were still about to create?

Since all the Foumban players were all males, several observers would now believe and pray that God bless Cameroonian mothers and sisters who, perhaps, might give the country something better when next it has to be done. Thus, although a minority of them would clearly not see why and how that should be,[112] the majority of writers have forcefully suggested that women would likely do better where men have woefully failed in Cameroon and enjoining the latter to cede place to the former. For instance, writing for the Association for the Fight against Violence on Women (ALVF), Chinje (1997) has posited that "After [more than] forty years of reign by the men and despite the fact that the women have shown proof of exceptional qualities, no female candidate ran for president [of Cameroon in 1997]."[113] As I have indicated earlier, Cameroon's Advanced Democracy is known to resist such proposals with all its might.

---

[112] See, for example, Napoleon Viban, "The Campaign by Women for Emancipation is Unnecessary" *The Herald* N° 427 (3-4 March 1997), 11.

[113] See also M.L. Lokanga, "Cameroon's Next President: A Dark Horse?" *Le Messager* N° 029 (18 July 1991), 5; Veronica Morfaw, "Men Have Failed in Leadership" *The Herald* N° 441 (4-6 April 1997), 11; and Bernadette Wendi, "Women are Naturally Good Managers" *The Herald* N° 452 (30 April-1 May 1997), 11. For further scholarly examination of the points raised in this section of the Chapter generally, see Susan Jackel, "Rethinking Equality and Citizenship" in David Schneidermann, *Conversations Among Friends << >> Entre Amies: Proceedings of an Interdisciplinary Conference on Women and Constitutional Reform* (Edmonton: Centre for Constitutional Studies, 1992), 43; Deborah L. Rhode, "Gender and Professional Roles" 63:1 *Fordham Law Review* (1994), 39-72; and Martha Chamalllas, "Questioning the Use of Race-Specific and Gender-Specific Economic Data in Tort Litigation: A Constitutional Argument" 63:1 *Fordham Law Review* (1994), 73-124.

But the women and other interest groups are not sitting back and waiting on the other sex to grant them their equal rights anyway. The ALVF is an association that has, since 1991, embarked on a permanent national sensitization and public education campaign for more effective participation of women in the public and political life of Cameroon. According to Ngobo Ekotto Ndoumbe, it principally targets women, organized women's groups, political parties and the public and private media: with its programme being "to strengthen the capacity of the female Cameroonian citizen to participate effectively as a voter and candidate at the various elections since 1992."[114]

Cameroon's system of advanced democracy (if one must keep the word 'democracy' alive) could only be best described as 'inverted democracy'. This inversion is easily reflected in those who can have equality or be patriotic in it. Females constitute about 52% of Cameroon's population but Chinje's (1997) report holds that they have been excluded by the same 'pre-multiparty' "discriminatory provisions in the laws of the land" from being patriotically interested in the country's past, present, and future, as can be seen in (a) the total absence of females in Foumban in 1961, (b) the number of females in the 'multiparty' National Assembly, (c) their membership within the executive branch, and (d) their presence even within those non-governmental organizations in Cameroon claiming to be after gender equality.

One might want to get into all these by citing another good instance of particularly sexing equality at the same time as one is 'advocating' equality. To Biya (1986: 37), "It is necessary to make every Cameroonian feel that he is fundamentally equal to all other Cameroonians." Several critics are still wondering just how this could be done when, quite apart from the official *second-classing* of the English-speaking of this country, females are clearly excluded from 'advanced democratic' equality. It is quite intriguing that females who

---

[114] N.E. Ndoumbe, "ALVF and the Cameroonian Woman in the Electoral Process" *The Herald* N° 521 (10-12 October 1997), 7.

constitute more than half of Cameroon's population can simply not be patriotically interested in the country's past, present and future. This is one of the myriad of things that would give advanced democracy its unsavoury 'flavour'; a flavour that would seem to have eaten through the entire fabric of the Cameroonian society to an extent that its single-sex one-party system is comfortably masquerading as multiparty democracy.

A report in April 1997 indicated that about 37 women were expected to be in parliament after the May 1997 legislative elections as opposed to the last parliament's 23 females out of the 180 parliamentarians (as per article 15(1) of 1996 Constitution). For the said April election, the report continues, the ruling CPDM had about 15 substantive and 40 alternate female candidates, the Social Democratic Front (SDF) 15 substantive and 16 alternate, while the National Union for Development and Progress (UNDP) had 8 substantive and 12 alternate, candidates.[115] Yet, after that election, the number of women in parliament dropped from the 23 before it to just 10; with Muabe (1997) reporting how Yaou Aissatou, the then minister of Women's Affair, lamented that "From the 23 female deputies in the 1992-1997 parliamentary mandate here we are today reduced to only 10 women." This lack of gender awareness in the midst of the singing of gender equality would not only end in parliament.

Claiming to be aiming at "a more just, balanced and harmonious society," female ministers and parliamentarians therefore met at the Yaounde Conference Centre on June 20, 1998 and formed an association called *Le Commité des femmes ministres et parlementaires du*

---

[115] See "Female Representation" *The Herald* N° 446 (16-17 April 1997), 3. See also A. Nzangou, "Municipal '96: les femmes ne sont pas sorties du ghetto" *Dikalo* N° 196 (29 juin 1998), 9; and Diane Lamoureaux, "Un majorité. Encore oubliée" in David Schneidermann, *Conversations Among Friends << >> Entre Amies: Proceedings of an Interdisciplinary Conference on Women and Constitutional Reform* (Edmonton: Centre for Constitutional Studies, 1992), 58.

Cameroun (CFEMP).[116] Was that creation to confront the problem? One cannot exactly tell; but among some of the various reasons advanced for this phenomenon (block to women's political growth in Cameroon), Muabe (1997) has identified "women who were enemies to their fellow women [and] Political parties and men."[117] The fact of well-placed Cameroonian women only paying lip service to female empowerment might explain why Mrs. Garga of the Alliance for Democracy and Development (ADD), in making a critical examination of the present situation of the woman in Cameroon, according to Chinje (1997), "even went further to condemn the newly created CAUCUS of women as being a white elephant, empty of substance." Others see illiteracy as also contributing. Thus, a journalist from Conakry in Guinea, who was one of the coordinators of the Forum for African Women Educationalists (FAWE), lamented that two-thirds of Africa's illiterate population are women; and urged men especially "to look at women as unique beings and to give the girl-child the same type of education given to boys."[118]

As far as concerns the role of political parties, there is much to be decried by Chinje (1997) regarding "the role the woman has played within political parties, serving [only] as dancers and cooks for occasions." This ALVF report (Chinje, 1997) took particular note of the programs envisaged by each of the nine 1997 presidential candidates for the betterment of the Cameroonian woman. It began by lauding all the candidates for admitting that the Cameroonian woman faces peculiar problems that require special attention. But it

---

[116] See "Cameroon Female Politicians" *The Herald* N° 624 (24-25 June 1998), 6. See also Takwa Suifon, "The Future of Feminism" *The Herald* N° 508 (10-11 September 1997), 6.

[117] See also Peterkins Manyong, "Well-Placed Cameroonian Women Only Pay Lip Service to Female Empowerment – Aseh Dorothy, College Proprietress" *The Herald* N° 597 (20-21 April 1998), 14; and Rositta Fualem, "The Real Enemy of the Woman is the Woman" *The Herald* N° 419 (12-13 February 1997), 11.

[118] Peter Ngea Beng, "People Should Look at Women as Unique Human Beings – Madelein Kaba, Guinean Female Activist" *The Herald* N° 631 (10-12 July 1998), 13. See also Diane Acha Morfaw, "Women are Transformed into Workers Right from Childhood" *The Herald* N° 449 (23-24 April 1997), 11.

expressed regrets (1) that none of the candidates' wives gave them a helping hand in the campaigns; and (2) that none of them put forward any concrete, practical program even for the growth of the woman, "who all of them used as mere pawns to read out their respective programmes for the woman." Cases are given by the report to illuminate this point.

For the CPDM, for example, it was Dr. Mrs. Dorothy Njeuma (then Vice-Chancellor of the University of Buea) who spoke on behalf of her candidate, claiming that the incumbent has done a lot for the promotion of the woman since his accession to power in 1982. To illustrate this, Chinje (1997) pursued, Dr. Njeuma said President Biya created a ministry to take care of women's issues as far back as 1984 and that for the past 15 years many women have held responsible positions in the administration. She also said that there were forty women in the CPDM central committee with four in the political bureau. But either by design or by error, the ALVF report concluded, "Mrs. Njeuma did not say what these figures really represent. I therefore feel that her failure to provide a complete data to back her claims is only meant to mislead people." Mr. Paul Ndemhiyembe, another CPDM speaker claimed that if re-elected their candidate was going to "improve on the situation of the woman." But the word 'improve', to Chinje (1997), "can be taken to mean that this candidate is yet to realize that men and women need to participate fully as equal partners in ensuring effective economic growth."

The ALVF writer (Chinje, 1997) therefore called on "all Cameroonians and gender-sensitive men as well as women, in particular," "to examine their consciences and vote only the candidate who proved prepared to address their most cherished demands with commitment." The conclusion of this incisive report is that women feel strongly that the current practices of making them dancers and cooks for parties continue to tarnish their image. The ultimate ambition is to eventually have the woman integrated as an equal partner in development, for persistent inequality between women and men constrains a society's productivity, and, ultimately slows its growth. Women have the competence and should fully participate in the running of Cameroon.

The whole rhetoric of equality and of people's rule in Cameroon would appear to be soundly corroborated by another poignant illustration. As one researcher on the NGOs (non-governmental organizations) in Cameroon has also discovered, in almost every development project, the word *gender* is echoed. Given that women make up a large proportion of Cameroon's population (as I said earlier over 52%), there is need for gender-balanced development, the study recommends.[119] It is for this reason and many others, the research proceeds, that many NGOs have cropped up to cater for gender issues in development. Paradoxically, the findings posit, some of these NGOs that advocate gender-balanced development are gender biased. This is the case of Helvetas and the Women's Information and Co-ordination Office (AWICO) in Bamenda. Though directly involved in gender and development issues, Ms. Mufua concludes in her report, they are neither gender sensitive nor gender aware; for there is only one female worker in Helvetas and no male worker in AWICO which clearly shows that there is an imbalance. This imbalance does also heavily exist in the political arena, making the ruling CPDM irreplaceable long before the arrival of "paper" multipartism.

The 1990 Multipartism Law and the Irreplaceable One-Party System

Genuine politicians must simply have realized that the legalization of political parties in the early 90s in Cameroon was too good to be true and effective. A number of plainly simple indicators are there for even any savvy elementary school pupil to grasp. The first is that it is not the one-party in power that has to authorize other parties to exist. There just has to be a condition in the generally accepted constitution (such as the acquisition of a certain number or

---

[119] Jane Frances N. Mufua, "Creating Gender Awareness" *The Post* (24 October 1997), 6.

percentage of the seats in the national parliament) in order to be recognized as a national party. Which means also that anyone can form their political parties and restrict themselves to village, city, or provincial, politics; levels that would all also have their own conditions of recognition. The Germans and Canadians have available models to show the way to those interested in learning. For instance, to eliminate splinter parties and to further the state's interest in the stability of its political system, the Basic Law (German Constitution) requires parties to win at least 5 per cent of the total vote as a condition for entering the national parliament. Canada requires a minimum of not less than 12 seats in the federal parliament. The idea behind these 5% of votes & 12-seat requirements is just the opposite of what is desired in Cameroon, with all the submarine parties, as I show below. All this is possible because it is the person who is in power who makes the rules, not the generally drafted constitution. I think it would not be wrong to state that only a non-human would lose a match in which he or she is also the judge or referee.

The other indicators revolve around the manner through which those parties are even brought into existence. It is now obvious that the people that are "trying" to unseat the Cameroonian Emperor-president are just as culpable as the dictator insofar as they are not prepared to have a system that will make it possible for others to later challenge them (should they ever get in). Could Mr. Biya then not be right in charging, as he clearly does, that all these people are not interested in effective change and are only out to take his job? Sungmini explains it better when he discusses "Mr. Paul Biya's loud cry against Mr. Fru Ndi: *'Il veut changer quoi? Il veut [seulement] ma place'*."[120] That being so how does anyone expect the incumbent administrators not to suspect that they will all be ruthlessly hung as soon as others take over? It is not speculation on my part because the 'politics of the inside' and 'outside' clearly tells the story and Biya

---

[120] Njemuchar Sungmini, "CPDM-UNDP Accord: What Lesson?" *The Post* N° 0040 (23 December 1997), 6.

(perhaps, more than those he is dealing with) is intelligent enough to understand it.

Not surprising, having listened to the 'utilitarian calculus' of some Anglophone 'politicians of the inside', an expert has openly cried for the beloved country that should have been. An "honourable" parliamentarian is said to have given another rendition of the "*notre tour de bouffer politics*" (alias 'politics-of-the-inside') argument, according to Dr. Nantang Jua, when "he argued in one instance that now that from the inside they do not see anything wrong with the [Ahidjo-Biya] system... they may see something wrong with it once they become outsiders. In the face of this utilitarian calculus, I would not blame anyone who cries for the beloved country that would have been!"[121] The absence of sincerity/patriotism is thus at the heart of the difficulty of effecting genuine change (by both 'insiders' and 'outsiders') in Cameroon particularly and Africa generally. No one is willing to ask and address the right and fundamental questions. Perhaps that is what Protais Ayangma Amang must have realized when he advised that 'it is essential that political parties in this country exist and operate in the usual manner they do in other democracies.'[122] This advice would equally apply to a lot of issues in this country, including that of the implacability and intolerability of those already in power. It will be better to say something about the supposed justification of the system before looking at the recent law that has come only to perpetuate this system while camouflaging political pluralism – the system's 'pluralistic democracy in an entirely democratized single-party'.

---

[121] Charly Ndi Chia, "Why Gov't Is Bent on Destroying North West Traditional Authority – Dr. Nantang Jua." *Cameroon Post* N° 0274 (December 11-18, 1995b), 6.

[122] "*Il faudrait que les partis politiques banalisent les consultations dans ce pays pour en faire un processus normal.*" See Protais Ayangma Amang, President of Association of Cameroon Insurance Companies (ASAC) in interview with Michel Eclador Pokoua in *Le Messager* N° 590 (3 mars 1997), 6.

On The Justification of the Single-Party State

'Advanced democracy', as seen in Biya's *serene and disciplined community* (in Chapter 2), assumes one where there are simply no conflicts and discussions and compromises; as observed in the considerable length Biya (1986: 43-47) would go to justify the so-called "temporary" and "imperative" need (who decides this?) for the perpetuation of the one-party farce he calls advanced democracy. (Note also always that the single-party is incompatible with federalism and, therefore, multiculturalism.) Among such imperatives, the One-Party, Biya (1986: 43) claims, has not only spared Cameroon from the political chaos plaguing other countries in Africa, but, Biya (1986: 44, emphasis added) rhetorically concludes,

> is also necessary for the mobilization of human resources, especially intellectual resources which, though so invaluable, are still scarce in our country. *For, how could we ensure the efficient running of the State machinery if the political leanings of the few senior officials Cameroon now has were to be torn between several opposing parties thus creating for any ruling regime an insurmountable crisis of power?*

The experts are however quickly dismissing this as a nonsensical justification. In a modern age that stresses realism and political pragmatism rather than strict dogma, Fombad writes, the doctrine of separation of powers facilitates unity, cohesion, and harmony within a system of checks and balances. It is clear that while the separation of powers on its own cannot guarantee constitutional democracy, he continues, where, as in Botswana, it exists and is allowed to work, it does so reasonably well and creates a more sustainable and feasible constitutional democracy.[123] In addition, I would add, the doctrine of separation of powers is not meant to promote serenity and

---

[123] Charles Manga Fombad, "The Separation of Powers and Constitutionalism in Africa: The Case of Botswana" 25:2 *Boston College Third World Law Journal* (2005), 301 at 342.

discipline but to generate said 'insurmountable crisis of power' that would then necessitate mandatory negotiation with, and compromise of, the parties concerned. That is essentially the American Founding Fathers' idea behind the United States system with its fixed term of office and rigid checks which St. John-Stevas (1968: 11) and Loewenstein[124] say have led more to paralysis of government than anything else. These experts are here inferring the advantage of the parliamentary system.

The greatest (and at the same time weakest) feature of the parliamentary system is the flexibility and close collaboration it allows between the legislative and executive arms of government, especially in the legislation-making area. This is also one of the main distinctions between the two systems of government in North America (Canada and US). Flexibility is thus characteristic of the parliamentary system which brings to the service of the state what Bagehot has called "an unrivalled average of continued ability" (St. John-Stevas, 1968: 8). This means that it avoids an unnecessary stalemate; it further prevents corruption and checks, if it does not exclude injustice (as against totalitarian states[125]). This is because St. John-Stevas (1968: 9) thinks that the knowledge and/or fact that action can be taken at any time that a government is no longer wanted by the electorate (as opposed to the fixed "term-of-office" systems) are/is continued check. The flexibility of the Canadian system is absent in the American system marked by paralysis of government that necessarily results from rigid separation of powers. Examples to substantiate St. John-Stevas' assertion on the paralysis of the American system are not hard to give; notably, President Franklin Roosevelt's attempts to pack the American Supreme Court

---

[124] K. Loewenstein, *British Cabinet Government* (London: Oxford University Press, 1967) at 151.

[125] But both R.H.S. Crossman, *The Myths of Cabinet Government* (Harvard University Press, Cambridge, Mass., 1972) at 55 and Moorhouse (1977: 113-139) would think the corruption check is now otherwise in Britain.

when it frustrated his New Deal Economic Recovery Programs[126] and Thomas Jefferson's tireless insistence that the executive also has the right (like the Courts and Senate) to pass upon the constitutionality of the acts of the other branches (see Commager, 1958: chapter 2). But why are American presidents not always crying out loud against the paralysis and hotly seeking a 'serene and disciplined community'?

The paralysis issue cannot even be restricted to the congressional system. Even the parliamentary system is not devoid of it as can be seen clearly in France before 1958 (See Blondel, 1985). As a federal parliamentary democracy could better serve Africa's need, it is essential that I say something about the instability of the parliamentary system right now. Some experts like Mallory have posited that, unless there is a strong bond holding King, Lords and Commons together, the British parliamentary system is essentially unstable.[127] Mallory's thesis is easily propped up by France before that country's 1958 Constitution; a constitution which Radamaker says

> Was an invention of De Gaulle, an expression of that powerful individual's determination to govern France unencumbered by the parliamentary factionalism which had resulted in the total paralysis of the government of the Fourth Republic at the time of the Algerian crisis. The constitution of 1958, tailor-made, as it were, for De Gaulle, limited the sovereignty of Parliament, not vis-à-vis the citizen by subjecting legislation to review for conformity to libertarian norms, but rather in relation to the

---

[126] See Kenneth M. Holland, "The Courts in the United States" in J.L. Waltman and K.M. Holland, eds., *The Political Role of Law Courts in Modern Democracies* (New York: St. Martin's Press, 1988), 6 at 27; and Harvard Law Review Editorial Board, "Round and Round the Bramble Bush: From Legal Realism to Critical Legal Scholarship" 95 *Harvard Law Review* (1982), 1669 at 1674-76

[127] J.R. Mallory, *The Structure of Canadian Government* (Toronto: Gage Publishing Company, 1984) at 6

executive branch of government.[128]

Important to note is the fact that it is bond, and not bound that is needed to hold the system together.

To begin with, as Cameroon is neither parliamentary nor congressional, the instability and paralysis that are characteristic of these systems would be a non-issue for it. Cameroon can simply not hide behind the instability of the parliamentary system per se. One must, furthermore, have to go beyond that and ask why, and if actually, there is no strong bond that holds Cameroonians generally together, let alone the traditional branches which some critics have discovered do not even exist in Cameroon, let alone any exclusive domain for the Legislature;[129] this applying also to the 1961 "Federal" Republic of Cameroon that effectively baptized, confirmed, and territorially extended the 1959 *pleins pouvoirs* law which had effectively destroyed parliamentary democracy and ushered in advanced democracy. Some of the critics of the *pleins pouvoirs* law like Sibafo have then not failed to ponder if to the French, for instance, democracy means clothing a single individual with open-ended emergency powers.[130] Sibafo has come to the conclusion that this is

---

[128] Dallis Radamaker, "The Courts in France" in J.L. Waltman and K.M. Holland, eds., *The Political Role of Law Courts in Modern Democracies* (New York: St. Martin's Press, 1989), 129 at 140.

[129] See Georges Burdeau, *Traité de science politique*, Tome V, at 38, cited by F. Mbome, "Les empéchement du président de la république au Cameroun" *R. Jur. Pol. Ind. Coop.* T.32 (Paris, Sept. 1978) at 905, translated and quoted by Anyangwe (1989: 34 n.32). See also J. Gicquel, "Le présidentielisme négro-africain: l'exemple camerounais" in *Melanges Offerts à Georges Burdeau* (Paris: LGDJ, 1977) at 701. As Fossungu has also told strangers to advanced democracy, "'Executive' in this democracy would properly connote executive as normally obtains elsewhere *plus* elsewhere parliament: although not in their combination; simply the *Président de la République*. In other words, it refers to nothing else than the president in his all-embracing, Janus-like, trio capacity of sole law-maker, law-enforcer, and chief justice" Peter Ateh-Afac Fossungu, "Doing *Noddometrics* in the Advanced School of Democracy" *The Herald* N° 608 (15-17 May 1998f), 10 (underlining as in original).

[130] "*[L]a démocratie[française] consiste-t-elle à donner les pleins pouvoirs à un seul homme sans l'accord de tous?....un homme peut-il, lui seul, prendre toutes les décisions relative au*

not democracy as is in place in France.

But Blondel (1985: 117) does think Sibafo's conclusion is somewhat inaccurate because he considers France to be, without doubt, the most mysterious of Western countries most probably because it is the French way of life to have a one-person show in matters of governance. As he argues further, even France's political "stability has been acquired only through a political system which is very different from those of other Western countries in that it gives the [French] president not merely executive powers but a dominance over the whole system which exceeds by far the authority of the American president." Through this type of governmental set-up, Magstadt (1991: 103) thinks the French president (from whom the intellectually sloppy Cameroonian copying is being done) "can exercise emergency powers (which make him a virtual dictator) by simply declaring a state of emergency."

Nevertheless, if those open-ended emergency powers were scrapped and Cameroon becomes a federal parliamentary democracy today, it could be one of the most genuinely stable nations on God's earth. It is now clear that the realization of the federal parliamentary system of governance in Cameroon cannot at all be difficult, if only the will and zeal are there. From the way the 'painfully myth-consuming and peace-loving' Cameroonian people have so far coexisted in their Mosaic Tower of Babel, it is clear that most of the so-called sources of instability and paralysis associated with the parliamentary system cannot even apply in Cameroon (see Chapter 5). The bond needed to hold the system's organs together, of course, is the "national interest" which is clearly absent in the thinking of the unpatriotic and uncharismatic ruling elite in Cameroon, but very much present in France since 1958.

It is well known from both Magstadt (1991: 102) and Mensah-gbadago (1991: 4) that in both Cameroon and France the PORs are in a position to manipulate the system and achieve desired results.

---

fonctionnement d'un [pays]? Est-il à même d'apporter, lui seul, les modifications nécessaires à l'appareil du [pays]? Quel non!" J.D. Sibafo, "Des questions et d'autres: la démocratie façon RDPC" *La Nouvelle Expression*, (30 août 1996), 9.

The sole difference in their manipulations however is found in the very simple fact that the interest of *la patrie* is the point of departure in France, but not in Cameroon (where it is *only* the interest – and an illegitimate one for that matter – of the manipulator and his masters that is overriding). That is why I often pity French-speaking Africans a lot when they go about hoping and even rejoicing that a certain person as president of France would mean a change in France's policy towards its neo-colonies in Africa. They simply do not understand what *la patrie* means to the French. It pays to note that this is what makes the French neo-presidential system (seen by Magstadt (1991: 108) as a built-in time bomb) to smoothly work rather than explode, to the utter amazement of most people, some of whom could not help declaring like Blondel (1985: 117) that "France is, without doubt, the most mysterious of Western countries." France's divisive political tendencies are there for all to see. But it is only because no party, personal, regional, and other interests whatsoever, must compromise that of *toute la nation entière*, that the apparently unworkable system, according to Teubner (1992: 1444), has come "to remain in the comforting twilight of closure and openness, separation and interwovenness, autonomy and interdependence in…[political] pluralism." That is, indeed, the whole mystery about the French mystery. There is a bottom line; that is why the French prime minister's effective powers are not illicitly regarded as threatening 'the integrity of the [French Head of] State' who, on many issues, remains an arbiter rather than an actor (Magstadt, 1991: 102; and Blondel, 1985: 166). In Cameroon no iota of powers must be left in any other hands other than the POR's to the extent that even 'legalized' political parties must remain mere empty shells.

The 'Cameroon is Cameroon'("*Le Cameroun c'est le Cameroun*") boastful attitude of the regime is quite understandable, for the killing or abandonment of multiparty politics is, of course, the destruction of democracy (that permits the striking of a balance between justice and order) as was done by the English-speaking in the 'Federal' Republic of Cameroon through their 'unified single national party' in what some critics (Zang-Atangana[131]; Benjamin, 1972: 54-55; Bjornson, 1991: 112-114) have lengthily described as "The Mad Rush Towards Ahidjo's Union Camerounaise". Konings and Nyamnjoh (1997: 210) tell the story in more straightforward and clear terms when they posit that Ahidjo looked upon federalism as an unavoidable stage in the establishment of a strong unitary state, and employed various tactics to achieve this objective. After becoming President of the Federal Republic of Cameroon in October 1961, he played Anglophone political factions off against each other, eventually persuading them to join the *Union nationale camerounaise* (UNC), the single party formed in September 1966, and was able to penalise any anglophone leader like Prime Minister Jua who remained committed to federalism. This One-Party federation of theirs has been and is being passed under the name of national unity, order and tranquillity. This is just as nonsensical as their single-party advanced democracy and experts on Democratic Federalism have all stiffly challenged it. Dawson (1970: 415) thinks there must be the existence of parties in the plural, for it is obvious that democratic government as it is understood and practised in Canada cannot function without the aid of more than one party; the communist and fascist idea of a single party and the rigid suppression of all dissenters has clearly no place in a democracy. The question is: Has the situation changed today in Cameroon with the law on multipartism?

Deconstructing the Multipartism Law

Could there be an effective Opposition party (let alone strong third parties) in Cameroon today: with the selfish and corrupt attitude of Cameroonians? Put differently, can the ADD, for instance, effectively ensure that its federalism contribution (which appears to threaten West-Central African political geography and peace) is imputed into the government's program? I would like to answer this

---

[131] Joseph-Marie Zang-Atangana, *Les forces politiques au Cameroun réunifié: Tome 2 - L'expérience de l'UC et du KNDP* (Paris: L'Harmattan, 1989) at 95-119.

question through a detailed look at Cameroon's current single-party multipartism. Very briefly then, I would say NO; because the regime is indeed still the One-Party System which is clearly the synonym for dictatorship, defined by Pearson and Rochester (1984: 593) as a closed, authoritarian governmental system in which the free expression and flow of ideas is severely curtailed and political opposition severely restricted. This definition also captures the "paper system" because multipartism can clearly not be effective where there are simply empty shells being called parties, most of them with no platform or issues except the insatiable filling of the belly.

The 'platformlessness' or 'issuelessness' of the myriad of 'opposition' political parties in Cameroon has, *inter alia*, been well orchestrated by the unilingual 1990 Parties Law (*Loi N° 90/056 du 19 décembre 1990 relative aux parties politiques*), carefully designed by the incumbent president who is very desirous of preserving himself as life Emperor of the U.K. (Unconstitutional Kingdom-republic) of Cameroon. The stark reality is simply that Cameroon has only been silently legalizing hundreds of paper parties. In Cameroon (which copies from France but not its effective multipartism and unique divided executive), there is hardly any separation. There is only fusion to a degree that even political parties must remain mere shadows. Thus, as Canada and others are *Legalizing Politics*,[132] Cameroon will only be silently legalizing myriad of empty shells called political parties. "If that just about covers it," Mewett (1996: 386) has questioned, then "why invent a concept [called multipartism] that does not exist?" Why do so except for confusion? An elaborate examination of the sham creation of the multiparty concept itself will help the experts' charge.

By the Parties Law (article 5(1)), political parties are created by first having a *dossier complet* or complete file or application. The

---

[132] See Michael Mandel, *The Charter of Rights and the Legalization of Politics in Canada* (Toronto: Wall and Thompson, 1989).

completeness of the application necessitates (I will indent them so that they can stand out):

> (1) a stamped application that indicates the names, addresses, as well as the complete identity, profession and residence of those to be at the helm of the party; (2) a certificate of non-conviction of the prospective leaders; (3) three copies of *le procés verbal de l'assemblée constitutive;* (4) three copies of the statutes; (5) written, signed and legalized undertaking to respect or abide by the enumerated principles of article 9 below [to be seen later]; (6) *un mémorandum sur le projet de société ou le programme politique du parti;* and (7) an indication of party headquarters.

(The law is, as it is usual in Biya's Cameroon, only in French and I have cautiously avoided translating where the sense/effect may be lost.) By article 5(2), any change or modification in any of the above requirements must be communicated to the governor's office concerned (*gouverneur territorialement compétent*). The complete application is then filed with the Minister of Territorial Administration through the said governor's office (article 4(1)), the said governor then has to issue, to the depositing party, *"Une décharge mentionnant le numéro et la date d'enregistrement du dossier"* (article 4(2)); also having *"quinze (15) jours francs"* within which to forward the same to the said minister (article 6); with this minister being the only competent person to decide on and authorize the existence of the party being requested (article 7(1)).

How does one know if the requested party has been legalized in Cameroon? It is very silently simple indeed, by article 7(2): *"En cas de silence gardé pendant trois (3) mois à compter de la date de dépôt du dossier auprès des services du gouverneur territorialement competent, le parti est réputé exister légalement."* This provision is simply saying that no news is good news. Hence, three months of silence from the date the complete application is submitted to the concerned governor's office signifies that the requested party has been legalized. Unlike in the toilet where 'yes' means occupied and, therefore, 'You can't come in', this time it is silence that means yes. The *silent* nature of this article 7(2) of the Parties Law is effectively the commencement of the *sous-marins* (submarines) strategy that is just one of the several methods that have been carefully designed solely to flush effective multiparty politics down the drain, where it appears, in the estimation of the Biya regime, to properly belong. Who in Biya's position would voluntarily give up the unrestrained powers he enjoys?

Success in the strategy of perpetuating his iron-fisted rule has been greatly guaranteed by the greed of Cameroon "politicians".[133] The submarines are political parties with no agenda or following (headed by 'former' CPDM stalwarts) that the ruling CPDM silently legalizes so as to conveniently dilute and stultify any effective opposition. Who then said Biya could be besieged by the opposition? According to an un-authored piece in 32:15 *Africa Confidential* of 26 July 1991 titled "Cameroon: Biya Besieged", these parties are known as submarines, "because they dive underwater to torpedo the big ships." But that is not the only potent arm because, where those big ships cannot be torpedoed in that fashion, there is another more potent weapon. According to article 17(1) of the Parties Law, the territorial administration minister can, for reasons of *"l'ordre public"*, suspend the activities of any of these parties; with possibility of his decision being taken to court as per article 8 of the Parties Law (article 17(2)). These parties can, in similar manner, also be dissolved, with such dissolution not barring legal proceedings against their leaders (articles 18-20).

---

[133] See A.A. Nyangkwe, "Antar Gassagaye Says Creation of Many Parties Encourages Tribalism, Hatred" *The Herald* (11-13 October 1996), 2; M. Aleni, "Cameroon is Cracking Because of Selfishness" *The Herald* (27-29 May 1996), 4; Shey Wo Fonkui, "Is Cameroon a One-Party State in Disguise?" *The Herald* (13-15 September 1996), 4; Amugwa Paul, "Wouldn't There Be Multipartism Without Arm-twisting?" *The Herald* (4-6 October 1996), 4; Nkuku Nwige, "A Helpless Call for a True Multiparty Democracy in Cameroon" *The Herald* (3-4 March 1997), 4; T. Dibussi, "To the Leaders of the Cameroonian Opposition" *Cameroon Post* (28 December 1990 – 4 January 1991), 4; and George Cheba Ntenga, "Who Will Save Cameroon: Multipartism or God?" *Cameroon Post* (30 May-6 June 1991), 6.

All this, I am inclined to think, should have clearly led anyone genuinely desirous of change in Cameroon to question a lot. For instance, by article 5(2) of the 1996 Constitution (which is just the continuation of previous ones since the federal) the Cameroonian president "is the symbol of national unity" – with this becoming even more disastrous when that president alone (by this same provision) decides/defines what that elusive concept entails; ensures respect for the Constitution; is the guarantor of the independence of the Nation and of its territorial integrity; etc. This should unmistakably and inevitably signify to anyone with the slightest amount of brains that *anything* that tends towards unseating this president must simply become a threat to "national unity". That being the case, the ultimate question that any of the so-called opposition party leaders (if they are/were really out to fix Cameroon for their children) should be posing, rather than madly rushing to create shadow parties, is this. Just how can anyone ever unseat the incumbent, without threatening "national unity"? This question should have as goal the unconditional call for a complete clean slate to begin with, as happened in most other francophone African countries, notably Benin, with national conferences that laid down new ground rules.[134]

The question is even more especially important as these same opposition leaders must have also initially undertaken in the Parties Law's article 5(1) that has been set out above to respect the principles of article 9 of the Parties Law by which: 'No legalization would be allowed for any political party that: - threatens the state's territorial integrity, national unity, the republican nature of the state, national sovereignty, and national integration, especially by way of any kind of discrimination, be it based on ethnicity, province of origin, linguistic group or religious belief; - leans towards violence or envisages having a military or paramilitary organization; - receives foreign financial support or whose leaders (one or all) resides abroad; - favours

---

[134] See Filip Reyntjens, "The Wind of Change. Political and Constitutional Evolution in Francophone Africa, 1990-1991" 35 *Journal of African Law* (1991), 43–55.

internal strife or war with other nations.'[135] This would effectively mean in Canada, if the same model of legalizing parties is adopted there, that the government in Ottawa would have been crazy to have legalized the Bloc Québéçois.

Brought back to Cameroon, could this law actually be representative of the confluence of, or war between, dictatorship and democracy in the preservation of international peace and frontiers? I ask this question because it is not exactly clear what the ADD president means by Ahidjo's enlargement of the federal system in 1972 in Cameroon (see Azeng, 1997, as discussed in Chapter 5 below). Could the ADD president actually be referring to the realization of the *Kamerun Idea*? That is, is he alluding to the regaining of former German Kamerun by reuniting all its severed parts, including British Northern Cameroons (that is now part and parcel of Nigeria) and other territories that France had ceded to its adjoining colonies, as indicated by Lantum (1991: 20)? Or is he instead alluding to Ahidjo's rumoured annexation of Spanish-speaking Equatorial Guinea in the late 1960s to form a trilingual federation, as Rubin (1971: 192) has suggested? Which of the two possibilities could be the enlargement of Cameroon's federation that Garga Harman Adji would be referring to? Could he be having both situations in mind?

Either or both ways would clearly still involve the redrawing of West-Central African political geography as well as affecting international peace, all of which Biya's dictator-perpetuating law here seems to have excluded. In other words, articles 9 and 17-20 (requiring dissolution for reasons of "*l'ordre public*") of the internal

---

[135] *Ne peut être autorisé, tout parti politique qui:*

- *porte atteinte à l'intégrité territoriale, à l'unité nationale, à la forme républicaine de l'Etat, à la souveraineté nationale et à l'intégration nationale, notamment par toute sortes de discriminations basées sur les tribus, les provinces, les groupes linguistiques ou les confessions religieuses;*

- *prône le recours à la violence ou envisage la mise sur pied d'une organisation militaire ou para-militaire;*

- *reçoit les subsides de l'étranger ou dont l'un des dirigeants statuaires réside à l'étranger;*

- *favorise la belligérance entre les composantes de la Nation ou entre des pays.*

dictatorial multipartism law in Cameroon would appear to have served to avoid the implementation of the ADD federation enlargement agenda because that would involve "threatening" not only "the [Cameroon] state's territorial integrity" (through incorporating 'new' territories) but also those of neighbours (Central African Republic, Gabon, Nigeria, and Equatorial Guinea); thus necessitating the application of the nullifying dissolution arm of that law. Is there any court in the country to which the ADD can then turn for umpiring on the issue? Yes. That court is judge and party – Biya. Should international law and community begin to turn a blind eye to this real problem because of the wars and the like that Dictator Biya has (inadvertently) taken care of, then I would like to invite them to this other side of the coin. Imagine Biya being the one with the Kamerun Idea agenda, who or what organ is there in Cameroon to put a break on his war-mongering agenda? Is Bakassi not a clean case to this issue of undemocratic administrations making themselves the synonyms of the state?

Whatever the case, the attitude of Cameroonian politicians who have formed and are still creating all these shadow political parties is even more incomprehensible especially as the one-party-perpetuating Parties Law itself very clearly states in article 8(2) that 'in case of disagreement the person seeking the legalization of a political party can sue the authorities refusing such legalization in the administrative branch of the Supreme Court in accordance with the laws in place.' One of such laws is specifically the much-regulated Ordinance regulating the Cameroon Supreme Court (*Ordonnance N° 72/6 du 26 août 1972 fixant l'organisation de la Cour suprême*). The story of the dependence of the 'apex' court in Cameroon can be considerably cut short by the manner the country's Supreme Court has itself been brutally regulated, as seen in this *Ordonnance*, which Fossungu says provides the "appetizer to the [confusing] story of amendments in Cameroon."

Indicative of the trouble the judicial institution in Cameroon is in, according to Fossungu, this legislation was amended barely two months later by *Ordonnance N° 72/21 du 19 octobre 1972 modifiant l'Ordonnance N° 72/6 du 26 août 1972 fixant l'organisation de la Cour suprême*: with this modification being itself re-modified six months later by *Ordonnance N° 73/9 du 25 avril 1973 modifiant l'Ordonnance N° 72/6 du 26 août 1972 fixant l'organisation de la Cour suprême*. There was then a bit of *Ordonnance*-converting space of three and one-third years before the Olympian affirmation of executive almightiness resumed with *Lois: Loi N° 76/17 du 8 juillet 1976 modifiant l'Ordonnance N° 72/6 du 26 août 1972 fixant l'organisation de la Cour suprême* was followed successively by *Loi N° 83/3 du 21 juillet 1983 modifiant l'Ordonnance N° 72/6 du 26 août 1972 fixant l'organisation de la Cour suprême* and *Loi N° 89/817 du 28 juillet 1989 modifiant l'Ordonnance N° 72/6 du 26 août 1972 fixant l'organisation de la Cour suprême*.[136] Only after 17 years of application and modifications, as the author of this appetizing story indicates, was it realized that the 1972 Ordinance had all through been incomplete; and it was supposedly then *completely modified* by *Loi N° 89/019 du décembre 1989 modifiant et complètant certaines dispositions de l'Ordonnance N° 72/6 du 26 août 1972 fixant l'organisation de la Cour suprême*. But is that the end of its modification? Then what about the recent avalanche of laws that are still modifying this *Ordonnance N° 72/6 du 26 août 1972 fixant l'organisation de la Cour suprême*?[137]

Could a court like this one be able to say a decision taken by the executive agent (the minister of territorial administration) must be reversed and the solicited party legalized, or that the party-legalization process in Cameroon be changed? By article 8(3) of the Parties Law, certain provisions of this 1972 Supreme Court Ordinance have been set aside *("Par dérogation aux dispositions...")* to permit those whose envisaged political parties have been refused legalization to have recourse to court action 'by simply presenting a request for a determination before the president of the administrative branch of

---

[136] Peter Ateh-Afac Fossungu, "The Cameroonian Judiciary in the Decree-Ordinance Trouble" *The Herald* N° 667 (30 September-1 October 1998), 10.

[137] *Id.* See also Pougoué, Paul-Gérard and Maurice Kamto, "Commentaire de la Loi N° 89/018 du 28 juillet 1989 portant modification de la Loi N° 75/16 du 08 décembre 1975 fixant procédure et fonctionnement de la Cour Suprême" 1 *Juridis Info (Revue de la Législation et Jurisprudence Camerounaises)* (1990), 5.

the Supreme Court.' Anyangwe (1996: 824-25) has shown that administrative justice in Cameroon is a total sham; being tied largely to the dependent status of the court.

Shouldn't any right-thinking person have first made sure that this un-supreme court becomes effectively supreme before launching into creating a political party? Where are the likes of Daniel Kemajou (who would rather die in dignity than live in slavery and dishonour) in this country? Have all the authentic democrats of this country been slaughtered by *pleins pouvoirs*, leaving only Laski's ignorant democrats? As Laski has very competently explained their attitude, ignorant democrats simply cannot defend democratic principles because they usually only know what they have lost after they have lost it, at which time it is too late to halt, let alone eliminate the dictatorship.[138] And where are the 'Anglophones' that boasted so profusely about teaching their French-speaking 'brothers' across the Mungo River the essentials of responsible governance? What is responsible government but another name for one that is marked by separation of powers and constitutionalism?

This confusion called Advanced Democracy is essential in Cameroon because democracy, to Biya (1986: 41), is pluralistically "real", "successful and lasting" only because the demons of irredentism have been neutralized:

> Indeed, every Cameroonian must be fully conscious of the fact that the past does not give us any example of a successful and lasting democracy other than those communities which have neutralized the demons of irredentism and of those centrifugal forces likely to threaten its [sic] existence as a socio-historical unit.

---

[138] "*Des démocrates ignorants ne pourront défendre la démocratie, tout simplement parce qu'ils sauront trop tard ce qu'ils auront perdu.*" Harold-J. Laski, *Le gouvernement parlementaire en Angleterre* [Translated by Jacque Cadart and Jacqueline Prélot] (P.U.F., Paris, 1950) at 323.

The Cameroonian authorities are quite right in this (see Franck, 1968: 184, quoting Alexander Hamilton's warning to the new states of Africa and Asia; and Shenoy, 1974: 10). But they are hardly correct when it comes to the *methods* of achieving such neutralization. The correct method is through genuine national unity which tolerates dissent and rejoices in diversity. Real national unity is rather promoted in multiethnic societies by federalism. In the proper words Bayefsky (1989: 443), "Real unity tolerates dissent and rejoices in variety of outlook and tradition, recognizes that it is man's destiny to unite and not divide, and understands that creating proletariats and scapegoats and second-class citizens is a mean and contemptible activity. Unity, so understood, is the extra dimension that raises the sense of belonging into genuine human life."

It is thought that a relentless pursuit of their desired Perfect-Nation/New-Ethnic-Group course is tantamount to trying to eliminate politics, which is an exercise in vain because Antonio Cassese has pointed out how the plain "fact is that conflicts and discussions cannot be simply swept under the carpet. They resurface again no matter how skilfully they are glossed over."[139] They can thus only be skilfully managed, not eliminated. The management of conflicts is the *art* called politics. Trying to eliminate conflicts, therefore, others have cautioned, is tantamount to being dead and alive at the same time. As Banfield and Wilson (1963: 20-21) have written,

> Whether one likes it or not, politics, like sex, cannot be abolished. It can sometimes be repressed by denying people the opportunity to practice it, but it cannot be done away with because it is the nature of… [human beings] to disagree and contend. We are not saying that politics arises solely from the selfish desire of some to have their way, although that is certainly one source of it. The

---

[139] Cited in Peter Ateh-Afac Fossungu, "The ICAO Assembly: The Most Unsupreme of Supreme Organs in the United Nations System? A Critical Analysis of Assembly Sessions" 26 *Transportation Law Journal* (1998), 1 at 24 n.97.

fact is that even in a society of altruists or angels there would be politics, for some would conceive the common good in one way and some in another, and (assuming the uncertainties that prevail in this world) some would think one course of action more prudent and some would think another.

It can thus be seen that being dead and alive at the same time is the fate of the bulk of Cameroonians, but it is even worse for the English-speaking minority. The Perfect Nation/NEG exercise then is nothing but part of the generalized confusion in Cameroon, an exercise that assures that the confusionists stay forever in power in their perfect nation; a perfect nation with a perfectly confusing multiculturalism that embodies a type of culture that does not encapsulates history, as Chapter 4 elaborately shows.

Chapter 4

Colonialism And The Leadership Mess In Africa: When History Is Not Historical – From Cameroon To Njangawatar?

People's culture must, of course, embody their history and vice versa. Hopefully there must be substantial, if not general, agreement on this. We have seen Lantum (1991) largely praising the efforts of the 'Intellectuals in Politics' who brought forth the current State of Cameroon now under review. As it happens too often in Cameroon that is 'blessed' with what the critics call an illegitimate foundation, the Yaoundé University professor of medicines (like many others) might not have known that he was doing just the opposite by citing from Professor Seeley's rhyme on fruitless political science without history. That is, condemning those 'Intellectuals in Politics' for having neglected history in Foumban, and thence bringing about the fatality that has since plagued Cameroon generally and its English-speaking community in particular.

I would want to borrow the professor's rhyme and similarly posit here that culture without history is not worth calling culture; history without culture is fruitless; and culture without history is rootless. Whichever of the two that exists without the other does not indeed exist, for a very simple reason. Since a vital and successful mobilization of internal cultural norms to support international human rights must recognize change as an integral part of culture Clifford Geertz, according to Toope (1997: 180), has defined culture as "an historically transmitted pattern of meanings embodied in symbols." Culture cannot therefore properly exist without history and vice versa; this holding, notwithstanding the Cameroon administration's threatening ambivalent posture that seeks to confuse the uniting of one history for the attainment of national unity.

The Cameroon regime would think that culture without history is not worthless; and has also defined what is meant by culture especially for Cameroon, as seen in Chapter 1. The regime seems however to flatly disagree with Geertz's definition of culture. But they do not disagree in the normal straightforward way but in camouflage, as usual. That is, there is an 'advanced democratic agreement' in the sense that while defining culture in Cameroon to include history, history is paradoxically being denied there. For illustration, Cameroon's teachers and other intellectuals have been instructed by Biya (1986, 9-10) not to "focus on" or study "the past [because] this could hinder a clear appraisal of the present and appropriate preparation for the future. We know that what requires our energies today is the future of our country." Why wouldn't the badly educated youths then remain utterly lost on critical political and constitutional issues that they ought to be able to grapple with in the future? How are they going to ever develop without their proper or authentic history?

On The Importance of History to Development

The name-change justification in this country is a clear denial of history, or least, the one that is created by human beings. Regression is thus the word that properly describes any development or nation-building which is carried out without authentic history. A people's uncensored history has a direct link to their development. To be useful to development, history must be the people's proper history. Only then does history play the role that is its own. Those in power cannot therefore create history that is unknown to the people and impose it upon them. Bjornson (1991: 160) cites Philombe as pointing out in *Le Livre Camerounais et ses auteurs* (1984) that the only true story of a people is the one they themselves tell. Ikeda (1987: 187) also cites the late Chinese Chairman Mao as categorically stating that "the people, the people alone, are the motive power that creates history."

Cameroonians are still to create history or, at least, one that is properly theirs; this book being meant to assist in that creation. On 9

June 1984 (the same year of the name-change that ushered in the worrisome atmosphere that is currently still dangerously rocking the National Unity Boat), Ikeda (1987: 186-91) delivered at Fudan University in China an important lecture titled 'History Is Made by Human Beings'. Because this is not the case in Cameroon, the country has simply become the best case in the study of political, cultural, and constitutional regression in Africa. It also principally explicates why countries like Botswana beat Cameroon in the continental nation-building match (as detailed out in the next Chapter). This regression is incongruously called 'advanced development' whose handmaids are 'balanced development plans', a unique kind of development that critics have found to be ironically not balanced on history and/or the country's undeniable cultural diversity. National regression is the correct appellation for it, since that is exactly what occurs when rather than unite two or more histories one 'unites' one history – all in the yearning for the totalitarian and discriminatory 'perfect nation'.

The instruction in the Hinge of Africa for history to be neglected is unimaginable and regrettable for any community that hopes to progress or develop or nation-build. There are several reasons that could each fill small volumes but presently two could be given. Absent confusion and its corollaries it is not clear how anyone can conceivably chart the path of the rational and methodical development of any country in Africa (or the world), without a sound knowledge of that country's past and present. I say this especially because Cameroonians have been invited and challenged by the same people giving them the interdiction on history to "today, more than ever before...take up the compass to chart the path of the rational and methodical development of Cameroon" (Biya, 1986: 9-10). If this is not confusion or regression, then it is hard to know what it is. Moreover, a year later a university professor acted in response to the challenge when he put his book at the disposal of the authorities, in which Anyangwe (1987: 269) clearly advocated that "[t]he task before us is to produce a legal system which in essence answers to Cameroonian needs, fits into Cameroonian circumstances and synchronizes with Cameroonian culture and aspirations in the modern world. It is strongly submitted that any rule of law which passes this test must be included in the Cameroonian legal arsenal irrespective of where such a rule originates from." This is indeed shrewd advice.

Eleven years after Anyangwe, Fossungu emphasized the point by amply illustrating how Quebecers who are of French stock are abandoning or remodelling French models like its Code Civil that do not fit into their realities but 'Francophone Africans tenaciously cling to them like the oxygen they breathe' even when these French things just do not fit into their situations.[140] Fombad also followed up in 2008 by clearly explaining to them that the main reason why the prospects for constitutionalism have been far better under the constitutions of Anglophone African countries rather than those of Francophone African countries is that whilst reforms in all these countries have drawn a lot from their colonial legal heritage, Anglophone African countries have approached these reforms with more openness and have looked far beyond England for inspiration and guidance. Members of constitutional reform commissions have travelled to Europe, North America, Asia, notably India, in order to learn more about modern constitutional developments. Many Francophone African constitutional draftsmen by contrast have continued to seek inspiration from and rely almost slavishly on what they perceive as the most reliable and unassailable constitutional model: the Gaullist Fifth Republic constitution and the timid amendments that have been made to it in the last fifty years.[141] These experts are always available to help but the inviting authorities have for their part only given their contributions to the dustbin. If

---

[140] See Peter Ateh-Afac Fossungu, "When Frenchmen Throw Away French But Non-French (Africans) Hold It Sacred and Immutable" *The Herald* N° 638 (27-28 July 1998), 10.

[141] Charles Manga Fombad, "Constitutional Reforms in France and Their Implications for Constitutionalism in Francophone Africa" Paper for Open Society Institute, Africa Governance Monitoring and Advocacy Project (June 2008) 1-5 at 1, available at www.AfriMAP_Fombad_Eng.pdf (last visited in March 2011).

not for the sake of confusion, why invite people to contribute when their contribution would not be welcomed?

Neglecting history is incredible for any society that hopes to progress because Ikeda (1987: 188) has posited that "history is fraught with didactic import and is a living reality in the present." The contradiction or confusion involved in the instruction to teachers in Cameroon may properly expound why this country, supposedly to be overflowing with cultural values, would appear to have no known values (since "Values are a deposit of experience in time past"[142]). The importance of the values of a society would not need to detain us, but it is stressed that these values influence the norms of the society concerned. Robertson (1987: 64) has thus indicated that if a community values education highly its norms will make provision for mass schooling. If it values a large population, its norms will encourage big families. In principle at least, all norms can be traced to a basic social value. Values are then a deposit of experience in time past. That is the basic element of a community's history; and no history effectively means that there are no values for the concerned community. One cannot then underestimate history's importance in any meaningful development.

By the way, is it not commonly said that one cannot know where one is heading to until one knows where one is; and that, to know where one is, one must know where one is coming from? How can one then know where one is coming from without knowing one's history? The only issue therefore has to do with how (not whether) to learn from the past. History is a crucial aspect of a people's development and there is no point in trying to deny that. As Schuartz has more expediently put it, "once one agrees about the importance of aiming at moral [and societal] improvement, the crucial issue becomes how (not whether) to [learn from history]."[143] Every

---

[142] Sim (1971: 172). See also J.B. Darby, "Cameroon – A Country of Forgotten Values?" *The Herald* (24-28 December 1997), 4.

[143] Joel Schuartz, "Moral Reform – Learning from the Past" 131 *The Public Interest* (1998), 71-91 at 72. *See* also Ikeda (1987: 193-94).

sociologist (or the social scientist who offers that crucial sense of options and choice that is essential to human freedom (Robertson, 1987: vii)) tells the same story about a people's history as part and parcel of their culture and values, a requisite for nation-building. But sociologists are not alone in the history story.

A rhetorical critic, Gold writes, need not necessarily be a historian, but he or she will be well off being armed with history if his or her contribution to the study of a given event has to be anything to go by.[144] The Cameroonian authorities cannot continue to feign ignorance here because Gold's view is also shared by Enonchong's (1967: xiii) book in which "A studied attempt has also been made to indicate the sources of the principles operating in the Cameroon system." Also recognizing the significance of the knowledge of constitutional history and of the socio-political data to an adequate understanding of constitutional law and its interpretation (*ibid* at xii), Enonchong (1967: xii) has included in his book "a historical conspectus of the constitutional evolution of Cameroon from 1884 to the Great Reunification Day." This 'conspectus' is his chapter 2 titled 'The Historical Conspectus of Cameroon Constitutional Evolution' (*ibid*: 45-82).

Enonchong (1967: 87, 88) firmly posited as far back as 1967 that any juristic appraisal and determination of the implied terms of the Constitution of Cameroon must take into consideration all the factors which accompany and explain them. These factors are in the nature of intrinsic and extrinsic aids. Among the said extrinsic aids, he indicated, may be included first, the historical panorama of the Cameroon people; second, the *travaux préparatoires* of the framers of the constitution; third, the social conditions of the time; and fourth, the purpose to be achieved. The historical panorama of the Cameroon people, I would think, cannot mean that of only the French-speaking people of Cameroon (especially when, as seen above in Chapter 1, 'the highest priority' undertaking of national integration

---

[144] Marc Gold, "The Mask of Objectivity: Politics and Rhetoric in the Supreme Court of Canada" 7 *Supreme Court Review* (1985), 455 at 459-60.

is with *all Cameroonians*), except confusion and regression are the purpose and goal to be achieved.

It is not surprising then that there is a clear opposition to the Biya regime's stance on history, coming notably from the main opposition party, the SDF. The SDF instead believes in the entire uncensored history of the country being rejoiced in. "History has a place for every one of them [because] The SDF believes in the oneness of Cameroon and the equality of citizens in rights and obligations, freedom to settle and own property anywhere within the national territory under the protection of the Constitution, the supreme law of the land."[145] Such a constitution, it must stressed over and over, must be clearly and properly drafted; otherwise, it cannot afford the said protection, nor be the country's most powerful document and law. As the experts have said, it must then also be meaningful to all citizens, capturing what they represent as a country and what they desire to become as a people. Capturing all this would necessarily call for a joint and sane decision regarding the cultures and/or histories that have to go into the multiculturalism basket because the plain fact is that the English-speaking people's history has to go into the basket of multiculturalism in Cameroon, if that term has to have any real meaning there, and thus also make national unity purposeful rather than fake and confusing. 'Uniting one culture' is not multiculturalism; and neither is it national unity. It is assimilation and, as things presently stand, can only lead to national disintegration; this, mostly thanks to the unnecessary claim of 'snatch' independence where none exists.

The Cameroonian administrators would even seem to have completely forgotten themselves (as is most often the case when one is engaged in confusing what Bjornson (1991: 118) calls an untenable "justification for maintaining the status quo") when they continued to vehemently argue with the "recalcitrant" teachers in the following words of Biya (1986: 140): "The independence of our country was

---

[145] Quoted from "New SDF Action Plan Will Be More Devastating – Fru Ndi" *The Herald* N° 327 [8-9 July 1996), 6.

snatched from the colonial powers through desperate struggles by the contending forces who used all the means they could imagine. Their common denominator was the Cameroonian identity." Obviously, Cameroonians and North Americans must certainly have to squarely face the "mystique" of independence that is involved here. Independence that is "not given", "not granted" – one that is "won" through being "snatched" – must be *real*: yes or no? Americans, of course, would quickly say "Yeah" while Canadians[146] would somewhat hesitate and try to qualify.

Whatever qualification the United Empire Loyalists may give for their stance,[147] the plain fact in Africa can hardly be camouflaged to anyone who has even a fleeting understanding of the real inner meaning of *la démocratie avancée* that is practised in Cameroon where yes-no has become the usual way of doing politics with naive "brothers". Cameroon is a country where anyone opting for the normal democracy and self-determination is guilty in the same way as those teachers who defiantly tell school children the truth about their country. On can begin to comprehend what living in an 'advanced democracy' is actually all about. There must obviously be something in "the past" that frightens the regime so much. So, what I am now doing on history must be unlawful or illegal as there is even a truth-telling offence in Cameroon.[148] That is how the regime frightens,

---

[146] "These 'conservatives' [who] sought an alternative to the liberal individualism of the United States and committed themselves to a regime dedicated to the pursuit of 'peace, order and good government' in the style of English parliamentary democracy." Corbett (1995: 623). For extensive discussion of P.O.G.G. (Peace, Order, and Good Government), see Hogg (1996: chapter 17).

[147] Corbett (1995: 621-22) has stated that "According to the standard account the Americans rebelled against their imperial masters, declaring themselves to be independent in the name of popular sovereignty. The United Empire Loyalists, on the other hand, moved north and waited for the right moment before asking for a degree of independence to be conferred upon them through an act by the parliament of the mother country. Thus, if the Americans achieved their freedom by symbolically killing the father, Canadians – Anglo-Canadians – established an awkward relationship with a distant uncaring mother."

[148] See Cameroon Penal Code (1965-67), section 153(3).

imprisons, and kills truth-tellers while it unites one history under the pretext of hating colonialism and solving problems 'created' by it. What might be frightening these people about our knowledge of the past would seem to have freaked them out to the extent of confusing them in their attempt to be patriotic and sincere and yet evolve without that patriotic "past". Chapter 1 above accorded a failure grade to the name-changing theses from the minority. Can the administration's name-changing justifications obtain a pass mark from genuine intellectuals and/or without their drawing the necessary consequences from them to convincingly justify the F-grade?

Theories Drawn From Name-Changing Justifications

The infamous instruction in Cameroon to teachers and writers to leave history alone was in furtherance of the justification for changing the URC to the 'Republic of Cameroon', and for altering the city of "Victoria" in Debundschazone to 'Limbe' (to name just these). The confusion and denial of history would be studied and explicated here through (1) justification of the name-changing based on the hatred of, and solutions to, colonialism which is the one that would have to move Cameroon to Njangawatar. Through the player-judge's confusing justification of the contested change, one can also see clearly (2) that history in Cameroon is not made by the human beings called Cameroonians but by the [head of] State alone, a fact that hinders development since the perfect nation (from the other justification of only one Cameroon people) unites one history rather two or more. I am going to show (1) that their name-change justification (the country's), if indeed serious and patriotic, would necessarily have moved us from Cameroonians to Njangawatarians and (2) that the Victoria to Limbe one, unmistakeably makes the talk of biculturalism nonsensical.

From Cameroon to Njangawatar?

This is not exactly what I am proposing for Cameroon as such but merely indicating it would be the logical thing to do for those who are seriously trying to "solve colonialism's problems through mere name-changing", as claimed by the authorities in place. If the hatred for colonialism is as real and serious, as claimed, then Cameroon should (have to) become *Njangawatar*. Confusion apart, the important question posed before (in Chapter 1) regarding the type of Cameroon to be passed on to progeny would obviously require Cameroonians deciding on (1) a lively, multicultural, legally bilingual (and why not with a unique uniting national indigenous language?), tri-jural, diverse, rights-respecting, enviable and genuinely proud Cameroon that would then, in Biya's (1986, 37) words, truly "occupy a choice place in the co[mmunity] of nations."

Or (2) a Cameroon that would be so denaturalized and vandalized that, were the spirit of Fernao Do Pôo (the Portuguese explorer and "discoverer") to revisit, it would not even recognize it as what its human form had named *Rio dos Camarones*. Whichever of the alternatives that Cameroonians decide on here will also simplify progeny's task. According to Cameroon's lawyers (who mostly only talk human rights when one of them is concerned), "When it will be time for posterity to judge our actions, it will first judge our judges here...."[149] Cameroonians and their lawyers in particular must not therefore continue fooling themselves by thinking that only the dependent judges would be judged by posterity for the mess they are left with. The simple truth is that said posterity might have to be wise enough to ask: 'Why were the judges not independent, and is the fact

---

[149] See *Cameroon Post* (20-25 May 1990), 5-8 (reporting the trial of some of their own, Me. Yondo Black and Ten others by the Military Tribunal in Yaoundé for attempting to create a political party). *Yondo et al* is also reported in R. Brody, ed., *Attacks on Justice: The Harassment and Persecution of Judges and Lawyers July 1989-June 1990* (Geneva: Centre for the Independence of Judges and Lawyers of the International Commission of Jurists, 1990) at 15.

of their not being independent not solely responsible for the POR being both party and judge in the game of governance?'

Correctly responding to this question from posterity would require a word or so on the discoverer thesis, a theory that also throws light on the amazement surrounding the Cameroon 'federation', a nice glimpse of which is also seen in the name-change solution-justification which denies history. It has been held that national unity, if that is essentially the goal in Cameroon, must not only tolerate dissent. It has, as Enonchong (1967: xii) sees it, to also properly address some important questions such as: "What common ground exists between the Cameroon common-law and civil-law approaches and what is their point of departure?" That is effectively what is done in polities properly claiming biculturalism, such as Canada. In Cameroon there is only the drive to assimilate the common law and yet be conspicuously pinning biculturalism to the chest. "Even honest Francophones [in Cameroon]," one is told, "admit that the President's chest beating attitude over a constitution that treats the Anglophones shabbily is a betrayal of the latter's commonwealth dream and Cameroon's long overdue bicultural awakening."[150] That is very unlike Canada which, according to Ofege (1995b), being sensitive "about its cultural origin, long ago banished such attempts at uniformism from its constitution" and this, to Bayefsky (1989: 441), has propelled Canada in its spectacular upward movement along "the same flight of stairs toward the destinies reserved for us in the world."

That painting of Canada does not represent the true picture if one has to go by Bayefsky's (1989: 438) thesis that a country's constitution, to be proper, has to be meaningful to all citizens, capturing what they represent as a country and what they desire to become as a people. To this effect, Canada is also guilty of confusing or ambivalent multiculturalism. Discussing this issue a little bit

---

[150] M. Obi, "In End of Year Address: Biya Provokes Anglophones" *The New Standard* N° 24 (4 January 1996), 1. See also Alfred Melow, "Making a Mockery of Anglophones" *The Herald* N° 451 (28-29 April 1997), 4.

further would be important though in not simply lumping Canada and Cameroon (with almost similar colonial 'pasts') in the same confusion basket. Since 1988, 'multiculturalism' is very noticeably and proudly declared every year to be the rule in Canada by its Multiculturalism Reports. The 1988/89 Multiculturalism Report, being the first of annual reports on the operation of the *Canadian Multiculturalism Act*, Bill c.93 (July 12, 1988), that was unanimously passed by both Houses of Parliament in July 1988, informs us that by

> combining multiculturalism with the traditional values of Canadian citizenship, Canadians of all origins are finding new ways to take pride in themselves, in their roots and in helping shape the Canadian identity. Beyond this, as the world is shrinking, we are awakening more and more to the advantages our rich cultural and linguistic heritage give us commercially, diplomatically and as concerned members of a world community.[151]

This is quite a laudable goal except that this acclaimed multiculturalism, as aforesaid, is confusing or ambivalent; an ambivalence that leads us to (1) "intellectuals in politics" and questioning of the discoverer theory and (2) the question of whether to move from Pidgin to Njangawatok.

"Intellectuals in Politics": Questioning the Discoverer Theory?

Canada's proud declaration of multiculturalism as well as discussions of Quebec as a 'distinct society' do seem not to even bother about the exclusion of Native Peoples' "unique culture, distinct and different from that of any other race of people on the

---

[151] Minister of Supply and Services Canada, *Operation of the Canadian Multiculturalism Act – Annual Report 1988/89* (1989, Ottawa: Minister of Supply and Services Canada) at ix (being the 'Foreword from the Minister', *id.* at vii-x). The minister in question was Gerry Weiner, Minister of State for Multiculturalism and Citizenship.

continent [which] has been the strongest common bond of these people in spite of all kinds of pressure."[152] The *Canadian Charter of Rights and Freedoms* that some writers have described as the most robust of Canada's human rights protection does furnish a subtle kind of this pressure. Writing about the preamble of this *Charter* that holds that Canada "is founded upon principles that recognize the supremacy of God and the rule of law," Turpel, (1991: 505) affirmed in 1991 that it "is both inaccurate as a historical matter, and insensitive to cultural differences at least with respect to Aboriginal peoples." The *Charter*'s reference to "the supremacy of God and the rule of law" has been the subject of much controversy. According to Corbett (1995: 627-28),

> These phrases raise questions of the utmost importance for human beings, questions for which there have never been easy answers. It is in our openness to the difficulties of these questions rather than in our willingness to opt for the security of traditional answers, that our best hope for the future is to be found. If we pretend that there is no disagreement over the word 'God; or succumb to the temptation to identify the word 'law' with one particular legal tradition, or, worse still, question in public what in private we would never challenge, then we will have closed ourselves off to the possibility that the solutions to our problems may lie elsewhere than in those places we have become accustomed to looking for them.

---

[152] Jean Goodwill, "A New Horizon for Native Women in Canada" in James A. Draper (ed), *Citizen Participation: Canada* (Toronto: New Press, 1971) 362 at 368. See also Carolyn Tuohy, *Policy and Politics in Canada: Institutionalized Ambivalence* (Philadelphia: Temple University Press, 1992); Edwards Rogers, "The Indian and Euro-Canadian Society" in James A. Draper, ed., *Citizen Participation: Canada* (Toronto: New Press, 1971), 331-350; and Marlene Castellano, "Out of Paternalism into Partnership: An Exploration of Alternatives in Social Services to Native People" in James A. Draper, ed., *Citizen Participation: Canada* (Toronto: New Press, 1971), 351–370.

Turpel (1991: 503), in concluding her "unapologetic critique of the Canadian Charter of Rights and Freedoms," has stated that

> the culturally hegemonic reading [of the *Charter*] is accurate insofar as Canada is believed to have been 'founded,' that is, discovered, by the dominant culture, and the authors of the preamble, descendants of the 'founders,' share the conception that God and the rule of law reign supreme in Canadian society. Aboriginal peoples would strongly contest this rendition of the founding of Canada, and the suggestion that their spirituality could be incorporated under the notion of the supremacy of God and the rule of law. [Turpel, 1991: 503, note omitted].

There is again agreement from then Dean of Osgoode Hall Law School who also makes it clear

> that the Charter was made in Canada, not in heaven; that the Charter's precepts reflect a set of values that have been selected by imperfect human beings, not by God or reason or natural law; that the Charter's precepts do not include all the values upon which Canadian society sets store, and not even all of the values necessary for the achievement of individual liberty and equality; and, finally, that extravagant claims for the Charter's moral authority, or deep-seated opposition to the use of section 1 or section 33, are entirely inappropriate.[153]

---

[153] Peter W. Hogg, "The Charter of Rights and American Theories of Interpretation" in R.F. Devlin, ed., *Canadian Perspectives on Legal Theory* (Toronto: Emond Montgomery Publications Limited, 1991), 375 at 376.

Quoting a lengthy passage from Joseph Magnet, [154] Turpel (1991: 511) makes an incisive point when she charges that "Canada pins multiculturalism to its chest [while] the dominant European culture continues presumptively to set the terms of tolerance for collective differences."

"When academics get together to talk about anything," according to a political scientist of the University of Toronto, "they tend to cheerfully disagree about everything. That is the politics of academic discussion. There is no constraint on the participants to agree. On the contrary, participants justify their existence by demonstrating their ability to put forward positions held by nobody else."[155] Whatever disagreement for agreement (orderly discord which is only possible in a democracy) Canadians may have about the rendition of their Charter and its implicit discovery theory, it is without doubt that Canada is predominantly bicultural. *Bi*culturalism is *multi*culturalism at least. Is it the same with Cameroon? Find out for yourself from my analysis of the name-change solution-to-colonialism justification.

The regime seems to have a lot of support for its hatred theory on colonialism. And this we clearly see through finding out if the Foumban actors were intellectuals in political science or in something else. Could Dr. Fonlon (the Foumban translator who has been specifically described by the phrase – 'intellectual in politics') possibly

---

[154] The passage in question runs as follows: "People who do not dream of national greatness together cannot survive as a state. Changes in the world system conspire against the multinational state as an organizing unit of politics. While Canada's system for sub-cultural accommodation tends to produce dull and uninspiring politics, it nevertheless works, fostering a growing sense of Canadian nationality, albeit slowly. The Charter makes accommodation between the sub-cultural communities much more exacting, but also more perilous. It is therefore crucial to consider entrenched collective rights carefully. We, who set the terms of debate, should strive to assist Courts expounding the Charter to devise a modus operandi that will fully protect the collective rights of semi-autonomous minorities, while keeping peace in the Canadian family." Joseph Magnet, "Collective rights, cultural autonomy and the Canadian state" 32 *McGill Law Journal* (1986), 170 at 175.

[155] Peter H. Russell, untitled Comments in David Schneiderman, ed., After Allaire and Bélanger-Campeau (being a Symposium) as reported in 3:1 *Constitutional Forum Constitutionnel* (Winter 1991) at 14.

have been an intellectual in the art of politics? An affirmative answer here would be doubted because Hong Kong legislator, Christine Loh, has posited that "The whole experience of colonialism, and what it has done for us as a people, is hardly talked about. The British were very good at giving their system of control a semblance of legitimacy. And until the mid-70s, one simply didn't question this. *Studying politics at school was illegal.* The entire colonial system was designed to disempower people. And it has created a very tame populace."[156] This passage is very helpful in the understanding of the vague description of people in Cameroon as *intellectuals in politics*; and it must play into the hands of the critics of the Foumban *intellectuals in politics* as well as of those currently trying to cover up their acts. The idea that is embodied in the Hong Kong legislator's statements would seem to point to the fact that the Foumban actors were intellectuals in something else than *politics*.

In keeping with Legislator Loh's thesis, Southall (1974: 22) makes it clear that Lugard's famous principle of indirect rule was not only administratively economical but, most of all, "an approach which encouraged co-operation with a traditional elite rather than the creation of a group of talented, able and educated men with new ideas, who might be potentially subversive of the existing order." Northrop Frye has also considered colonial status to be a kind of frostbite on the roots of the Canadian imagination. "Colonialism," Newman (1975: 386) quotes him as having written, "produces a disease for which I think the best name is prudery. By this I do not mean reticence in sexual matters. I mean the instinct to seek a conventional or commonplace expression of an idea." Eleazu has lengthily discussed the British indirect rule approach[157] and

---

[156] Quoted in Mark Abley, "Caged in the City of Gold" *Montreal Gazette* (Friday December 20, 1995), A1 at A11 (emphasis added). See also Julia Gallagher, "Healing the Scar? Idealizing Britain in Africa, 1997-2007" 108 *African Affairs* N° 432 (July 2009), 435 at 441-446; and I.J. Mowoe and R. Bjornson, eds. *Africa and the West: The Legacies of Empires* (New York: Greenwood Press, 1986).

[157] Uma O. Eleazu, *Federalism and Nation-Building: The Nigerian Experience, 1954-1964* (Elms Court: Stockwell, 1977) at 76-82.

concluded at page 79 that "Lugard was very suspicious of missionaries and very prejudicial against any African who had acquired European type education… [because this] proved difficult to fit into the philosophy of indirect rule."

It could perhaps be argued with Lantum (1991: 21) that it was Dr. Fonlon's knowledge (from the study of politics) that led to "the strange message during his unexpected send-down from the Major Seminary at Enugu that his brains would be more useful in the wider world than in the confines of the priestly profession." Priesthood and civil society are even unavoidably bound (see Ikeda, 1987: 87-98; and Mbuy, 1996). Either way then Dr. Fonlon had to earn Lugard's suspicion and prejudice because of his being in the seminary and of his having acquired European type education. As Lantum (1991: 20) indicates, Dr. Fonlon was soon appointed as Executive Officer (Administration) in the Prime Minister's Office in Buea on his return from further studies. Does this fact mean then that he was an intellectual in the art of politics?

Christine Loh of Hong Kong would object strongly, based on her thesis on British colonial attitude. Most people in Cameroon would appear to have realized the logical implication of Legislator Loh's thesis on British colonial attitude. But Lantum (1991: 22 & 13, respectively) would instead prefer to further compound the confusion by declaring from time to time that "Dr. FONLON was an intellectual in politics" but concludes "from a double perspective, to wit, the political and the intellectual, and may be [sic] a third, namely, that he was not an intellectual in politics." So now there is also a third meaning appearing, namely, the IPM (intellectual in process manipulation)? In fact, this type of 'he-is-and-he-is-not' position is not the only confusing characteristic of the whole Foumban Enterprise in Cameroon; such yes-no posture not being limited just to the country's PORs who are always saying yes-no to important human rights issues.

Cameroon's intellectuals in politics, if they are to be known as intellectuals at all, are only good to be known as intellectuals in process manipulation (the IPMs); or better still, intellectuals in the personification of public debates. That is precisely what the employment of the vague 'intellectualism in politics' is meant to conceal; a fact that would largely explicate Mensah-Gbadago's (1991: 4) thesis that "What makes Cameroon a unique case in the political evolution of Africa, is the manner in which the leadership has always succeeded in manipulating the process and achieving the results, in spite of the cleavages that underline the socio-political set-up." The easiness in this manipulation has been especially propped up by what some critics describe as "cowdung" journalism and intellectualism.

The issue of vague or 'cowdung' *intellectualism in politics* is not limited to the situation in West Cameroon though. Ofege (1995a) has also traced the roots of the continuing and worsening human rights atmosphere in Cameroon to the dubious training received by most of the country's French-speaking leaders from "this French-Contraption for [N]egroes called the *École-d'outre-mer* whose specialty is to fabricate mediocre cadres for Tropical Africa." But most of the "intellectuals" that Cameroon politics is today infested with did not study only in France, let alone in the 'Contraption'. A lecturer at the Department of Law and Justice of Laurentian University in Sudbury, Ontario, Canada, has made the point, wondering why people known for their intelligence and brilliance while out of Cameroon change overnight on reaching the country.

> I read… [my father's] mail with some interest. He alludes to the enormous talents of Cameroonians who live outside the confines of Cameroon. His perception cannot be refuted – there are numerous talented Cameroonians abroad. However, Biya [the current president] was once a 'talented' student abroad, Agbor Tabi [then Higher Education Minister] studied in the [United] States… short, the mass of those presently in power in Cameroon studied abroad and in their days, they were similarly situated as we are now – claiming to possess lots of talents. So what happens to that talent when you take it to Cameroon? Why does it suddenly disappear and monsters start growing out of

people who were once talented? Is it our attitudes? I am tempted to think so.[158]

It is really 'our selfish attitudes' that would be responsible because it would be hard to be convinced that all these people (graduates of the 'Contraption' and other foreign institutions) are only taught how to go back home and starkly bend plain facts in broad daylight to further selfish and secretive dealings in public affairs. Can democracy, a condition sine qua non for federalism, then function in this kind of environment? The experts do not think so; because a call for democracy and/or federalism here will very easily be twisted and equated with a call for secession. But can the twisted equation stand the test of genuine intellectualism? And can the distinction being made between the 1972 and 1984 name-changes hold up a candle to genuine intellectuals? And can the name-changing justifications pass by without serious implications drawn by such intellectuals?

In addition to its discussion so far, this dehumanising practice referred to as colonialism, according to Ngefac (2010: 150), involved the total domination and transformation of African and Asian nations by some Western nations. Through this practice the political, economic and social life of the colonised nations was invaded, transformed and controlled by the colonisers; the worldviews, cultures and languages of the colonised people were eroded and subjected to an inferior position; their minds and cosmic visions were upset and they were finally made to understand that everything of theirs was barbaric, satanic and inferior. An American sociologist (Robertson, 1987: 305-306) confirms Ngefac's charge when he also states:

> On an objective analysis of the facts, the invading whites were morally in the wrong in their dispossession of the Indians, but

---

[158] See email sent out by Nicoline Ambe, nambe@nickel.laurentian.ca, on Thursday, 26 September 1996 to multiple recipients of list CAMNET camnet@vm.cnuce.cnr.it.

since American history has been written primarily by whites, a grossly distorted picture of the events has been handed down as the true story. The ethnocentricism of the standard historical accounts is remarkable: the whites are described as 'pioneers,' not 'invaders'; the native peoples' defense of their way of life and economic assets is 'treacherous,' not 'courageous'; the military successes of the whites are 'victories,' but those of the Indians are 'massacres.

As already seen also above from Hong Kong's Legislator Christine Loh and others, colonialism and assimilation are obviously problem-creating institutions. However, the problems that they create cannot, for sure, be 'solved' through mere name-changing. But, since this is the only solution the Cameroon regime knows or has adopted, one has to legitimately wonder why said regime has not also changed the name(s) 'Cameroun' and/or 'Cameroon(s)' too since these are also from colonization. I am trying therefore to show these administrators (using only their own preferred mode – name-changing) how to better decolonize Africa.

Political and constitutional historians (Tixier 1974, 16-18; Nelson et al 1974, 9-10; Fombad 2003, 88 n.16) have it that in 1472 a Portuguese explorer called Fernao Do Pôo, in expressing amazement at the abundance of just one type of its myriad of natural endowments, jumped to call one of the territory's rivers *Rio dos Camerones* (the Shrimp River – which is currently known as the Wouri River).[159] (The proposed state name of Wourizone derives from this historic river.) As Dunton would put it, "The farcical story of Bismarck's Germany seizing the territory from under the noses of the hapless British has been told many times, but Gaillard tells it well, as he does the history of incursions into central and northern Cameroon, when three European countries [Britain, France &

---

[159] See also 'Histoire du Cameroun': http://www.camnet.cm/celcom/histoire/histoire (last visited on 12 August 2011).

Germany] criss-crossed the land as if possessed."[160] Through colonialism's crisscrossing metamorphosis, the Shrimp River is now Cameroon (English) and/or Cameroun (French), both having passed through Kamerun (German) – alias The Land of Plenty of Confusion; confusion that is nowhere more accentuated than in the arena of history and independence/dependence. Absent the abundance of confusion, Cameroonians' disgust for colonialism (if genuine) must logically entail their sagacious digging into history (that they deny denying) so as to locally-rename the country to what the Portuguese 'Discoverer' called it (for instance, *Njanga Watar*) before the colonialists 'named' it Cameroon/Cameroun or Kamerun. The discussion of this issue of renaming the country to its pre-colonial 'local' name, will not only entail (1) moving from Pidgin to *Njangawatok*; but also (2) the change of a city's name solely to eliminate colonial vestiges: from Victoria to Limbe.

From Pidgin to *Njangawatok?*

Njanga Watar is the correct common local lexicon for 'Shrimp River', gotten from the *lingua franca* known as "Cameroon Pidgin English, which is now known as Kamtok" (Ngefac 2010, 151). This Pidgin is a language that has already been the subject of much academic or scholarly discussion, with some considerable emphasis on its grammatical characteristics.[161] This is a 'language' that is generally understood in Cameroon, even by the French-speaking who will not usually comprehend the same thing (e.g., shrimp river) said in

---

[160] C. Dunton, "Book Review of *Le Cameroun* by P. Gaillard" *West Africa* (March 30-April 5, 1992), 567.

[161] See, for instance, Daniel A. Nkemleke, "Must and Should in Cameroon English" 14:1 *Nordic Journal of African Studies* (2005), 43-67; Yves Talla Sando Ouafeu,"Politeness Strategies in Colloquial Cameroon English: Focus on Three Pragmatic Particles: na, ya and eihn" 15:4 *Nordic Journal of African Studies* 536 (2006) 536-44; and Kelechukwu U. Ihemere, "A Basic Description and Analytic Treatment of Noun Clauses in Nigerian Pidgin" 15:3 *Nordic Journal of African Studies* (2006), 296-313.

the Queen's English. This language is described by Ngefac (2010, 151) as "a major lingua franca known today as Kamtok." The name Kamtok, he explains, means 'Cameroon Talk'. Since in this book I am moving from Cameroon to Njangawatar (as a logical theory drawn from the name-change justification), it has to necessarily become 'Njangawatar Talk' and, hence, Njangawatok. This appellation is preferred for a number of reasons advanced by Ngefac (2010, 152 & 151). Principally, it has existed in Cameroon for over five hundred years and has adapted itself significantly to the ecological and socio-cultural realities of the country, having systematic linguistics that are very different from those of the languages from which it originated. Hence, it is now a Creole and must no longer continue to carry the pidgin label, which suggests a marginal and simplified language that serves only limited and temporary communicative needs. The language is thus no more a pidgin, given that it displays most, if not all, creolistic traits; transcending furthermore most ethnic, educational, geographical, professional, religious and other social boundaries; and having incredible communicative potential, given that it has served the communicative needs of Cameroonians for more than five hundred years and today, he concludes, it remains one of the most widely spoken languages in the country.

Since they seem to hate the 'German-English-French' colonialism so much, adopting a language like this (and, perhaps, renaming it Njangawatok) should be an important step towards decolonizing. Implementing this language also excludes the controversy surrounding and bedevilling adopting an indigenous language of this and not that ethnic group. Njangawatok is already common to almost all Cameroonians. In spite of the widespread nature of Njangawatok, Ngefac (2010, 152) has noted, "and the fact that it is a lingua franca that has penetrated the hearts and minds of most Cameroonians, there are many attempts from the government sector to discourage and even ban its use." How is this language a common language to most Cameroonians? I think this commonality could be further seen through two factors: no need for prior knowledge of English and/or

French for its use, and its constructive use in the 1961 reunification talks.

Although the "linguistic features of this contact language are drawn from the colonial languages spoken in Cameroon and the indigenous languages" (Ngefac 2010, 151), there are a lot of Cameroonians who will understand and speak neither the Queen's English nor continental Europe's French but do speak and comprehend Njangawatok (or what some might want to call Njangawatarian Creole) so well. For illustration, I will just navigate the reader to the towns of Manjo or Nkongsamba in the French-speaking Wourizone (Littoral Region).[162] While there, talk all you can about 'Mercredi' or 'Wednesday', and rest assured that many of the fathers and mothers there would not have grasped anything.[163] Anyone who wants to be understood by them should rather talk of *Mindro Work* (literally deriving from 'the middle of the work week'). That is the 'Wednesday' or 'Mercredi' they know as being preceded by *Agfta Monday* (that is, 'Mardi' or 'Tuesday').

What is even more significant is that even those of us who speak one or both of the two foreign languages (that those fathers and mothers do not seem to comprehend) do also understand Njangawatok. Of course, a lot of so-called 'intellectuals' do pretend here. The pretence that would come forth is not new and has already been exposed by Ajulo (1997: 27-42, 35-36) through the ridiculousness of a Nigerian judge requiring an interpreter ('like a

---

[162] Some critics would be quick to point out that Njangawatok is not known in the northern portion (current Adamawa, North, and Extreme North Regions of Cameroon; which are the proposed Njangawatar states of Adamowazone, Benouezone, and Logonezone). My response to that (quite apart from the second point below – Ahidjo coming from this region) is to emphasize that Njangawatok is not the only language that is not widely spoken and understood there. French itself stands in no better position as Westernized schooling and/or foreign influences were/are widely resisted there due to the change-resisting nature of the culture and religion there as can be seen in Nelson *et al* (1974: 80-84).

[163] I talk mostly of fathers and mothers here because the youths (of both linguistic groups) through what some now call 'varieties of Kamtok' such as Camfranglais and Mbokotok would not be that lost. See Ngefac (2010: 152-53).

colonial district officer') to be able to 'understand' his own tribesman speaking their native African language in court; as well as by Bokamba's 'ukolonia' tendency that is discussed in Ngefac (2010, 151 & passim). It is usually said that experience is the best teacher. I do vividly remember how my French-speaking colleagues at both the Universities of Yaounde and of Douala have always been at a loss when I talked to them through the Queen's English but always perfectly understood everything I said when it came through Njangawatok. This is in fact the uniting language in Cameroon that is neither solely indigenous to any one part of the country nor wholly foreign. This 'indigenous-uniting-language' issue alone could be a topic for a whole volume of its own (and, of course, it has already filled lots of pages of many journals/books on African languages); but it suffices here to merely add that musicians like Lapiro de Mbanga are as popular as they are principally because of their almost exclusive use of this language's varieties like Mbokotok in their music, as Ndawouo would lengthily attest.[164] Again, since they seem to hate the 'German-English-French' colonialism so much, adopting a language like this one (and, perhaps, renaming it *Njangawatok*) should be an important step towards decolonizing. So why not formalise its use for the national interest?

Having very elaborately surveyed Language Politics in Post-Colonial Africa, Ajulo (1997: 31), a prominent member of the Presidential Advisory Committee in Abuja, Nigeria, has come to the inevitable conclusion that

> ambivalence would seem to characterize the language policies of post-colonial African states. Most of their national constitutions certainly took note of the existing 'babel' in their respective states; hence the nationalists voluntarily adopted their colonial linguistic heritage. That accounts for why all Commonwealth

---

[164] See Martine Fandio Ndawouo, "De la subjectivité et de la délocutivité comme stratégie argumentative : lecture pragmatique de la chanson populaire camerounaise" 18:1 *Nordic Journal of African Studies* (2009), 91-109.

African countries, (except for Tanzania and now Cameroon and Mozambique) adopted English as their official/national language.

It is significant that Cameroon is not left out in the list (of post-1996 writings) of African countries that have not adopted English as their official language(s). The camouflage of bilingualism in the 1996 Constitution thus seems not to be selling as it has been castigated by Kouega, cited in Ngefac (2010: 162), as a "one-way expansion of bilingualism, with speakers of English operating increasingly or fully in French, but their French-speaking counterparts remaining largely monolingual." This is what was defined by some critics in 1998 as *Ngoa-lingualism* (see section B below).

No one would doubt Biya's (1986, 31) assertion that 'Language-wise, Cameroon is a real Tower of Babel'. The need in this country for a common uniting language (clearly also necessary even for the so-called 'perfect nation' that has been defined in Chapter 2) becomes even more axiomatic. Faced with a similar situation, Das (1996) narrates how the patriotic and visionary Indonesian leadership chose a minority language (Bahasa Indonesia) as a national language, choosing from some 80 distinct languages and about 240 dialects because they realized (a thing which is most often possible only in the midst of patriotism and independence) that "they could not build a nation by imposing the majority language on dozens of minorities. Today, Bahasa Indonesia is well established and spoken as a second language by most Indonesians." In Cameroon, the task has been made very easy by the existence of Njangawatok. This lingua franca is therefore a unique God-given uniting national 'indigenous' language. The leadership of the 'real Tower of Babel' (if they were as patriotic as they claim and had any vision like the leaders of Indonesia) would have very easily elevated it to the place that is its own. As Ngefac (2010, 162) has noted, "[t]he widespread use of this language by Cameroonians from different social backgrounds, in spite of the official efforts to ban it is indicative of the importance Cameroonians attach to it."

The importance and uniting capabilities of Njangawatok do not just come from what has been said above. Above all, it was through this language that Cameroon, as we know it today, was created. According to Benjamin (1972, 124), the Talks in Foumban (a city that has too often been acclaimed as Cameroon's Philadelphia) were conducted most of the time in Njangawatok. One of the main, if not dominant, participants there was President Ahidjo from northern Cameroon. I may not be the best advocate of Njangawatok; but what is language but an effective means of independence, of cultural transmission and/or communication, etc? What is Creole that is widely spoken in the Caribbean today but what one might call 'pidgin French'? Is it not today the national language of, say, Haiti? And do Haitians not still study and know French and other foreign languages? What could properly account for the gapping failure of Cameroon's administrators in this made-easy field of common national language? The answer is intimately tied to the issue of whether there can even be effective biculturalism in Cameroon; a matter that is also heavily embedded in continuing colonialism, as the Victoria name-story can prove.

From Victoria to Limbe: Biculturalism in Cameroon?

Still emanating from the hatred of colonialism in Africa, should one be wrong in audaciously demanding that the case-study country be no longer called Cameroon but Njangawatar, and its people not Cameroonians but Njangawatarians (speaking Njangawatok)? Of course, this is what should logically have to be done if the story of 'Cameroon/Cameroun' is actually to be devoid of its colonial past, as the Biya regime also claims in the change of the name of the city named after Britain's Queen Victoria to Limbe. To them, the original name simply smacks of the country's colonial past. One must have to clearly point out that only in an 'advanced democracy' would this justification be tenable: since Kubuo has found it to be "gun-powder or democracy of the baboon [used] to stifle justice and exalt cruelty."165 This cruelty is particularly accentuated towards those (teachers, writers and journalists) who discuss the history of (in)dependence and/or the (in)dependence of history.

Why does one even have to use the term 'history' if the past is not to be part and parcel of it? Is there any nation in the world that hates being under colonial rule than the United States of America? The USA, for example, cut itself free from British colonial rule by declaring its independence. Corbett (1995, 622) tells us that Americans, unlike Canadians, "achieved their freedom by symbolically killing the father." But why haven't Americans since gone around changing all names of states, counties, cities, streets, etc. that would remind them of the colonial epoch? Why hasn't American history been re-written to commence only from the 1776 Declaration of Independence? The answer is so uncomplicated. If colonialism is part and parcel of one's history, there is absolutely nothing one can do to make that portion of one's history go away: unless one does not want to have a history at all or one that is properly one's own.

The American Declaration of Independence of 1776 is completely meaningless without the colonial period preceding it because Ngefac (2010, 150) has stated that "postcolonialism cannot exist without colonialism." You cannot therefore talk of your independence (if you have it at all) without talking of/about the one who was keeping it before you seized it and why (which the USA Declaration lengthily dwelled on by submitting "Facts" "to a candid world"). It is as straightforward as that. In fact, as Joanne Meyerowitz has been quoted in Okafor (2005: 181) for saying, "history never rips in two. 'Before' and 'after' are never entirely severed, even in the moments of greatest historical rupture. ... In fact, historians devote entire careers to placing the *seemingly new* in historical contexts." (Omissions and emphasis are original.) Trying to challenge this thesis could only wind up confirming it, as is usually the case in Cameroon when the bold questions on independence are posed. It is only in an

---

165 John Kubuo, "Is the Mentality of Some Politicians Akin to that of Honourable Baboons?" *The Post*, October 24, 1997, 4

'advanced democracy' that leaders would be talking of 'our independence' when none exists; be talking of colonialism in the past when nothing has in fact passed.

Is it even an issue of hating colonialism, as it is claimed by the Cameroonian leadership? One can only comprehend what all the justification against colonial past actually signifies in the Hinge of Africa if one is bold enough to ask a sane question about statues of French generals and the numerous schools, avenues, etc. that are still now being named after French people (in commemoration of that same "colonial past"). At this point, one would then be astonished by what the same regime does give in answer to the question, now that they have only the French-derived part of that 'past' in mind. They vehemently oppose its being effaced, with Biya (1986, 133) ordaining: "It is not right for our country to wipe out all traces of its recent past. An effort has, therefore, to be made to safeguard historical sites and monuments which merit being maintained as such throughout the country." Is the regime not really just confusingly saying what the hard reality is? That is, that the colonialism in question is not yet in 'our past' as far as the French are concerned? Otherwise, what exactly is or is not historical about Cameroon's history? Le Vine (1986) appears to have generally taken care of the Political-Cultural Schizophrenia involved here. I would then merely add that the real answer to the query could be found in the mystiques of independence in this country, mystiques that are effectively responsible for Cameroon 'developing' or 'federating' without its history. The burying of "our colonial past" without there being a colonial "past" is a theory that results in (1) moving from bilingualism to Ngoa-lingualism, and from bijuralism to unijuralism; and (2) the well calculated use of epsi to prevent educational biculturalism.

From Bilingualism/Bijuralism to Ngoa-Lingualism/Unijuralism

The justification of the Victoria name-change but not the change of French-derived colonial names indicates in bold black that any talk of bilingualism and/or bijuralism in this country is just as nonsensical since the English language and law will stand in the same position as the name of their queen: Effaced. Southern Cameroonsians are one of most sizeable but also the most marginalized and forgotten minority in the world; it is hardly surprising, as I explain shortly. It is true that the politics of academic discussions, of its very nature, does not compel agreement from the participants. But I would venture to think that other minorities around the globe have succeeded solely because, when it comes to clear threats to their collective rights (be they cultural, linguistic, religious, ethnic), their academics and statesmen simply call a spade a spade. This community cohesion is graphically wanting in the case of Southern Cameroonsians, as even a fleeting look at the politics of bilingualism for national unity can show.

The genuineness of official bilingualism as a vehicle for national unity in Cameroon is an issue that is very controversial even within the (Southern Cameroonsian) academia. This is odd in a way but not very surprising when one considers, as tersely noted by Bjornson (1991: 110), that the system has co-opted a lot of these intellectuals who then have a vested interest in the defence of the system. For example, there are several theses from said academic community that would be buttressing, rather than fighting against, the confusion being called full citizen participation and cultural dualism in Cameroon. Particularly furthering the regime's unfounded claim are two notable theses, one on bijuralism (seen later) and the other on bilingualism from Lantum (1991: 22) that claims that "bilingualism… was enshrined into the Federal Constitution of 1st October 1961." Claims like this do lead one to ponder about what is genuine: confusion or multiculturalism?

I clearly fail to see how bilingualism was entrenched in Foumban in 1961 when by article 59 "The revised Constitution shall be published in French and in English, the French text being authentic." This 'Second Fiddle Syndrome' has been maintained in all the many and confusing constitutions (article 44 of 1972 and article 39 of 1984 constitutions¹⁶⁶) until the 1996 (whose article 1(3) now makes both English and French versions of the constitution of equal status – though whether or not this includes their *authenticity*, is not clear). All this would vividly contrast with the language rights sections 16-22 of the 1982 Canadian Constitution that clearly makes both English and French versions of texts not only authentic but also of equal strength.¹⁶⁷ The international level is no exception because Ajulo (1997: 29) points out that article 104 of the 1991 Treaty establishing the African Economic Community makes all four texts (Arabic, English, French and Portuguese) "equally authentic"; and article 111 of the United Nations Charter recognizes the official languages of the Organization (Chinese, English, French, Russian and Spanish) as "equally authentic". Has the 1996 formula in Cameroon actually alter the position then?

Ofege (1995a) thinks article 1(3) of the 1996 Constitution "is a sure vista of official hypocrisy... an ongoing farce. How exactly does Mr. Biya intend to make English and French as official languages, equal in status [?] Why did he not show the example by reading his entire speech in English first and then in French later[?] Jean Chrétien of Canada does it every day." Dr. Paul Nkad Mbangwana, Head of the Department of English of the University of Douala, has also answered the question, stating (according to Bangsi, 1997) that in this country "there was [always] no harmony between declarations made by the establishment and actions taken by the executing agents." Bangsi (1997) indicates that the head of the English department went on to also warn that "We can't speak of national

---

¹⁶⁶ By contrast to the Belgian Constitution (as noted in Chapter 1), viewing the vast numbers of constitutional instruments of the less-than-seventy-years-old state called Cameroon, some critics have concluded that confusion is inevitable and might even be the actual goal of the constitution-inflation. See Peter Ateh-Afac Fossungu, "Many Constitutions Create Confusion" *The Herald* N° 695 (4-6 December 1998), 4; and Ngalle Miano, "La constitution révisée répond-elle aux attentes de la Tripartite?" *Le Messager* N° 477 (6 février 1996), 9-10.

¹⁶⁷ For further discussion of the Canadian position, see André Tremblay, "Les droits linguistiques" in G-A. Beaudoin et E.P. Mendes (eds.), *Charte Canadienne des Droits et Libertés* 3é éd (Montréal : Wilson et Lafleur Ltée, 1996), 901.

unity and integration and at the same time preach minority and settler differences. Instead of putting competent people in positions of national responsibility, we have seen people ill-qualified given posts because they are 'sons of the soil' whose interests must be protected." This kind of appointment has obviously given rise to the infamous *Boss Code*, a notorious article of which holds that 'The Boss is always right.'[168] Bangsi (1997) also reports how at the launching of his *Look Up to the Mountain Top: Beyond Party Politics*, Ambassador Christopher Nsahlai did also call on Cameroonians to guard the country's special socio-cultural endowments, amongst which is its bilingual character; noting in regret "that while Cameroonians preached bilingualism, they were yet far from making it a living experience."

Some others have concurred; with Fossungu (1998a, emphasis as in original) even going on to posit that "any discussion of Cameroon's bilingualism/bijuralism, to my mind, is like discussing an invention that is yet to be realized as if it were already real. In short, it is like talking about a nothing. But, as there has already been too much talk about a *nothing* as if it is a *something*, I have now got something to discuss about nothing." And, to gain time and space by shortening the lengthy Much Ado About Nothing, Fossungu (1998a) has simply invited any doubting Mary to the Green-Red-Yellow Cover (of the 1984 Constitution that sparked off secessionist drives in Cameroon) where she

> would be flabbergasted to find that, on the portion supposedly to be the English version (*Constitution of the Republic of Cameroon*), she can identify all our ten provinces – assuming [of course] that she is at all Ngoa-lingual – only in French: PROVINCE DE L'EXTREME NORD, PROVINCE DU NORD, PROVINCE DE L'ADAMAOUA, PROVINCE DU NORD-OUEST, PROVINCE DE L'OUEST, PROVINCE DU SUD-OUEST, PROVINCE DU LITTORAL, PROVINCE DU CENTRE,

---

[168] See "The Boss Code" *The Messenger* (20 May 1996). 7.

PROVINCE DE L'EST, and PROVINCE DU SUD. Ngoa-lingualism, isn't it? [Capitals and emphasis as in original]

As Fossungu (1998a) makes clear, the side-by-side rendition would not even need having two maps but one. On that single map would be something like this: Province du Nord/North Province. It's that simple, if bilingualism were a reality in Cameroon.

It is therefore not bilingualism but in fact Ngoa-lingualism that is the sole goal; and the latter concept has been well elucidated again by Fossungu (1998b):

> What is Ngoa-lingualism? Perhaps only the experiences of some newly arrived to the Ngoa campus could better explain it to you. They would tell you Ngoa-lingualism means unilingualism under the camouflage of bilingualism. It should thus not be surprising to find that one of the newly arrived Anglophone male students to the unique Yaounde University would, for instance, go to the University's restaurant (*Resto*) and, on being handed a plate (*plateau*) of food without the usual pineapple (*anana*), would stare on, not knowing what to say, since he must speak French to be understood in his bilingual Cameroon. When those lined up behind him would shout out: *Allez-y, Anglo!* (anything that doesn't go well is Anglophone in this institution and country) his response, which would also confirm the charge, would come resounding: *No, moi pas le pinaple!* More demonstrations of this bilingual et al confusion could also be found especially at hospitals and police stations.

Fossungu's *Ngoa-lingualism* thesis could elucidate Enonchong's puzzlement why the Cameroon regime would not even bother "that prescribing French as the working language of OHADA Article 42 presents serious constitutional and human rights difficulties in

Cameroon."[169] It is not idle talking for this University of Birmingham law professor to want to know, for instance, how an English-speaking Cameroonian is going to obtain a position with and function in the OHADA (Organization for the Harmonization of Business Law in Africa). Now, bring it back to the national level and the same question props up in regard of the constitutional guarantees of equality, of cultural dualism, etc. vis-à-vis the mono-cultural 'national' bureaucracy. Effective multiculturalism implies full or collective participation in nation-building of both or all cultural groups, a participation that can only be assured through the federal formula of constitutional or liberal democracy. Can bijuralism be feasible where bilingualism is not?

The thesis on bijuralism comes from Nyambo, a lecturer in law at the University of Yaounde II at Soa, who posits that "At unification in 1961of anglophone and francophone Cameroon, each with a distinct legal system, *the idea of the co-existence of two legal systems was born.*"[170] I will only talk a little bit about this bijuralism without delving so much into the controversies and conflicts about Tamanaha's (1993) "folly" of legal pluralism that Teubner (1992) says is so much loved by postmodern jurists. What the intellectuals concerned could be hanging their bijuralism claims on will be the Federal Constitution's article 46 (which is the same as article 11 of *Federal Ordinance N° 61-OF-9 of 16 October 1961*) by which "Previous legislation of the Federated States shall remain in force in so far as it does not conflict with the provision of this Constitution." Intellectuals in politics indeed; I am talking about the Foumban Boys from Southern Cameroons.

It must be stressed, first, that it is (only the legislation and) not the *legal systems* of the said states that would have to remain in force.

---

[169] Nelson Enonchong, "The Harmonization of Business Law in Africa: Is Article 42 of the OHADA Treaty a Problem?" 51:1 *Journal of African Law* (2007), 95 at 114.

[170] Temngah Joseph Nyambo, "Adoption of Children under Customary and Statutory Law in Cameroon" 9 *Revue Africaine de Droit International et Comparé* (1997) 894 at 903. (emphasis added)

By contrast, Canada's British North America (BNA) Act effectively preserved the existing pre-Confederation "systems" in section 129.[171] Second, in the stark absence of an independent judiciary (federal article 32 making president guardian of judicial independence), who else but the POR (a Francophone) decides if there is conflict? Third, it is well known from Enonchong (1967: 81) that "Most of the articles of this constitution were directly taken from the French Fifth Republican Constitution, 1958." Ex hypothesis, it is pure madness to be talking of the birth at Foumban of the idea of co-existence of the two legal systems. It is that simple since it is hard to see how common law 'legislation' is not going to conflict with a French-civilian Constitution.

This point is very important since both legal systems seem to be opposites in almost every sense. Enonchong (1967: 20) posits that "Common law is of course to be distinguished from 'civil law', the Roman law based system, where uniformity is the fundamental objective by the promulgation of presumably all-inclusive Codes... Needless to say that these two legal systems differ not only in concepts but also in approach." In further illustrating the point, Enonchong (1967: 20-21) has indicated how "droit constitutionnel has one connotation to the French civil-law trained lawyer and another to the Anglo-American trained lawyer." How then, once more, are West Cameroon's common law legislation and principles not going to "conflict with the provision of this [1961] Constitution" in order to co-exist with it? This folly would duly account for Anyangwe (1987: 267) indicating that "[I]t is in the civil law area that law reform [in Cameroon] encounters the stiffest test – test of will, test of national interest, test of intellectual integrity and honesty ... [because] Some lazy, petty and misguided minds [in Cameroon] would rather choose the road of ease, wholly inappropriate in our

---

[171] For further discussion of this issue, see R.A. Macdonald and F.R. Scott, "Harmonizing the Concepts and Vocabulary of Federal and Provincial Laws: The Unique Situation of Quebec Civil Law" in Ministère de la justice Canada (ed) *L'harmonisation de la législation fédérale avec le droit québecois et le bijuralisme canadien* (Ottawa: Ministère de la justice Canada, 1997) 29.

national context which consists of taking the French Civil Code [for example], tinkering with it, having it translated into English and presenting it as a 'Cameroonian Civil Code'." It accounts as well for Taku (1995: 3) making it known that "Attempts by us to form a Cameroon Common Law Bar have been frustrated. The practice of the Common Law as it were has been systematically invalidated by piecemeal legislation and what is left is a mockery of the system. Anglo-[S]axon qualifications are still being subjected to the equivalence of inferior certificates from France." That should already also tell the tragic story of the educational systems, passing through *epsi*'s critical assimilationist role.

The Purpose and Objectives of Education plus Epsi as Preventing Biculturalism

This section generally critiques the country's education politics, using *epsi* or *bourse* ('scholarship') to demonstrate that the real purpose of the law on education is not the one that is stated but that of assimilation of the English-speaking minority. The section demonstrates that the laudable purpose and objectives of education in the law are only political gimmicks as the practice to date portrays a different story; also debunking the regime's somewhat 'benevolent' administrative devices such as *epsi* that might have been employed solely in preventing the establishment of a genuine bicultural educational base; illustrating how the 1998 Education Law has come only to camouflage assimilation for multiculturalism. I will first examine the purpose of education before its objectives.

On the Purpose of Education in Cameroon

The sphere of education very well makes the point on pointless biculturalism and camouflaged national unity in Cameroon for two interconnected reasons. First, the burning human rights issues of bilingualism and bijuralism (in countries like Cameroon and Canada) do radiate out of education. Second, as shown in chapter one, education now seems to be the only existing stronghold of Southern

Cameroonsian resistance to outright assimilation and, therefore, what now gravely threatens Cameroon's national unity. The reasoning then is that what brute force has so far failed to completely achieve, may perhaps be easily attained through the law. So it is now time to employ alluring terminologies (such as educational dualism and bilingualism) in the very laws that are specifically geared toward obliterating those very conceptions.

An undisputed "key factor of life – education"[172] is so vital to development in all its connotations that nations that are truly desirous of advancement have not spared any effort in taking the education of their youths very seriously. This accounts for Kanyongo's (2005: 65) indication that, soon after independence, most governments of developing countries reformed their educational systems to align them with new national goals. Cameroon, unlike Zimbabwe, is not one of such countries that have embarked on massive reforms of their education system in order to reflect and/or incorporate 'new' national realities. Cameroon's education politics does not augur well for development of any kind and must leave multiculturalism experts with more than enough to negatively talk about. Legal education must, of course, be topmost in any society. Anyangwe (1989: chapter 11 – 'Legal Education in Cameroon') has offered a general discussion and critique of the sorrowful state of legal education in Cameroon.

Education generally, according to a great and respected African human rights activist and president, is the great engine of personal development. It is through education that the daughter of a peasant can become a doctor, that the son of a mineworker can become the head of the mine; that a child of farm workers can become the president of a great nation. It is what we make out of what we have, not what we are given, that separates one person from another.[173]

---

[172] Sheri Wisnowski, "Letter to Editor" 44 *Canadian Business* (December 1996) at 11.

[173] Nelson Mandela, *Long Walk to Freedom* (Boston: Little Brown and Company, 1994) at 144.

Mandela really knows what he is talking about. It is trite then that it is only through its judicious handling of its education politics that Cameroon can become the leader of the greatly multicultural continent of Africa. It is truly what Cameroon makes out of the two dominant foreign cultures it has inherited, and not what any of those foreign powers would instruct it to do, that would separate success from failure. So how is Cameroon faring in the domain of purposeful education?

The impression is given that its 1998 Education Law has come to rectify things. This law in its section 4 sees the general purpose of education in Cameroon to be to train Cameroon's children for their intellectual, physical, civic and moral development and their smooth integration into society bearing in mind the prevailing economic, socio-cultural, political and moral factors. Has this law then come perhaps to actually correct the situation that had been prevailing in Cameroon's institutions of higher education before it? For instance, it is well known that most lecturers of the then unique Yaoundé University (to be specific, its Faculty of Laws and Economics that Anyangwe also condemns[174]), often, if not always, prefaced their lectures with: *Je sais très bien que les anglos aiment bien la politique; mais je vous avertis que mes cours ne donnent aucune occasion pour la politique.* This could be loosely translated as meaning: 'I am aware of the fact that you, Anglophones, are very fond of politics but I must warn that my classes do not provide any platform for any non-legal or political discussion or commentary.' Thus, politics and history, for instance, must be completely kept away from legal education, according to these lecturers. Is that instruction correct and consonant with the job of teaching people about knowing and firmly assuming their rights?

Cameroon might not be alone here; but Pirie (1987:580) has answered in the negative because he considers this to be a 'dog-

---

[174] Anyangwe (1987: xv) thinks "It is amazing, though by no means surprising, how much many of our law students and legal practitioners know of English and French law but only little [or nothing] of that of their own country. We here in the [Yaoundé University] Law Faculty are partly responsible for perpetuating this mischief....this unacceptable situation."

breeding' modus which, while effectively "sharpen[ing] the mind by narrowing it", can only aid in furthering the "false legitimacy to existing social and power relations." Pirie is not alone in condemning the strategy since Suifon (1997) declares that

> Opinion is divided whether the role of the University of Buea [UNIBU] as the citadel of Anglo-Saxon cultural heritage has so far been fulfilled since its inception in 1993. One fear which ought to be haunting Anglophone Cameroonians but which doesn't seem to be the case is the fact that UNIBU appears to be judiciously following the example of the then University of Yaounde which for years churned out stereotypes into the job market who are unable to prove that rather than pass through the university, the Buea University passed through them.

The dog-breeders that the UNIYAO had as lecturers, would partly, if not entirely, explain why some critics have posited that many graduates pass through the UNIYAO without the University passing through them since "a graduate of law," for example, "knows little or nothing outside law. He is a big illiterate in computer science, etc. The science graduate is no better as he knows little outside botany, geology and zoology."[175]

There seems to be disagreement with Mvondo though; as the UNIYOA-trained lawyer is said to have broader objectives than just the practice of law because the institution's Bachelor of Laws (LL.B.) degree, according to Anyangwe (1989: 201), "aims at broader objectives than just the practice of law. Which is why in addition to courses of a more strictly legal nature, courses in the political and social sciences are also taught: sociology, political ideas, political regimes, civil liberties, political economy, general economics, financial institutions, and introduction to accounting." This position in the UNIYAO would clearly differ from Kenya's LL.B. which Ojwang

---

[175] J.M. Mvondo, "On Graduating from the University of Yaounde" *Cameroon Post* (12-19 August 1991), 6.

and Salter say does not incorporate a "more societal perspective."[176] Gold would think this has also been the case in Canada (outside Quebec) where legal scholars by and large "lack rigorous training in anything but law [and] This training tends to incline the academic lawyer towards an identification with the bench and bar, in part as a way to rationalize what the academic lawyer can do best."[177] Pirie (1987: 579) also regrets "the failure of legal education [in Canada] to include important political perspectives in the curriculum" The important question would thus become that of knowing why the Cameroonian intellectuals, especially the lawyers (with all the wider scope and the like), unlike their Canadian and Kenyan counterparts, would be such "societal illiterates" and be very sheepish. Is this due to other factors or to the decried educational dog-breeding?

The 'dog-breeding' strategy in Cameroon's educational institutions may largely explicate why many of the students eventually get to public or political positions without knowing how the political game is supposed to function, principally because they were never groomed to know, for example, that in politics, self-control is a necessity. This lack of self-control is exhibited in various ways, including, for example, in the training or recruitment for the civil service; with teachers (of all people in society), according to Bodo's report, passing the *concours* or competitive examinations into ENS (*École Normale Supérieure*) where they are trained: without even having sent in their candidature, let alone sat for the examinations. On top of all this is the other awkward fact that some of these 'passers' would not even be holders of the first degree (e.g., LL.B., B.A., or B.Sc.) that is required for taking the examinations.[178]

The Executive Secretary of the Cameroon Anglophone Teachers'

---

[176] J.B. Ojwang, and D.R. Salter, "Legal Education in Kenya", *Journal of African Law* 33-1 (1988-89), 78 at 90.

[177] Marc Gold, "Constitutional Scholarship in Canada" 23 *Osgoode Hall Law Journal* (1985), 495 at 498 n.11.

[178] See Damien Fouda Bodo, "Concours ou clientélisme?" *L'Effort Camerounais* N° 60 (1057) (14-24 décembre 1996), 6.

Union (CATU) in the person of Simon Nkwenti has also lamented about this awful situation.

> Look at the breed of teachers passing out of ENS today. ENS is virtually being sold at Mokolo market, Melen market, just anywhere. The result is that we have fake teachers sneaking into the profession. By all standards, ENS has been transformed into a comprehensive college. It is no longer a teachers' college. And what do you expect? A breed of teachers no better than the students they're sent to teach! The dividing line between the knowledge of teachers and students is so thin.[179]

According to Fohtung (1996, omission is as in original), "Since 'Ecole Normale' is the only professional institution admitting and churning out young students into the civil service, we can argue that a good number of these running-nose civil servants are the teachers...of our children!" How can any civil service or government department filled to the brim with people of this sort be able to know how laws have to be properly enacted, and be general and neutral in application (explaining why Atubah says "our parliament up to now is full of people who haven't the least idea of the law" so as to "enact laws suitable to our own society"[180]); and to know that educational opportunities should not be made available to citizens based on some unnecessary discriminatory criteria but be open to all who qualify without exception?[181]

---

[179] See "Admission into ENS Can Now Be Bought at Mokolo Market - Nkwenti Simon" *The Herald* N° 508, 10-11 September 1997, 6. See also Fon Peter, "Scandal in E.N.S Admissions" *The Focus* N° 0021 (22-26 September 1997), 1 & 2; and Akem Etang, "Teaching Has Become an Adventure in Cameroon, Says Headmaster" *The Herald* N° 590 (30-31 March 1998), 11.

[180] Awutah Philip Atubah, "The Legal Implications of Sections 11 and 15 of the Southern Cameroons High Court Law 1955" *The Herald* N° 430 (10-11 March 1997), 4.

[181] See Fidèle Muabe "Bamileke Students Petition Biya for Educational Discrimination" *The Herald* N° 334 (16-18 August 1996), 3.

It was also perhaps to eschew this situation and several others that the Education Law in section 7 has now also placed on the Cameroon state the duty to guarantee or ensure equal opportunities for education to all, without discrimination as to gender, political, philosophical or religious opinion, or social, cultural, linguistic or geographical origin.[182] And that education is not only a top priority of the Cameroon State (section 2(1)), but must also be apolitical (section 8), with the state firmly guaranteeing that public education be compulsory at primary level (section 9) and secular, neutral and independent vis-à-vis all religions (section 10).

These are very commendable policies except that they seem to be just French photocopies that do not only not reflect national realities but also end only on paper. For example, Cameroon's claim to secularity has been held to be just another instance of blind copying "from Metropolitan France" because "it is a contradiction in terms to what prevails in this country."[183] The regime could also not be right in saying that education in Cameroon is apolitical when Suifon (1997) attributes the current laughing-stock status of the UNIBU to a number of factors that principally include the

> political inclination of the top brass of UNIBU and the consequent squelching of the politically non-conformist lecturers; the suppression of an elected students' union body; the victimisation of its leaders, some of whom were simply dismissed; the avoidable tragedy resulting from the politicisation of the university by the authorities and the accompanying tribal cleavages [which] created a sense of betrayal especially as some of the indigen[ous people] perceived the university as nothing short of a tribal estate.

---

[182] There is a lengthy discussion of the requirements of this provision by Brunnell (2005); and Adams (2006: 4-8).

[183] Bonny Kfua, "What Does Being Secular Mean?" *The Herald* (4-6 October 1996), 4.

This would not be surprising to anyone who understands just how the Cameroonian POR himself deals with the country as one would one's private property. Why should anyone expect the plethora of his personal appointees to behave any differently? It is thus clear that the 1998 Education Law has not made any difference since the practices seem to be continuing in spite of the laudable objectives of education; laudable only in the name of confusion, as I will next demonstrate.

On the Objectives of Education and Epsi

Desirous of success in the domain of leading Africa out of the cell, it would seem, the Cameroon administration has taken steps to enact the 1998 Education Law that is geared towards "reaffirming our national option for biculturalism" in its section 15(1). Using *epsi* or *bourse* in the demonstration, this study however shows, through an informed and critical inspection of some of its objectives of education, that the reaffirmation of "our national option for biculturalism" is very far indeed from being the aim of that law. The objectives of education in Cameroon are specified in section 5 as being to:

(1) train citizens who are firmly rooted in their culture, but open to the world and respectful of the general interest and the common weal;

(2) inculcate the major universal ethical values which are dignity and honour, honesty and integrity, as well as a sense of discipline into pupils and students;

(3) promote family life;

(4) promote national languages;

(5) provide an instruction to the democratic culture and practice, respect for human rights and freedoms, justice and tolerance, the fight against all forms of discrimination, the love of peace and dialogue, civic responsibility and promotion of regional and sub-regional integration;

(6) cultivate the love of effort and work well done, the quest

for excellence and team spirit;

(7)   develop creativity, a sense of initiative and spirit of enterprise;

(8)   provide physical, sports, artistic and cultural training for the child; [and]

(9)   promote hygiene and health education.

These are noble objectives indeed but it is not clear if the authorities are genuine about them. This writer does not think they are for a number of simple reasons.

It is plainly doubtful that the Cameroonian authorities are serious about them when it is no longer a secret that teaching has become a dangerous adventure in Cameroon due to the very corrupt demeanours of school administrators and most teachers who are members of the educational community that is defined in section 32 as follows: "(1) The Educational Community shall comprise all individuals and corporate bodies that contribute towards the functioning, development and prestige of a school. (2) It shall comprise the following members: the authorities, the administrative and support staff; teachers; parents of pupils; students; persons from socio-professional cycles; regional and local authorities." Johnson-Hanks (2006: 125-31) has lengthily and critically discussed some of these members of the 'educational community', namely, 'The School and Their Teachers'. I cannot therefore see the administration's seriousness in those objectives which, by the way, are mere smokescreens. It is surely not this same administration that is out to do all the magnificent things that the Education Law purports to represent when, because of its lack of vision, private education establishments have now sprouted here and there, including what Boyle (1996: 620 & 622) calls "schools of increasingly dubious quality." Dubious schools with equally doubtful teachers who Fohtung (1996) says would quickly and sheepishly abdicate "when it comes to the Anglophone Problem or say, decentralization which can spare them the costly trips to Yaounde."

The authorities can basically not be serious about those

objectives of education when Boyle's (1996: 621) seasoned research has further clearly shown that "the state lacks the wherewithal and political will to direct [educational] change in Cameroon." A serious administration would not be wanting in this aspect because Mback (2007: 74) thinks only such political will, of course, "would have the potential to transform municipal institutions and, more widely, local governments into the new actors in development they should have been and remained since they were introduced in Cameroon [in 1996]." The much-needed political will is lacking principally because "Cameroon is a nation where, deliberately or otherwise, the political cart is placed before the horse."[184] The debilitating effects of this 'horse before cart' politics on human rights would not require any enormous amount of the stretching of the intellect to grasp.

Because of that gaping political will void, in the early 90s the then unique and overcrowded UNIYAO students' *parlement* surprisingly forced the birth of six universities that were created by the very controversial legislation on higher education reform.[185] The created universities included the long-suppressed Anglophone one in Buea. Because of the student *parlement*, Cameroon was hurriedly dotted with four more universities through decreeing previous *Centres Universitaires* (university centres) into full-fledged universities. These are the UNIBU (until then a professional school for translators and interpreters) in Debundschazone, University of Douala (Wourizone), University of Dschang (Bamboutouszone), and University of Ngaoundéré (Adamawazone). The unique UNIYAO was split into

---

[184] R.B. Sanjo "Did Ahidjo, Biya Suppress Foncha's Plan for an Anglophone University?" *Le Messager* (18 July 1991), 10.

[185] "*six universités crées par le très controversée réforme de l'Enseignement supérieure.*" Alex Gustav Azebaze, "Crise des Universités: Obounou limogé! Et la session d'Été alors?" *Le Messager* N° 513 (6 juin 1996), 8. See also Yvette Mbassi, "Fruits et leurres de la réforme" *Cameroon Tribune* (2 novembre 1998), 8. Langdon has written an interesting essay that elaborately discusses the factors accounting for, trends, consequences and nature of, this 'new form' of power (student-power) in Canada – with some very similar characteristics in the Cameroonian *parlement* situation. See Steven Langdon, "The Politics of Participation: A Student Case" in James A. Draper, ed. *Citizen Participation: Canada* (Toronto: New Press, 1971), 45-56.

two universities (for Sanagazone), namely, UNIYAO I (being the former university's two Faculties of Arts and of Sciences) which stayed-put on the original campus of Ngoa-Ékéllé from where *Ngoa-lingualism* is derived, and UNIYAO II with campus at the city's suburb of Soa (being the mother university's Faculty of Laws and Economics). Five of the proposed ten regions (one English-speaking, four French-speaking) are left without a state university: Benouezone, Guinean-Savannazone, Logonezone, Nyongzone, and Savannazone.

The UNIBU, the then lone state university in West Cameroon,[186] was established by Decree N° 92/74 of 13 April 1992. Decree N° 93/034 of 19 January 1993 organizing the UNIBU states in article 1(a) that the University is "conceived in the Anglo-Saxon tradition." But is the talk of Anglo-Saxon tradition and educational dualism in this country then genuine? The answer is no because this 'Anglo-Saxon' UNIBU whose creation was only "forced" by the student *parlement* must now be destroyed with much subtlety; subtleness that is particularly embedded in Part II of the education law itself (already examined in Chapter 2). The comprehension of the confusion that is being called higher education (or university) reforms and the reaffirmation of the country's biculturalism would still be aided by a further discussion of the activities of *parlement*.

The unprecedented activities of this student revolutionary body did not only come as a giant surprise to the authorities. It also shook the entire country to the root, with some wild rumours that the student body had plans to take over the running of the country (And what is wrong with that?). The whole enterprise of reform that followed the rise of *parlement* is brutally confusing and controversial. I find all this normal because that is what always happens when an administration has no clear vision or any at all and is overtaken by events it never foresaw coming. I would nevertheless attempt highlighting some pertinent points.

---

[186] The University of Bamenda (UNIBA) was recently created by presidential decree of 14 December 2010, unlike UNIBU that came along eighteen years earlier through presidential decree of 13 April 1992.

The first is that *parlement*'s only demands (contrary to the rumours that were spread around to 'justify' the barbaric measures used in trying to disband it) were inevitable wide-ranging reforms in the then 'one and only' and excessively overcrowded UNIYAO. Second, *parlement* was able to stand as firm as it did – in the face of the heavy deployment of the military – because of its cohesion or solidarity in purpose. There was the marked absence of the usual Anglophone-Francophone division that has always been noticed in the ill-fated fights against human rights violations, notably those regarding the G.C.E. system or those touching uniquely Anglophone interests.[187] These kinds of divisions were absent in *parlement* that seem to have understood that to begin by discriminating whose rights should be defended would eventually mean that nobody's rights are safe from the dictatorship. As Chapter 3 could show, the leaders of the paper political parties never understood this vital lesson and where they are today (begging for the crumbs or remains from Biya's meal table) tells the whole story. Third, *parlement* 'gave' Cameroon five (rather one) more hurriedly decreed universities not so much as a response to the students' demands. Public opinion, according to Anyangwe (1996: 826) does not count for anything to the Biya "government [that] is generally insensitive to public opinion and the demands of fairness." Furthermore,

> there is a growing disenchantment about commissions of inquiry [and new universities and/or constitutional organs] in the Biya regime. For one thing, they have always symbolised official deception at its most treacherous stage....[G]overnment

---

[187] As Tangwa (1996) has identified, the divisiveness involved in defending human rights in Cameroon could be attributed to a number of factors; one of them being "political parties and interest groups [which] could not rally behind Mbawa [an Anglophone] as was the case during the Monga-Njawe [Francophones] trial. Political parties and interest groups, whose manifestoes were espoused by Mbawa, shied away. Either these parties or groups did not react because they have already entrenched themselves in the political mainstream and, as such, did not see Mbawa's case as one of political show of force (as the Monga-Njawe trial was) or they were embroiled in crises."

sponsored commissions of inquiry [and universities and/or constitutional bodies]... have always tended to cloak rather than shed light on issues....Since he [Biya] came to power...[30] years ago, he has contrived to create commissions [and universities and/or constitutional organs] only when he intends to shelve an issue.[188]

The decreeing of those universities therefore, in the estimation of the authorities, had a double-edged purpose: first, a very nice means of diffusing the unprecedented student power; and, second, a way of not looking like succumbing to the demands of the English-speaking, as I will further expose.

The principle idea behind the creation of these universities is that of dispersing the exceptional student power that had 'dangerously' developed right there in the very heart of Yaoundé – Cameroon's alpha and omega which, according to President Biya, breathes and the rest of the country lives. (*"Lorsque Yaoundé respire, tout le Cameroun vit!"*[189]) That can also explain why any talk of genuine decentralization becomes heresy or subversion to this administration. To Biya then, that dangerous student power in the jealously guarded respiratory organ of 'his' Cameroon had to be swiftly eliminated. That is precisely why the 'nerve centre' of the overcrowded UNIYAO's *parlement* – the Faculty of Law and Economics – must have to be sent to the suburb of Soa, done even without adequate (if not actually no) infrastructure there. This theory becomes clear through a look at the consequences, for the students, of bringing about the unplanned creation of those universities.

As already noted, decreeing the existence of five more universities (rather than just one that should normally have to be in West Cameroon) provided a convenient way of not looking like

---

[188] M.L. Lokanga, "Student Leader Refuses to Talk to the Endeley Commission," *Le Message* (18 July 1991), 10.

[189] See "Cameroon: Crisis or Compromise?" 32 *Africa Confidential* (25 October 1991), 2 at 3.

"succumbing" to the long suppressed Anglophone demands for university institutions across the Mungo River. But as *parlement* had untimely brought that about, the students must pay dearly for it. How they are to be penalized, is interestingly telling to the thesis of one-culture biculturalism that is being developed. The punishment given to them, quite apart from the brutal response to the unexpected rise of *parlement*, came in two ways. The first was the abolition of *epsi* (or *bourse*) and the second was in the form of the imposition of university fees.

Epsi is the student-invented milieu name for the monthly grant that the Cameroonian administration had until then been spending in the name of *bourse* to UNIYAO students for no other reason than just to make unthinking drunkards out of them and, therefore, avoid facing and tackling the important issues of an authentic bicultural educational base. This *epsi* strategy would seem to have taken its toll on the Anglophone students who have also been largely frustrated by the UNIYAO educational language politics that is popularly known as *Ngoa-lingualism*. As just indicated, *epsi* and *Ngoa-lingualism* (the first attracting them to the second) have imposed their exacting levy on Anglophones to an extent that the following statement (in Njangawatok) has become very commonplace: "*Massa, leave man withi politics. If one beer dey, tell me I go follow you.*" This is Njangawatok for: 'I am not a politician and do not want to bother anymore about what the politicians are doing; if you have something else to offer, for example, a bottle of beer, then I am all yours.' Other familiar forms of this 'Massa leave man' are furnished by Fonkeng (1990: 20 & passim): "How we go do now?", "Dokta, weti man go do noh?" That is exactly what *epsi* might have been meant to achieve. Attract them with *epsi* and then frustrate them with *Ngoa-lingualism* as much as possible so that heroes are never born out of any of them, as Marian Chia has elucidated:

> Heroes build nations. Nations admire, encourage and revere their heroes, but in Cameroon, we ridicule, frustrate, imprison and kill heroes or chase them into exile….Do we have such people in

Cameroon? Yes! But they are all 'locked up in themselves'. They do not set the example we expect. They have become frustrated beings, drunks, con men, lecherous fornicators, adulterers, white-collar thieves, blatant liars and occult[] worshippers. These are the people our children are supposed to emulate. These are our heroes. This is our future.[190]

The *epsi* used to be classified in CFA francs per month as follows: 60.000 (*doctorat* students), 50.000 (*maîtrise* students), 40.000 (third year *licence* students), and 30.000 (first and second year *licence* students). In view of the university population then the amount of money dished out as *epsi* in just five years, for instance, could be more than enough money to have built at least two well-equipped and high quality universities in Cameroon (including or excluding the UNIYAO). But rather than confront the problems while they were still easily solvable, the authorities had thought that *epsi* was the 'magic portion'. In the words of a community development expert (Sim, 1971: 171-72), the administration,

> by avoidance of basic issues, has helped to promote the ultimate chaos that follows delay and postponement of facing up to fundamental problems, and has contributed to the deluge that comes when redress is too niggardly, when justice arrives too late. If history notices what...[this administration] has done in the past quarter-century at all, its judgment will be harsh. Posterity will [either] say it was innocent because it was too naïve to understand the consequences of what it had done, or it was guilty because it did understand, but feared the consequences of acting boldly, lacked the necessary nerve to fly into the eye of the storm.

The same thesis is also advanced in French by Eyoum Ngangue, "Fermeture de la BIAO: une mesure tardive qui sacrifie l'épargnant" *Le Messager* (16 septembre 1996), 8.

---

[190] Marian Chia, "Our Heroes" *Cameroon Post* (11-18 December 1995), 10.

Indeed, to think that *epsi* was the 'magic fix-all' was brainless enough because it does not take any great amount of intelligence to see that *epsi* would instead aggravate the issues since its links with the congestion at the UNIYAO (that mainly brought forth *parlement*) is plain enough. The overpopulation and the accompanying ills that gave birth to *parlement* would not be hard in coming because of Anyangwe's (1989: 199 n.7, emphasis added) discovery that "Every year hundreds of [high school] students register in the [Yaoundé] University *without any serious intention of studying but simply to acquire the status of University student and to receive the monthly grant which they consider as a kind of unemployment benefit*." As long as the students get this *epsi* money and drink their unemployment and frustrations to death, there will be no problem. That was the administration's line of thinking; which is perfectly normal for one that is well known for its policy dubbed *navigation à vue* (visionless policy). *Epsi* must then be purely and speedily scrapped off the books now that there is on the table the problem it has failed to indefinitely 'solve' or postpone. But its scrapping is not enough chastisement for the students.

The second penalty came in the form of the POR's *Décret N° 93/032 du 9 janvier 1993* that would impose university fees. This Decree instituted and regulated the payment of fees of 50,000 francs CFA an academic year. Thus, a student who was being paid CFA 40,000 francs a month without paying university fees, for example, is now required to pay CFA 50,000 francs a year as fees without *epsi*. Why? It is simply because the 'Anglos' now have a university, thanks to them. It should be noted that this introduction of university fees also came at the same time as their parents' salaries had been slashed to unbearable bits: not to mention the full effects of the French devaluation, leading to Waindim's cry of the destitute on discovering that change in Cameroon has always been

> in the form of old wine in new wine skins. Yet, that our docility and blind tolerance as future generations are being mortgaged, point to the impression that we may after all deserve the leaders we have. Were it otherwise, who, therefore are we? What have we

done when leaders force themselves on us? What have we done when our forests are raped; when pseudo law enforcement bandits contemptuously rape our daughters and wives without remorse; when bullets and grenades are hauled at children and women who deserve our protection; when salaries are non-existent and devaluation has made life unbearable; what have we done?... [Who is ever going] to inject some doses of courage into the inmates of the prison called Cameroon?[191]

Until the devaluation of the French franc (FF) in the early 90s, according to Clément *et al* (1996: 'Introduction'), CFA 50 francs were equal to 1 FF. Since then, the rate is 100 FCFA = 1 FF.

Furthermore, at the same moment of imposing fees on the students there was the introduction of too many taxes which, according to Boyle (1996: 618-622), would also strangely couple with the drying up of "public resources" and the stifling of "private initiative" of parents who are opting for better schooling of their children. All this would seem to be the punishment the entire student body in Cameroon must endure for causing the untimely creation of the 'Anglo-Saxon UNIBU' in particular, which must now be destroyed, one way or the other. This thesis can explain why the 1998 Education Law, which in the opening section 1(2) declares itself to be limited only to pre-university education, would wind up, in a very questionable manner, actually regulating "all levels of education" in section 14 of its part II. The UNIBU (and newly created UNIBA) could be a clear target and some critics have already warned that "[t]he word 'Anglo-Saxon' in the decree creating the University of Buea, to us, was not gratuitous. In fact, on that word hinges a people's lifestyle, indeed, legacy."[192]

---

[191] Jude Waindim, "Gwangwa'a's Cry of the Destitute," *Cameroon Post* (11-18 December 1995), 4.

[192] The Post Comment, "Five Years After: How Anglo-Saxon is UB?" *The Post* N° 0044 (23 January 1998), 4.

One cannot therefore speak of universities when one has not created appropriate infrastructures and other conditions necessary for the existence and smooth functioning of those universities. It is thus highly doubtful that the 1998 Education Law came to put a stop to (rather than fortify) the sad dog-breeding situation in education generally in Cameroon. That is why the absence of self-control in politics persists to date, as evidenced especially by both that Education Law itself and the 1996 Constitution. Both laws employ the terms biculturalism, bilingualism, and cultural dualism, when in fact their whole essence is the destruction of any semblance of the existence of those concepts. That is why the creation of a so-called Anglo-Saxon university in this country had to be an involuntary act, with these two pieces of legislation (among others) now being in place to ensure that the said institution remains 'Anglo-Saxon' only in name and on paper. In short, that they be Anglo-Saxon only in the *Ngoa-lingual* sense, as even the war between the two educational systems (in Chapter 2) has also largely portrayed. All this happens because of leadership non-charisma and non-challenge of historic trivia which the next Chapter shows to be directly and largely responsible for many countries (with far less natural and other endowments) beating Cameroon in the development game.

Chapter 5

Leadership Non-Charisma and Non-Challenge of Historic Trivia: The Uniting Of One History Is Why Cameroon Is Not Championing In the Development Business in Africa

We must start by telling the people the truth about their present catastrophic economic [and political] situation which is the product of [over] 14 years of unpardonable economic and political mismanagement. We can no longer lie to them just to earn votes. But we must tell them their true potential and where they are now and where they can be in the future if they mobilise themselves [SDF, 1996: 2].

This Chapter critically examines the human factor as it impacts Cameroon's political economy; showing that the country is blessed with everything required for speedy and sustainable development but for the lack of intelligent, efficient and patriotic managers. It starts by generally surveying the natural qualities of Cameroonians, spiced with Cameroon's unrivalled physical environment and other natural endowments that, with just the right push from the quality governors just described as being absent, would undoubtedly transform the country into a Paradise on Earth. This state of affairs has not yet materialized simply because of problems in leadership non-charisma and in non-challenge of historic trivia, and not the result of the country's unquestioned diversity, as its administrators would claim.

Political economists like Magstadt (1991: 50-51); and Baumol *et al* (1988: Part VII – 'The Government and the Economy') all seem to agree with Edwin Cannan in his *Wealth* (1930), as discussed in

Bladen (1956: 3), that how plentifully a community will be supplied with the "necessaries and conveniences of life" will largely depend on four factors, namely, (1) the natural qualities of the members of the community, (2) the original quality of the physical environment, (3) the heritage of accumulated improvement, and (4) the good judgment with which the efforts of the group are regulated. These four factors will be studied but the focus is on the first and fourth that are direct human factors that could shape or alter the others (or all four). The first part of the chapter will seek to expose some uniquely favourable characteristics of the political economy; the second looks at quality of the managers, accentuating the perfect nation (or the uniting of one history) and its impact on democracy and collective participation; highlighting confusion as a way of preventing an industrial economy that is very much required for the generally known democracy – liberal or constitutional.

Understanding the Political Economy of Cameroon

As previously noted in the Introduction of this book, a single but exceptionally instructive example, the experiences of the Republic of Cameroon, though a study of a single case, provides us with a lot of issues that are relevant to all of Africa and, indeed, to most of the new states of the world. These 'new states of the world' have generally been lumped up as the Third World, a class that is meant to set them apart from the 'old developed states' that already occupied the first two worlds – one capitalist and the other communist. William C. Olson in his *The Theory and Practice of International Relations* (1987), as cited in Fossungu (2010: 217 n.15), differentiates them as follows:

> The *first world* consists of highly developed capitalist/democratic countries; the *second world* consists of highly developed Communist states. The rest of the world was previously classified as *Third World*, but it now appears that there are large distinctions among these countries. *Third World* is defined today as those

societies, still underdeveloped, who possess the *capacity* to develop and modernize rapidly. But some countries are so poor that it remains doubtful whether they can develop, even with massive foreign assistance – the *fourth world*. There is, to some, even a *fifth world* absolutely hopeless of meaningful modernization.

Third World is used in this study to cover even those other worlds below it since they are all often referred to as 'developing nations'; with some experts even finding their gross disregard for human rights to be largely responsible for Neal Riemer's thesis, cited in Fossungu (2010: 217 n.15), that "most [of these] Third World nations are poor and developing, and sometimes not even developing." I would here venture to go further and posit that because of the gross abuse of basic human rights (the catalyst for development), some of these Third World states, championed by Cameroon that is not even poor as such, are not only not developing but actually regressing.

About twenty-five years ago Biya (1986: 97 & 27-28), recognizing Cameroon as "'Africa in Miniature' geographically, historically and culturally," clearly asserted that "I can affirm that a great destiny awaits Cameroon" because of "the human and material potential of our country." The graphical question has already been posed as to whether the Cameroon leadership (with all these potentials of the country) is up to the continental leadership task. It seems to have been in answer to the question as well as in allusion to the various strategies (such as the denying of history and the prevention of a strong industrial economy) employed by the ruling CPDM to frighten Cameroonians off democracy, that the opposing SDF (1996: 2) made the affirmation that opens this Chapter; a chapter that is obviously a segment of the truth that the Cameroon People and the experts generally would need to be told.

This part of the Chapter therefore reviews some of the human and natural characteristics that do give Cameroon the description of a complex, yet blessed society. It throws light on Cameroon's human and natural or physical endowments that, with proper management, ought rightly and easily, according to political economists, to put the country far ahead in terms of development. The term 'development' has already been more elaborately defined in a degree-earning study on sustainable development;[193] with Couloumbis and Wolfe (1986: 335-346 and the copious literature cited therein) also offering an extensive discussion of its various forms (economic, social, political, and intellectual) in the Third World. On the economic side of development as concerns Africa generally, Dzidzornu (1995: 445-446 n.21) has offered an impressive list of sources. It is already well established that development is the synonym for nation-building.[194] It is hard to gainsay that human rights (including those to good health and authentic education) are the invisible hand behind any meaningful development or nation-building. Education has already been analysed in previous Chapters of this book but it pays to emphasize here with Brunnell (2005: 343) that bona fide "Education is the highway that propels America, driving its businesses, delivering opportunity, and fuelling its political, social, and moral conscience." There is thus a sacred relationship between respect for human rights (including rights to decent education and to health) and development, a link that has also been well established by Appiagyei-Atua (1999: chapter 2[195]) and would not need to further detain us here.

---

[193] See generally José Vincente Zapata Lugo, *Sustainable Development: A Role for International Environmental Law* (LL.M. Thesis, Institute of Comparative Law, McGill University, 1993).

[194] See Thomas M. Magstadt and Peter M. Schotten, *Understanding Politics: Ideas, Institutions, and Issues* (New York: St. Martin's Press, 1988), chapter 2 ("The Nation-State"), 29-54, cited in Magstadt (1991: 40).

[195] The chapter is titled 'Establishing the Relationship between Human Rights, Civil Society and Development'. See also Asbjorn Eide, "Linking Human Rights and Development: Aspects of the Norwegian Debate" in Irving Brecher, ed., *Human Rights, Development and Foreign Policy: Canadian Perspectives* (Halifax: The Institute for Research on Public Policy, 1989), 5-30; and Kwadwo Appiagyei-Atua, *Re-Discovering the Relation Between Rights and Development through the Theory of Community Understanding: The Experiences of Ghana and Canada* (LL.M. Thesis, Dalhousie Law School, 1994).

Cameroon is one of the least developed (though being the most 'advanced in democracy') on the continent. Illustrations on its least developed status are not hard to find. First, its Chief Delegate at the 29th Assembly of the International Civil Aviation Organization (ICAO) in Montreal in September-October 1992 stated that Cameroon is "the microcosm of Africa and a country with paradoxical contrasts, a varied economy and a dense population... [though regrettably still] an essentially agricultural nation."[196] Second, citing G.T. Kurian, *The Book of World Rankings* (1979), Couloumbis and Wolfe (1986: 383) have drawn attention to a 1979 Data of Levels of Absolute Poverty in Non-Communist Developing Countries that was compiled by the Overseas Development Council, Washington, D.C., showing that the per cent of population in absolute poverty in 1977 in Cameroon was 33 while only 16 in Ivory Coast. Third, Jubilee 2000 has listed 55 countries where debt payments are adding to problems of growing malnutrition and high infant mortality. About 15 of them, the report concludes, "including Haiti, the Ivory Coast and Cameroon owe Canada about 1.2 billion."[197] Ex hypothesis, Africa's Microcosm is a conspicuous member of what Couloumbis and Wolfe (1986: 344) describe as the "vicious cycle of poverty" whose membership Myrda says African states have acquired "with the encouragement of advanced countries."[198] Cameroon's underdevelopment is not in doubt; what is important therefore is the reason why Cameroon is that backward with all the potentials that most other countries in the world only

---

[196] *ICAO Doc. 9601 A29–Min P/1–14* at 117. Paradoxes or contrasts by themselves are not as bad as the Cameroonian authorities would appear to want to present. See Maneli (1994 : 26 & 14-18); and Suzanne Kola-Lobé, "Peut-on gérer les conflits?" *L'Expression* (17 avril 1997), 11.

[197] Janet Vlieg, "Jubilee. A Call for Renewal: Churches Want to Offer the Third World A Second Chance" *The Edmonton Journal* (13 January 1999), F4.

[198] G. Myrdal, *Development and Underdevelopment* (1956) at 65, cited in Tixier (1974: 62). See also Appiagyei-Atua (1999: chapter 3, titled 'African Development 1960-90: The Impact of Western Policies and African Socialism on Human Rights').

dream of. Many reasons have been advanced but I think the root of the matter is the uniting of one history under the cover of national unity.

Specialists would agree that respect for human rights in culturally diverse societies like Cameroon would necessitate the federal structure as well as the entrenchment of multiculturalism as has been intelligently done in Canada, Switzerland, and Belgium; and that the concept of federalism is nonsensical in the absence of effective multiparty politics and other forms of separation of powers. These rights respecting vehicles were clearly absent in Foumban in 1961; absences that are at the heart of the entire human rights and nation-building crisis in Cameroon particularly and Africa generally. The failures of Foumban (where the FRC was created) are even greatly magnified by Cameroon's enviable geopolitical bearing among other factors, including the original quality of its environment.

Original Quality of Cameroon's Environment

The controversy on its total territorial size and population, though impinging on its environment in a way, has already been surveyed in Chapter 2. I will here just highlight the encouraging original environment and enviable geographical position (already seen in a previous Chapter). Cameroon is blessed with four natural regions which Nelson *et al* (1974: vii) enumerate to be the northern plains, central and southern plateau, western highlands and mountains, and coastal plains. Cameroon's climate and vegetation are as diverse as its population and ethnic groups. The climate is sub-arid and hot in the northern plain area, with seventeen-month dry season. The central plateaus and western highlands are slightly cooler because of elevation and have much shorter dry season, shading into year-round rainfall in southwest. On the other hand, the coastal lowlands are monotonously warm and humid throughout the year (Nelson *et al* (1974: 42-46, vii). Cameroon's wildlife and settlement patterns are no less sources of enchantment (see Nelson *et al*, 1974: 48-52; and Zuhmboshi, 1997). It is simply futile to think that one can even sufficiently catalogue all the intriguing natural and physical endowments of this unique West-Central African country. In short, according to French (1997), Cameroon is so profusely and variably "rich in natural resources [that it is considered] to be Central Africa's [P]romised land."

As to the original quality of the environment of a country like Cameroon, political economists like Baumol *et al* (1988: chapter 34 – 'Environmental Protection and Resource Conservation'), Jua,[199] and Bladen (1956: 5) tell us that the importance of the physical environment is also obvious. The significance of a fertile soil, a convenient topography, availability of such natural resources as wood, minerals, fur and fish, and the presence of resources of water power must simply require no over emphasis. The climate, Bladen (1956: 5) has indicated,

> is also of great importance, affecting needs as well as productivity because a long cold winter, for instance, makes necessary better houses and fuel to heat them, better stabling for the cattle and more work to care for them; it means shorter growing season for annual vegetation and winter killing of perennials; and it precludes the performance of many kinds of work, for example outside construction, for several months in the year. Adequate rainfall in the growing season and sufficient sunshine for ripening are clearly important.

Are people not truly blessed in Cameroon (and Africa)? Winters are unknown to most of Africa especially south of the Sahara, Cameroon therein included. With all these human and physical potentials that even the blind can see, why is Cameroon one of the least developed on the continent? Why is this otherwise 'African Paradise-on-Earth' in the camp of Prodigal Sons? What else, apart

---

[199] Nantang Jua, "Small Is Not Always Beautiful: A Case Study of the Njinikom Area Development Association" 11:3 *Nordic Journal of African Studies* (2002), 336-358.

from the staggering lack of good and patriotic managers, can explain the misery of Cameroonians in particular and Africans in general? These questions are even more important to ask in view of this country's enviable continental geo-political-cultural position that couples so well with the natural qualities of the Cameroon people.

The Natural Qualities Of The Cameroon People

The natural qualities of the members of the community will be examined to show how, spiced with the equally development-oriented original quality of the physical environment, patriotic and efficient managers would have little or no problems in transforming the country into an enviable place of bliss. No one doubts that Cameroon is a wonderful land inhabited by a wonderful people, as ably described by a French-speaking journalist, Eyoum'a Ntoh (1996): "*Le Cameroun est un grand pays. Cela ne fait aucun doute. Un grand pays habité par un grand people. Cela non plus ne fait pas de doute.*" As I have already said, the instability and paralysis associated with the parliamentary system (that I am advocating for, to go together with federalism, in this country) cannot even apply in Cameroon but for their deliberate orchestration by the leadership to justify personal power. Ethnic, religious, and cultural tolerance is the order of the day in Cameroon because inter-ethnic, inter-religious, and inter-cultural (*anglophone-francophone*) marriages are very common and regarded as perfectly normal in the country.

This is one of the many things (including abundant availability of food and alcoholic drinks[200]) that make Cameroon stand out. The type of religious clashes between Christians and Moslems that one often witnesses in neighbouring Nigeria (to leave out faraway Indian sub-continent and the Middle East), are absent in Cameroon. This is not so much because the followers of those faiths cannot clash; nor that there are no Christian and Moslem people in this country; far

---

[200] The 'hungry man, angry man' adage would seem to have no place in this country. What about the 'drunkard, unthinking man' adage?

from it. Like Indonesia and Alaska in the United States, Cameroon "is a place with great variety of [ethnic patterns,] cultures, beliefs, and attitudes, yet there is a substantial commitment to tolerance."[201] This is probably because in Cameroon, as Johnson (1970: vii) has discovered, the "family has [simply] become a kind of cultural crossroads: some of its members have adopted Christianity, while others profess Islam." In this country, the spirit is different – tolerance as usual: with both groups (and the non-believers) all going about their businesses as brothers and sisters of the same family and society: Cameroon.

All this is further topped by the dynamism and positive developmental attitude of Cameroonians, characteristics that are no secret even to the uninspiring leadership: As Biya (1986: 11) has declared, "I think the reason why most citizens in this country strongly reject destabilization attempts orchestrated by adventurers at home and abroad is that they are imbued with the strong conviction that only in an atmosphere of peace and stability can they hope to develop this potential wealth in the country and enjoy it in the most honest manner possible." This is a very unique element that many countries only crave for and dream of (all in vain) but which Cameroon's administrators get for free; and yet they cannot utilize as well as they should in propelling national development. This characteristic of Cameroonians standing all by itself does indeed make the realization of the largely cherished 'Paradise in Africa' there very easy. During Ahidjo's visit to Buea in 1960 – a year before the 1961 unification of the two Cameroons – one of this unification's principal architects, John Ngu Foncha, according to Stark (1976:

---

[201] J.H. McComas, "And Justice for All: A Northern Exposure" 9:2 *Criminal Justice* (1994), 8 at 8. Indonesia's 14,000 islands is home to some 200 million people of diverse ethnicity who share all the major religions of humankind and speak some 320 distinct languages. But, as Das (1996) reports, there are unifying forces in this melange – the first being religion. Despite the diversity, according to the report, nine in 10 Indonesians are Muslim, making Indonesia, therefore, the world's largest Muslim country. However, Das cautions, "it is an Islam that's much more tolerant than the image evoked in the Middle East [because] Islam coexists with Christianity, Hinduism and Buddhism."

428), declared that "given the time and the opportunity a united Cameroon can be transformed into a paradise in Africa." Exactly how much time and opportunity does reunited Cameroon still need to lead Africans out of the dungeon and onto their Promised Land? Can the current Cameroon leadership be trusted to actually perform this sacred mission when they are persisting in their highly centralized Unitary State that is heavily punctuated by their Single-Party Multipartism? Are these not some of the notorious mechanisms that have been employed to negatively change the amazing people of this country?

One of the negative effects of Cameroon's dictatorial and culturally and economically exclusionist policies is that most of its citizens have generally been conditioned to be frightened even by things that should not scare anyone. The SDF (1996: 1) has thus posited in their 'An Economic Blueprint to Challenge 14 [now 31] Years of Unpardonable Economic, Political Mismanagement' that Cameroonians are a frightened people. Unlike others such as Canadians who do look forward to the 21st century and beyond with excitement, Cameroonians look to the same thing with fear. This fear, the SDF (1996: 3) Economic Blueprint explicates,

> is the emotion which is shared by that half of mankind which finds itself ill-prepared for this moment because they live in economic and social circumstances which make them believe that their future as well as that of their children is going to be worse than what it is now. It is this half that has suffered economic decline as a result of their failure to structure their societies in a manner which enables them to become efficient players in [the] emerging global economy of the 21st century. These societies have lived beyond their means for too long and now find themselves trapped in a cycle of dependency. They are ill-equipped to survive in the competitive world of the 21st century. Some are doomed to disappear as sovereign states and shall be absorbed by more economically powerful nations.

The SDF theory on Cameroonians' fright cannot be lightly contradicted; otherwise it would then be hard to comprehend Cameroon's backwardness. It is craziness indeed to think that the development level of Cameroon would be otherwise with frightened and brutalized citizens. These are important statements that in a way bring to the foreground the important role of the human factor in development, with human health and intelligence standing out.

Health and Intelligence in Development in Cameroon

Many writers on development have tended to ignore this human factor when assessing a country's resources. The stress put on physical resources in many development studies that classify states into 'Worlds' seems to be misleading. For instance, according to Magstadt (1991: 55), Fourth World nations, "comprising of the poorest of the poor", are defined as those that lack the resources needed for development. In practice, however, this distinction is difficult to make. Indeed, 'resources' can be almost anything, and very few developing nations lack at least one vital resource, namely human beings. Yes indeed; and as I have said earlier this human factor is topical as it can determine the path of the others. But what types of human beings would be necessary for development: freethinking or frightened ones? Does development require healthy or sick people? This is where the *natural quality of the people* will become much more significant to development politics since it greatly impacts on the fourth factor, namely, the good judgment with which the efforts of the group are regulated, discussed below in part two. The *natural quality of the people* will hinge on the health and strength, intelligence and character of the people concerned. Thus, it is not just enough to have people but to have healthy, strong, intelligent and upright people with an authentic history and/or culture. These matters, according to Bladen (1956: 4),

> are too obvious conditions of wealth to require discussion

[because] One has to contemplate the time wasted in sickness (health it should be noted is a major part of well-being as well as a condition of increased production of wealth), the job left undone because the man's strength is unequal to them, the jobs done slowly because clumsily, the jobs done improperly because carelessly.

Discussing the health of Cameroonians,[202] Nelson *et al* (1974: vii, 106-112) have postulated that the fairly high incidence of disease in Cameroon could be reflecting nutritionally inadequate diets, insufficient medical care, and poor sanitation. Endemic diseases, according to their report, do include malaria, various parasitic infestations, and kwashiorkor: with malaria and tuberculosis being Cameroon's chief health problems.[203] These health problems are exacerbated by the undemocratic nature of the medical profession itself, capped by the bossy and fraudulent attitude of some of its personnel.[204]

Cameroon's modern medical services are, however, proving capable of coping with the country's major epidemics and have been

---

[202] For further discussion of the health of Cameroonians, see P.R. Awah *et al*, "Perceived Risk Factors of Cardiovascular Diseases and Diabetes in Cameroon" 23 *Health Education Research* (2008), 612-620; Susan Weiger and John Akuri, "Cameroonian Women's Perception of Their Health Care Needs" 16:1 *Nordic Journal of African Studies* (2007), 47-63; Biya (1986: 76-77); Nelson *et al* (1974: chapter 6); and Sammy Lysonge, "Sound Mental Health in Cameroon: A Sine Qua Non" *The Herald* (22-23 July 1998), 10

[203] See also Randy J. Sa'ah, "WHO Expert Recommends New Methods to Treat Tuberculosis" *The Herald* (13-14 July 1998), 6; Collins J.B. Akwo, "Gov't Should Reinstate Health Inspectors" *The Herald* (22-23 October 1997), 4; and Jean-Marie Kémajou, "Douala étouffe sous le poids de ses déchets" 173 *Jeune Afrique Economie* (novembre 1993), 46.

[204] See Chiabi Achuosih-Nyoah, "Doctors Call for Liberalisation of Medical Profession" *The Herald* N° 597 (20-21 April 1998), 11; A.A. Nyangkwe, "Doctors Denounce Medical Malpractice at French Embassy in Yaounde, Sue Illegal Medical Practitioner" *The Herald* N° 447 (16-17 April 1997), 3; "Resistance of Health Personnel to Implement Health Policy" *The Herald* N° 632 (13-14 July 1998), 4; and Kum Set Ewi, "WHO Worried About Discrepancies in Medical Lab Results in Cameroon" *The Herald* N° 636, (22-23 July 1998), 1.

providing fairly good modern care especially in southern urban centres, but only very limited care is said to be available elsewhere.[205] Muabe (1998) reports that in March 1998, Minister of Health (Professor Monekosso) launched "an emotional appeal to all health personnel, be they private or public, donors and partners in the health sector, all opinion leaders, religious or traditional, as well as to all Cameroonians to join in efforts towards a decisive improvement of the health system in Cameroon."[206] During that appeal, Muabe (1998) pursues, the minister described the Ahala and Mendong integrated health posts and the renovated Biyem-Assi District Hospital (all of them in Yaounde, the capital) as some "of the first [projects] to be financed by the World Bank in the health sector in sub-Saharan Africa." The six-year objectives of this ambitious health project (which would require the construction of 18 district hospitals and 150 integrated health centres throughout Cameroon) have been identified as follows. The project, according to Muabe (1998), has, first, to lend institutional support to the national population policy and ensure the rapid implementation of the family planning strategy. Second, it has to ameliorate the quality and coverage in primary health care to the poor and to advance the decentralization of health services. And, third, it is to democratize access to primary health care by taking it nearer to the most underprivileged.[207] Folk medicine that at times has been regarded with almost total disrespect is now also making a very great impact

---

[205] Nelson *et al* (1974: 111-112). See also "Use and Protect These Hospitals Jealously – Pr. Gottlieb Monekosso" *Cameroon Tribune* N° 6559-N° 2848 (16 mar. 16 1998), 8 [interviewed by Irene Morik].

[206] See also Tendong David, "Health Personnel Urged to Serve Selflessly" *The Herald* N° 585 (18-19 March 1998) 11.

[207] See also Ngalah Edward, "Building a Solid Health System in Cameroon" *The Herald* N° 682 (4-5 November 1998), 4; and Irene Morik, "Health, Fertility and Nutrition Project: Reaping the Fruits of an Ambitious Health Project" *Cameroon Tribune* N° 6559-N° 2848 (16 mar. 16 1998), 8.

on the health of Cameroonians[208] – a development that is just as healthy for economic development as is the original quality of Cameroon's environment. But why is underdevelopment instead the case?

Confusioncracy Passing for Balanced Development

This part of the chapter critically examines nation-building regulation and other strategies of the Cameroon administration, positing that the unbending schizophrenia toward the obliteration of the history and culture of the English-speaking minority is not only inconsistent with the ceaseless singing of biculturalism (as already elaborated on above); but also principally what is (1) responsible for some African countries (with far less economic and other natural endowments than Cameroon) being ahead of Cameroon in the development or nation-building game and (2) precluding this otherwise 'Paradise in Africa' from truly advancing and assuming its legendary role as Africa's pathfinder. An extensive critique of the regulatory schizophrenia is carried out to also show, first, that the policy does not reconcile national interest and (foreign) investors' interests; with the authorities paradoxically equating their excessive and arbitrary regulation with the very definition of a democratic society. Second, it is portrayed that the dirigisme is solely geared toward preventing the existence of a sound economic base that is so vital for democracy – a form of governance that would necessarily ensure the effective rejoicing in the histories/cultures of both cultural segments of Cameroon. It is because of the resulting unnecessarily imposed fear on the citizenry, capped by the absence of suitable and durable societal structures that Cameroon remains backward despite its enormous potentials – all being intimately tied to the drive to deny history and to assimilate.

---

[208] For further discussion, see Emily Hillenbrand, "Improving Traditional-Conventional Medicine Collaboration: Perspectives from Cameroonian Traditional Practitioners" 15:1 *Nordic Journal of African Studies* (2006), 1-15.

When Democracy and Economic Development wed each other, there is usually – if not always – advancement. But when either or both of these would be found in the same bed with Confusion (if they do couple at all where impossible remains impossible), one can only have Regression as the off-spring. Confusion is the unmistakable harbinger of regression; being usually capped by the human rights violations that are characteristic of Africa generally.[209] The particular case of Cameroon – a country that Biya (1986: back cover) says is "one of the most important countries of Africa" – is quite saddening. What makes Cameroon that important to Africa, it may be asked? It is argued that Cameroon has colossally failed in leading Africa towards the "great destiny" it promised the continent long ago; and this solely because the country's over-sung cultural dualism is a charade.

Whether or not the Cameroon leadership could be up to the African unity task can only be seen in its approach to human rights generally as well as its attitude towards the English-speaking minority specifically. Respect for basic human rights is a sine qua non for any meaningful development or nation-building. Federalism is seen and being proposed here as the appropriate channel through which to respect these rights in radically diverse societies like Cameroon. Centralization or concentration of powers (an extremely pronounced form of denying history) in this country can only beget regression. The historical scare in Cameroon is quite evident in its disastrous econometrics or political economy. This inevitable and direct result of nation-building that is void of history is a significant factor that gives other African countries the upper hand in the intercontinental nation-building match. Being a doleful loser, Cameroon has simply become the best case in the study of political, cultural, and constitutional confusion; and also, as far as concerns human rights (the invisible hand of development) in Africa, the best case for researching in regressive advancement. This fact will be seen in (1)

---

[209] See Daniel D. Nsereko Ntanda, "Victims of Abuse of Power, with Special Reference to Africa" 28:1 *University of British Columbia Law Review* (1994), 171.

the Anglophone factor and the absence of known rules and (2) the stifling of industrialization to promote the idea of Peace Must Work on Father's Land, the cloaked goal of some of the given instances of confusion in development and/or development in confusion.

The Anglophone Factor and Absence of Known Rules

The regression in this country is very intimately tied to fake biculturalism or multiculturalism. Biculturalism, of course, must entail more than one culture effectively operating on an equal basis of recognition; otherwise, there is only what the critics have called pointless multiculturalism or assimilation. Some recent studies like El Obaid's (1996: 15-18) that have advanced a theoretical framework for the recognition of cultural diversity and its impact on human rights have concluded that the ruling elite and those engaged in human rights violations (especially in Africa) have no claim of cultural legitimacy (El Obaid, 1996: i). That is, the ruling elite and their agents cannot, all by themselves, legitimately decree both the definition of culture and the cultures that go into making multiculturalism, as is the case in Cameroon. Regression, as already said, is the word that properly describes any nation-building that is carried out without authentic history. In Cameroon this regression is euphemistically called "advanced development" whose handmaids are 'balanced development plans',[210] a development that is paradoxically not balanced on history and/or the country's cultural diversity. As previously indicated, federalism is the form of state that will propel development in Cameroon, especially if the country's history is made by human beings called Cameroonians. As the contrary is the case in

---

[210] For a lengthy critique of these 'balanced development plans', see generally U.S.A.I.D, *The Tortoise Walk: Public Policy and Private Activity in the Economic Development of Cameroon* (Washington, DC, 1983); Peter Ateh-Afac Fossungu, "The Anti-Development of Cameroon's Balanced Development Policy" *The Herald* (9-10 November 1998), 10; and Charles C. Fonchingong & Lotsmart N. Fonjong, "The Concept of Self-Reliance in Community Development Initiatives in the Cameroon Grassfield" 12:2 *Nordic Journal of African Studies* (2003), 196-219.

this unique West-Central African state, here then is actually what most studies on development and nation-building have this far failed to adequately grasp about Cameroon, which is not only a unique case in the study of most, if not all, issues relating to Africa but also the best example of the African countries that should truly have no use for the Beggar Syndrome that is characteristic of the continent. I am here talking about the spiral initiated by "the World Bank and IMF [both described] as 'unfriendly agents of imperialism.'"[211] Why does Cameroon then still suffer from backwardness?

Many theories have been postulated in answer, including some like Tixier (1974) that pin the problem on dirigisme and Anyangwe (1996: 826) on the French-derived "culture where the legislature is in practice a mere extension of the executive and therefore at its beck and call, and also where the government is generally insensitive to public opinion and the demands of fairness." There could be no single straightjacket answer to the question but I would think the other responses are sort of missing the real issue, namely, the unbending drive to deny a portion of the country its authentic history. The plain answer then is simple: confusion (that in this case is rooted firmly in the drive to efface the history of the English-speaking people of this country) and development have never been comfortable bedfellows; and development without authentic history can only be regression. For demonstration, it would be essential to first elaborate on (1) the Anglophone Equation called national unity and (2) the fact of not playing by any known rules.

Turning the English-Speaking into the French

The thesis on history obliteration would largely explain why other French neo-colonies but without the 'Anglophone Equation' are

---

[211] J. Solheim, "Yoke of International Debt' Holding Africa Back" *Anglican Journal* (September 1999), 10. *See* also Couloumbis and Wolfe (1986: chapter 18: "The Gap between Rich and Poor: Reassessing the Meaning and Process of 'Development'"); and Michael Binyon, "After 50 Years, Outlook for Africa Still Bleak" *The Edmonton Journal* (15 January 1999), A18.

having some advantages over Cameroon notwithstanding that the latter far outweighs the others in terms of natural and other resources. Take *epsi* as a simple illustration. Just imagine only the astronomical sums of money spent over those many years as *epsi* to UNIYAO students (in Chapter 4 above) in an unrelenting effort to assimilate the English-speaking, and you would have grasped the point very well. Ivory Coast or Chad or Botswana, for instance, during that same time (that Cameroon is paying out *epsi* and creating lots of all sorts of confusion) would be putting just one-tenth of said sums to more progressive developmental use. It is this argument that can duly account for the differences between countries like Cameroon and, say, Ghana – to leave out South-East Asia's Indonesia where, according to Canadian Ambassador Gary Smith (quoted by Das, 1996), "You can get stinking rich in a hurry." This Indonesian case is getting rich without being *voyou* or *véreux* like in Cameroon – as has been elaborately catalogued by Eyoum'a Ntoh (1996) and others.[212] The honour in the Indonesian case, of course, not only results from being able to do business "playing by the rules" (Das, 1996), but also by rules which are known beforehand by (and encourage full realization of potentials, rights and obligations of) the parties involved: foreign or national (see de Jorge, 1993).

This is very unlike in Africa because "Cameroon and… [other Third World] nations need to do more in terms of the legal aspects

---

[212] See J. Nsom, "The Extent and Implications of Corruption in Cameroon" *The Herald* N° 597(20-21 April 1998) 10; Wamey Panky, "Santa Priest Attacks 'Chop Broke Potism'" *The Post* (24 October 1997), 8; Joe Bashi, "Who Is Corrupt in Cameroon?" *The Herald* N° 585 (18-19 March 1998), 10; Ngah Christian Mpipgo, "CBC Boss Laments Vice in Church, Promises Sanctions for Wayward Pastors" *The Herald* N°631 (10-12 July 1998), 2; Asong Ndifor and Peter Ngea Beng, "Gov't Threatens Court Action as Biya Regime Is Rated Most Corrupt in the World" *The Herald* N°.666 (28-29 September 1998), 1: Herald Editorial, "Biya Regime: Fight Corruption, Not Transparency International" *The Herald* N°.666 (28-29 September 1998), 4; and Simon Coldham, "Legal Responses to State Corruption in Commonwealth Africa" 39:2 *Journal of African Law* (1995) 115.

for attracting direct private investments into their economies."[213] Penn is quite right since it has been discovered by Zama (1992: 43) that Cameroon's legal arsenal is a mosaic confusion which no doubt "leaves the foreign investor who is coming to Cameroon for the first time wanting and confused since he cannot lay hands on this legislation within a reasonable time. Also, administrative bottlenecks and the constant referring to other legislative texts which might not be easily handy, makes the whole process cumbersome and time consuming." Not only the foreign investor faces this problem which is aggravated in the sense that he or she cannot be sure to rely on a local advocate or solicitor to safely navigate the confusing waters.

It is not very uncommon for even lawyers and judges not to know the law in Cameroon because Anyangwe (1987: 263) points out also that Cameroon's legislation is in an immensely unwieldy and confused state, a mosaic, a veritable labyrinth in which even those initiated in the law can easily get lost. What exactly is the type of justice that businesses (or anyone else) can hope to obtain in a society whose lawyers are ignorant about what exactly the law on any issue is? "And what is even more important," yet another expert (Enonchong, 1967: xiii) has declared, "especially for a developing nation, is that the people know the quantum of legal norms that govern their freedom of action within the State; otherwise the maxim *ignorantia juris non excusat* will end where reality begins." Some experts have therefore admonished that "as long as our enthusiasm to... [rectify this sad and strange legislative situation] is watered-down, there is little doubt that the judges will continue to work in an atmosphere of persistent confusion."[214] Once more, who is then

---

[213] Godfred A.E. Penn, "Legal Aspects of Foreign Investment in Cameroon" 1 *Juridis Info (Revue de Legislation et de Jurisprudence Camerounaises)* (1990), 55 at 55.

[214] Ephraim N. Ngwafor, "*Nicholas Nkewenun Ayafor v. Yongen Alexander and Two Others*: An Interpretation Question Re-Echoed" 1 *Juridis Info (Revue de Legislation et de Jurisprudence Camerounaises)* (1990), 32-36 at 36. See also Peter Ateh-Afac Fossungu, "Confused Cameroon Law" *The Herald* N° 659 (11-13 September 1998), 4; and Peter Ateh-Afac Fossungu, "Nonsense About Our Duress Law: Would Our Criminal Legislators Listen?" *The Herald* N° 541 (1-2 December 1997), 4.

hoping to get any justice from confused lawyers and judges? The whole idea behind this strategy is development in confusion which assures that frightened and 'peaceful' people of Cameroon must only work on the farms (a strategy that is examined in the next section).

That was a tip of the iceberg of the score board of the Asia-Versus-Africa development match but returning to and focusing on the intra-African game many others on the continent still beat Cameroon, a miserable loser – thanks to its unyielding drive to assimilate the English-speaking. As far back as 1972, some experts like Shenoy (1974: 10) loudly castigated its economic policies as "a case of holding the tiger by the tail", sternly warning Cameroonians that

> the prevailing policies cannot continue indefinitely. They are destined to take the country, via economic stagnation, social tensions and political instabilities, into the ranks of centrally planned economies, which the Communists within and outside Government ardently strive for. If on the other hand, the country should turn to liberal economic policies, [the situation might be arrested].... The need, therefore, is great for the Cameroons to retrace, and ... abstain from extending, dirigiste measures.

These *dirigiste* measures of an insensitive government are not healthy for development of any kind.

Thus, despite Cameroon's considerable economic potentials that far overshadow those of Ivory Coast, Tixier's (1974: 63) tested research on these two Francophone African states has portrayed that "it is the Ivory Coast, in general, which asserts itself as the plainest example of success among African nations which gained independence around 1960." Remember that this is two years after the 1972 'Glorious Revolution'. Before this name-changing event, Ivory Coast could not even have come close to Cameroon which was already surprising political pundits with its spectacular development, its cultural and historical diversity notwithstanding. Corroboration of the points I am making can be found in Cameroon's spectacular and admirable progress in the direction of 'national integration' during the first six years of its life as a bilingual, multicultural federation – questionable as that federation was. Both Johnson and Bjornson make this point exceedingly clear.

Interest, according to Johnson (1970: viii), also comes from the fact that Cameroon has, for the first six years of its life as a bilingual, multicultural federation, achieved steady progress in this national integration direction, while many African states, even with single colonial legacies, have barely held together if not actually lost ground to centrifugal forces. By the time the Federated Republic of Cameroon was transformed into a unitary state in 1972, Bjornson (1991: 108) writes, it had actually become a relatively stable, economically viable country. The developmental spectacle might be explained by the fact that federalism would, of course, prevent things such as the *compte hors budget*. After reviewing the achievements and shortcomings of what the SDF (1996: 3-4) calls 'The Economy under the First Republic (1960-1982)', the SDF (1996: 4) concluded that

> one of the most important mistakes which was committed by the Ahidjo regime was that he failed to introduce a system of transparent accounting for oil revenues. While accepting his concern for not budgeting all the oil revenues, in creating the *Compte Hors Budget*, which was not specifically covered by the finance law, he failed to bring an important component of fiscal revenues under the control of parliament. This set the stage for the abuses which occurred during the Second Republic [under President Biya] in the management of oil revenues and eventually wrecked the economy.

The tilting of the weight from 1974 in Ivory Coast's favour then could probably be principally because Ivory Coast (free of the Anglophone Factor) was simply not 'uniting one history' and therefore not as national-unity-crazy as Cameroon.

Like the political parties, many scholars have also been making federation proposals and there is an impressive recommendation of federalism from Etinge (1991: 7) that has clearly and neatly called for "a broad based federation of about ten States or less with autonomous powers and elected governors... taking into consideration that this country is a bilingual [and bi-jural] one." It is not idle talking on the part of this legal expert. The unfortunate situation in Cameroon has pushed some Canadian specialists to join the chorus in ardently calling for (a) 'Federalism as Expression of Diversity' and (b) 'Institutional Accommodation of Duality and Regionalism' in the country.[215] I would want to think they are right because anything that fails (like the SDF proposed four-state federation) to pay particular attention to the bicultural nature of Cameroon is just as good as no suggestion. Biculturalism does not necessarily mean a two-state federation, although those important facts (of election of officials & bi- or multiculturalism) must be emphatically made clear.

The two-state federation insistence is not helpful for many reasons but one is that it clearly shuts the door to the fact that French Cameroun, for instance, is not a mono-cultural entity, in the same way as English Cameroon is not. In Canada, to illustrate, the three provinces of Alberta, Manitoba, and Saskatchewan are known as the Prairies; so too are the four of Nova Scotia, New Brunswick, Prince Edwards Island, and Newfoundland and Labrador called the Maritimes. But why are the three provinces that constitute the Prairies not lumped up as one province in Canada? It is basically because while having some things in common, they also have their individual unique characteristics that are worth keeping apart from the others. The Bamileke, for instance, are territorially situated in the French-speaking part of Cameroon (precisely in Bamboutouszone); but why are French-speaking Cameroonians (as seen in chapter 2) hostile towards them because of certain aspects of their culture, if all

---

[215] Linda Trimble, "Federalism, the Feminization of Poverty and the Constitution" in David Schneiderman, ed., *Conversations among Friends << >> Entre Amies: Proceedings of an Interdisciplinary Conference on Women and Constitutional Reform* (Edmonton: Centre for Constitutional Studies, 1992), 87 at 88.

Francophones in Cameroon are considered as people of the same culture? Above all else, why must people from whatever part of Cameroon have to depend on Yaoundé to have any minuscule of a thing done?

Some political parties have also contributed in this same direction. To the ADD president, if the principle of federalism is instituted and respected in Cameroon, as a first point, "we will kill tribalism at the level of states." Secondly, it will propel development; and (like others similarly advising that Africans learn not to just see wood for wood[216]) Adji used Guinean-Savannazone to lengthily develop the point to Azeng (1997):

> Look at the East province and see the amount of unprocessed wood that is exported from there. If this wood were processed in the East Province, imagine the employment opportunities that would be available to Cameroonians. When you see wood passing in trucks, don't look at it in terms of wood, you should rather look at it in terms of employment opportunities that are being exported. Now, imagine that 33% of revenue from natural resources exploited in a state [would] belong to the Federal Government while 65% go to the state from where the resources are tapped. Of course the Federal Government will have a lot of money to carry out research and we will be one of the richest countries in Africa.

Accordingly, Adji posited that the federal form of state organization will propel development in Cameroon because it will enable each state or province to freely decide its own affairs while still belonging to one Cameroon.

Crossing over to West Cameroon again with his illustrations and specifically using Debundschazone, Adji took a critical look at the

---

[216] See G. Salole, "Not Seeing the Wood for the Trees: Searching for Indigenous Non Government Organizations in the Forest of Voluntary Self Help Associations" 6:1 *Journal of Social Development in Africa* (1991), 5.

intriguing case of petroleum (the subject of the *compte hors budget*) by stressing that, with federalism, the oil-rich Debundschazone would not be as backward as it is today, with the war in Bakassi also being excluded. Like others,[217] the ADD president explained to Azeng (1997) that "If the South West Province had even only 15% of our petroleum revenue, the war in Bakassi would never have come up. Roads, which don't exist in that province, would have been tarred. The misery in that part of the country wouldn't have been at that level." This is indeed pathetic since it is well known from Fonkeng (1990: 'Preface and Thanks', 3rd paragraph) that "the resources from this [minute West Cameroon] area [alone] account for about ninety per cent of the country's foreign exchange" although the territory remains until date the heart of "economic impoverishment."

Garga Harman Adji of the ADD is so infuriated by the current state of affairs resulting from the highly centralized unitary form, opining that, rather than fuse Cameroon in 1972, Ahidjo should instead have enlarged the federation. According to Azeng (1997), the ADD president (using two towns from Debundschazone and Logonezone) firmly stated:

> If people in Mamfe want a road and those in Kouseri want to dig a well, why must they depend on Yaounde? It's a nasty situation. And they're singing about a unitary state, about 20th of May [1972] and so on. It's a nasty situation. I have never agreed with that since the days of Mr. Ahidjo. What Ahidjo was to do on the 6th of May 1972 was to enlarge the federal system and not to fuse Cameroon into a unitary state. He didn't do it; but we have to do it. And we will do it. There is no way we can succeed in Cameroon if we don't go federal.

---

[217] See Bonny Kfua, "Federalism as a Solution to the Bakassi Crisis" *The Herald* N° 337 (31 July-1 August 1996), 4; and Christopher Sinju Motase, "Kumba-Mamfe Road: Will the Population Disappear before the Road Arrives?" *The Herald* N° 343 (14-15 August 1996), 4.

Yes, indeed; from all the debates the great question is not that of whether, but that of how, Cameroon should go federal. This is where the SDF's role in thwarting the people's wishes becomes graphical to the corrupt and corrupting Biya regime.

Other political parties and scholars are proffering sane solutions to the ethnic management problems of Africa. Tixier (1974: 87) had also advised, to no avail, in 1974:

> If the Cameroons finds a way to overcome the rather national[unity] attitudes of its senior officials who occupy themselves a great deal with *dirigisme*, it will preserve all its opportunities for progress towards harmonious growth. It is hoped that [the] President..., who had until now been above all concerned to secure the political unity of his country, [should] become conscious of the need to give more play to private initiative and to receive foreign investors [of countries other than France] more openly.

One can thus see that the other Francophone West African country (Ivory Coast) has even succeeded where 'national-unity-crazy' Cameroon fails solely also because of what Tixier (1974: 63 & 87) praises as "the prudence shown by the Iv[oirians] at the outset of independence" which has helped them to know (like the Asians[218]) "how to reconcile national interests and those of foreign investors."

Citing the examples of Japan and "Many mini-Japans in Asia, which pursued the Japanese pattern of resource allocation [and] benefited similarly," an expert at the Economic Research Centre in New Delhi, India (Shenoy, 1974: 10), has declared that "all economic miracles in the post-war world were made possible by the most effective allocation of resources." Do I need to cite Germany's well

---

[218] See Chan Jin Kim, "Foreign Investment and National Interests" 2 *Korean Journal of Comparative Law* (1974); 30; Young Moo Kim, "Legal Forms of Doing Business in Korea" 2 *Korean Journal of Comparative Law* (1974); 58; and Chan Jin Kim, "Legal Aspects of Foreign Investment in Korea" 1 *Korean Journal of Comparative Law* (1973); 2.

known Economic Miracle here? The simple reason for Cameroon's backwardness then is not hard to divine: confusion (or concentration) of powers in the presence of unparalleled diversity, concentration that has been easily installed "thanks to the [history-less] constitution promulgated on 1st October 1961 which marked the Reunification of Southern Cameroons and the Republic of Cameroon" (Lantum, 1991: 20). Thus, while the Ivoirian leadership would be busy trying (as the Asians and others) to do things right, their Cameroonian counterpart would be busy only in trying to transform English-speaking Cameroonians into 'French' people, and calling it national unity. National regression is the correct appellation, since that is exactly what occurs when rather than unite two or more histories you 'unite' one history through *epsi*. But the *epsi* strategy is not all that obstructs development in the Hinge of Africa; there are also some important absences.

Operating Without Local Governments and an Independent Umpire

Confusion is very unhealthy for progress of any kind, except progress in regression; and businesses love certainty and time well used. In addition to the mosaic confusion in this country that has been found to be very time consuming, there is also an avalanche of excessive taxes that come down hard on businesses (*"une quarantaine d'impôts frappent les enterprises"*) in Cameroon.[219] As there are no roads and other necessary infrastructures to propel economic development, what are all these taxes even used for, except for the unknown missions of the POR's personal appointees? The nature of the role of some of these appointed chiefs in Cameroon has left a lot of people wondering about a lot of things. In fact, many foreigners residing in

---

[219] Patrice Mandeng Ambassa, ministre camerounais du Développement industriel, « Le Cameroun aidera l'Afrique du Sud – Confidences: propos recuellis par Laurent Marcaillou » *Jeune Afrique* (18-24 mars 1993, 33. See also Tixier (1974: 44-45, 50-53, & 59-61).

the country have been particularly appalled not only by the arbitrary nature of regulating their stay;[220] but also by the dubiety of missions and the ever growing ministerial portfolios whose competence the tax payers hardly even know. Some of the puzzled foreign-resident experts have consequently recommended that

> The post of ministers in charge of [unknown] *special duties* should be scrapped. What makes the situation very alarming is the fact that, most of the citizens whose tax money is used in paying these people do not know *what these special duties are*. Is it going out for CPDM campaigns? Does it entail transferring public revenue from Cameroon to private accounts in the Swiss Banks?[221]

This expert's theory does many things. First, it, to a large extent, explains what is behind the burgeoning and astronomical number of ministers and rank-of-minister portfolios in this small triangular West-Central African country.

Second, it tells us that citizens and businesses pay too many taxes but do not get services in return. We all know that in business time is money and profit is usually the motivation. So what is there to encourage any foreign businesses that have tasted the confusion, unnecessary taxes and time-consuming process in this country to continue doing business here or come back for a second time? Would the institution of Free Trade Zones (FTZs) be the enticement? The Cameroon leadership would want to think so, hoping that their lies-fabricating machines or *Kontchoumeters* could effectively hide the fact

---

[220] See *Loi N° 97/012 du 10 janvier 1997 fixant les conditions d'entrée, de sejour et de sortie des étrangers au Cameroun.*

[221] Lord W. Degaulle, "Retrench Ministers to Fight Economic Crisis" *The Herald* N° 356 (13-15 September 1996), 4 (emphasis added). Despite the numerous suggestions for reduction, more ministries and more posts in them would rather be created. See Fidèle Muabe, "Biya Restructures Government to Compensate CPDM Hawks, Contrary to Advice" *The Herald* N° 545 (9-11 December 1997), 8; Denis Nkwebo, "Le Sud, L'Est et Centre : l'argument tribal faussera le partage" *Le Quotidien* (27 octobre 1997), 3; and *Decret* N° *98/043 du 13 mars 1998 portant nomination des secrétaires généraux de certains ministères.*

that their FTZs are 'cut off like a monad'. But no matter how hard they try the critics do not think they could succeed because businesses would also have discovered the trick, namely, that these FTZs are only in name. Some researchers have thus found out for the business community that the Cameroonian Free Trade Zone has not succeeded like was the case in the Mauritius because of several factors which include the "no secret to any businessman that current administrative procedures provide the most disincentives to investment in Cameroon in spite of an attractive and Liberal Investment Code."[222] The Investment Code (like most other legislation) in this *Kontchoumetered* country is liberal indeed on paper but the practice is a complete different story. In addition to that should be added what Zama (1992: 44 & 45) condemns as the "bureaucraphobia that is very prevalent in Cameroon" and which results in there being no one out there "to verify whether environmental protection is adhered to by the industries concerned." By 'Bureaucraphobia' the experts (Zama, 1992: 44-45; Shenoy, 1974: 9-10) are defining the fact of "every person want[ing] to remain in the office."

All this is because of the absence of the normal type of democracy that is punctuated by an independent and impartial arbiter. Citing J.A.G. Griffith's *The Politics of the Judiciary* (1977), Anyangwe (1989: 22) indicates that democracy necessarily requires

---

[222] Godfred A.E. Penn, "Commentary on Ordonnace N° 90/004 du 29 janvier 1990 créant le régime de la Zone Franche au Cameroun" 3 *Juridis Info (Revue de Législation et de Jurisprudence Camerounaises)* (1990), 66 at 74 Some critics have pointed out the evil intentions behind having a highly centralized system. "These uncalled for bottlenecks that one finds here leaves no doubts in anyone's mind that it is this CPDM government's intention to make some Cameroonians live for others. Make people desperate so that they can accept just anything. It equally reveals the hollowness and the inefficacious [inefficient?] nature of a highly centralized and monolithic system." Aseh Andrew, "Finance Ministry Degenerates into a Super Market" *Cameroon Post* (20-26 August 1996), 3. See also Mystic Johnson, "Monopoly and Its Paralysing Agents" *The Herald* (24-25 June 1998), 10 (outlining and critiquing some of the gross misdeeds of SONEL – the national electricity corporation – that do not also encourage foreign businesses setting up in this country).

that some group of persons acts as an arbiter not only between individuals but also between governmental power and the individual. Businesses have been calling for the liberation of the court system that currently does not encourage investments, especially in regard of litigation. It is also noted that the alternative mode of arbitration that the business community is craving for, finds a place in the *Charter of the Organization for the Harmonisation of Business Law in Africa* (OHADA) which is based in Abidjan, Côte d'Ivoire. Cameroon ratified OHADA in September 1996 and yet "they [the businessmen] observed that the present [1996 constitutional] system made no provision for specialised tribunals to handle cases between business establishments", which results in "the high costs of litigation which hampered and frustrated actions by business enterprises."[223] It is simply hard for the courts in this country to be independent when the administrative system is ultra-centralized; all in the name of uniting one history.

Without local government and the independent judicial institution, no one can think out of the conformists' box. It is only normal that, as conformists cannot encourage free thinking, the bulk of Cameroonians (not abroad) find themselves cowed into selves, not exhibiting their potentials that are supposed to power the economy and nation-building. A society with such citizens clearly has no core, a necessity for development. As an expert on civil society has pointed out, people are the core of civil society, not the people who make and impose decisions, but those who are often kept out of the decision-making process through various overt and subtle processes or who themselves opt out of the decision-making process due to frustration or indifference or an inadequate appreciation of the role that they can and should play.[224] It is hard to expect anything better from people

---

[223] See "Businessmen Flay Judiciary, Say It Is Ineffective" *The Herald* (13-15 June 1997), 7. See also Boniface Forbin, "A Court System the People Can't Trust" *The Herald* (6-8 June 1997), 4.

[224] Kabir Chowdhuri, "Civil Society: A South Asian Perspective" 43:1 & 2 *Religion and Society* (1996), 63 at 63. See also Femi Osofisan, "Warriors of a Failed Utopia? – West African Writers Since the '70s" (being a lecture delivered at The

without an authentic history and culture – what the experts (called political economists) would be referring to as the heritage of accumulated improvement.

Specialists have all pointed out that the only true story of a people is the one they themselves tell. Effective local government is the proper medium for the people to effectively tell their own story because it is suitably through local government that voters can scrutinize local officials' performance and hold them accountable for not paying enough attention to their culture and/or history. Some able writers have brandished this argument in trying to combat further centralization of power.[225] One of such able writers (Eyinga, 1996: 7) has skilfully argued that at a time when democracy and decentralization are the talk of the day it is unacceptable that governors, mayors and other local officials be all still appointed by the POR. Local officials, as he sees it, must be elected by the local population if we have to genuinely talk of democracy and decentralization which are very important instruments for communal progress.[226]

Also elaborating on 'What Makes A Democratic System Work', the then Canadian Minister of the Department of National Health and Welfare (Ottawa), in a paper presented at the Canadian Conference on Social Welfare held in Toronto, June 1970, posited that

> A democratic system, to succeed, must be much more than a general vote one day out of every three or four years. It must be a

---

Second Annual African Studies Lecture given at the University of Leeds on the 24th April 1996) *Leeds African Studies Bulletin* N° 61 (1996), 11.

[225] Henry Aubin, "Bourque's Lasting Legacy May Be the Further Weakening of Montreal" *Montreal Gazette* (15 January 1997), B2.

[226] *"Je ne peux pas admettre qu'au moment où on parle de démocratie, au moment où on parle de décentralisation on procède à la nomination d'un maire! Un maire doit être élu et je crois que notre pays a fait des progrès qu'ont fait les autres pays modernes. Ce progrès a consisté à quoi dans le domaine communal? .... L'aboutissement de l'évolution c'est que les gens qui président aux destinées des communes soient élus et c'est ça la décentralisation."*

vital, on-going contact and exchange between governments and their constituents...all of them, not just the rich and the powerful. This is the crucial role of citizens groups – to organize and mobilize their people into a political force, so that their views can be heard in their own right, not filtered through a massive super-structure of agencies and committees and officials.[227]

Anyone with just sufficient elementary education would not deny that only effectively elected officials (as opposed to those through unfettered presidential appointments) are those that Ikeda (1987: 239-241) says can be "Always Young and Always Eager to Learn" about what the people desire. That in a democracy, this learning means listening carefully to the people; that doing this is the effective way of "growing" or developing or nation-building. And that one can only validly talk of nation-building when the learner (nation-builder) goes to, lives among, learns from, serves, and plans with, the people in question.[228] No one can correctly do all of these without knowing and taking into consideration the people's uncensored history.

The task is considerably made easier when (as should always be the case) the nation-builder is one of their own; thus justifying local government with locally elected officials at all levels, including cities and rural areas. Mback (2007: 74) could not have said it any better:

> The city is the centre as well as the lever of development. It is also the place where peoples intermix, where a feeling is born of belonging to a nation, a feeling that goes beyond that of

---

[227] Wilson A. Head, "The Ideology and Practice of Citizen Participation" in James A. Draper, ed., *Citizen Participation: Canada* (Toronto: New Press, 1971), 14-29 at 17.

[228] See Michael Nelson, "Bureaucracy: The Biggest Crisis of All" in Charles Peters and Nicholas Lemann (eds.), *Inside the System* 4th ed. (New York: Holt, Rinehart and Winston, 1979), 315 at 324-325 & 320; and James A. Draper, "Introduction." in James A. Draper (ed.), *Citizen Participation: Canada* (Toronto: New Press, 1971), 5–9 at 5-6. See also G.A.W. Mbi, "Can the Lion Learn from the Leopard's Demise?" *The Herald* (20-22 June 1997), 4.

belonging to a community. Therefore, it, as well as rural areas, should be a privileged place for the exercise of basic democracy. The opposite choice that Cameroon has made is not consistent with the construction of a legitimate governance system. But, the question is larger: Is Cameroon ready to consider local governments as part of the national system of governance, and consequently, decentralization as a requirement for its modernization as well as for the efficiency in the operation of its public services?

To an administration that is truly desirous of advancement, the answer to this 'larger question' would, of course, be YES: because local government is the best way out of underdevelopment, since it is the technique that would assure the increasing capacity to make rational and reasonable use of natural and human resources for social ends.[229]

Stifling Industrialization

To the Cameroonian leadership, however, the answer to Mback's graphical or larger question has always been negative because they do regard any call for this form of governance that is the best way out of underdevelopment only as a call for secession; a view which is in reality just another way of denying the people's history. Denying the people's authentic history while creating confusion surely assures that they remain forever on the farms since democracy and underdevelopment have never been comfortable bedfellows. To shorten the lengthy story on disastrous econometrics, the impression is given that Cameroon's leaders do not intend to see it become a country with a credible industrial economy since they are only interested in seeing peace work on fatherland at all costs.

---

[229] J.H. Mittelman, *Out of Underdevelopment* (New York: St. Martin's Press, 1988), at 22, cited in Magstadt (1991: 40).

Africa has a unique type of democracy in Cameroon that, for obvious reasons, clearly sees no importance of a viable and industrial economy (and authentic educational system) to communal progress. A comprehensive review of the economy until the advent of Biya has been effected by the SDF (1996: 3-4) ('The Economy under the First Republic') and Tixier (1974) generally. According to the findings of French (1997), Cameroon's economy was booming with inter alia an expanding petroleum industry when then 49-year old Biya took over at the helm from 58-year old Ahidjo in 1982. Biya promised that the generational change in leadership would bring about a national rebirth and "Western investors briefly considered Cameroon… to be Central Africa's [P]romised land." But what did Biya do instead? French (1997) says he "presided over unprecedented decline, marked by official corruption, ethnic cronyism and administrative drift."[230] Experts seem to agree that Ahidjo's astute "Ethnic Arithmetic" in his unfettered appointments, at least, saved Cameroon from the naked institutionalized tribalism that is now the rule under his successor.[231]

---

[230] For a general review of the economy under the Biya regime, see SDF (1996: 5-6) ('The Economy under the Second Republic (1982-1997)'); and John Mukum Mbaku and J. Takougang, eds., *The Leadership Challenge in Africa: Cameroon under Paul Biya* (Trenton, N.J.: Africa World Press, 2004).

[231] For more on this "ethnic arithmetic", see Delancey (1989: 58-63). "*Jamais*," a Université de Montréal professor explained the 'arithmetic' as far back as 1972, Mr. Ahidjo "*n'a [cependent] commis la faute grave – fréquente dans de nombreux pays africains – de s'entourer exclusivement de ressortissants de sa propre tribu. Dans le choix des ministres [...] il a procédé à un dosage extrêmement sage pour que toutes les régions, toutes les tribus, tous les groupes religieux soient équitablement représentés.*" Benjamin (1972 : 28), citing B.C. Baeschlin-Raspail, *Ahmadou Ahidjo, Pionnier de L'Afrique moderne* p.78. A Fulani and Muslim, Ahmadou Ahidjo (one of the founders of the Union Camerounaise party that later became the country's principal, if not only, active political party) was born in August 1924 in Garoua. He attended the École Primaire Supérieure in Yaoundé. From 1942 to 1946 he served as a radio operator for the Posts and Telegraph Service. In 1947, he was elected a delegate to the first Cameroun Representative Assembly (ARCAM). When that chamber became the Cameroun Territorial Assembly (ATCAM) in 1952, he was again elected to serve in it; in 1956 he was re-elected to the Cameroun National Assembly (ANCAM) and also in 1960. From 1953 to 1957 he served as a member of the Assembly of the French Union. In 1955 he was elected Vice-President of ATCAM, and in 1957, became President of ALCAM (*Assemblée Législative du Cameroun*). In May 1957, he

With the Biya regime, Konings and Nyamnjoh (1997: 213) have notably advanced "the increasing monopolisation of key posts by members of the President's ethnic group who appeared to be much bolder in staking out claims on the state's resources than had Ahidjo's *barons*. As of August 1991, according to Joseph Takougang, 37 of the 47 senior *préfets* were Beti, as were three-quarters of the directors and general managers of the parastatals, and 22 of the 38 high-ranking bureaucrats who had been appointed in the newly created office of the Prime Minister." This 'tribalization' of 'national' institutions by Biya has largely contributed in wrecking the economy.

Well-documented facts clearly show how the tourism industry in Cameroon (despite all its potentials and the popularity brought about by the country's soccer World Cup performance in Italy in 1990) has instead declined. The number of tourists that came to this country ("like butterflies visiting a hibiscus to enjoy the beautiful Savannah scenery" (Zuhboshi, 1997)) between 1975 and 1994 dropped from 152,000 to 90,000.[232] The industrial sector, according to the research, is no exception and statistics can show a marked contraction of over 30% within a thirteen-year period. Using Syndustricam as an example, the SDF critical document reveals that in 1985/86 the sector reported total sales of FCFA 534.8 billion and a work force of 57,715; but by March 1993 its combined sales had declined to FCFA 346.864 billion with a work force of 17,779: representing a 36% drop in sales revenue and a 70% fall in work

---

was appointed Vice-Prime Minister in the cabinet of the first Cameroon government of André-Marie Mbida, acting as Minister of the Interior. Upon Mbida's resignation in February 1958, Ahidjo became Prime Minister. In May 1960, he was elected President of the Cameroun Republic. Le vine and Nye (1964: 3). Following the unification of the two Cameroons, Ahidjo remained as the President of the Federal Republic, and was re-elected over and over. In November 1982 he surprised most Cameroonians with his controversial resignation, handing power to Biya – his hand-picked successor. For some of the controversies surrounding the resignation, see Ahidjo (1996: 12).

[232] SDF (1996: 13). See also Ngah Christian Mbipgo, "North West Tourism Delegate Urges Government to Give Priority to Tourism" *The Herald* (10-11 September 1997), 7.

force; and the overall decline in the sector is put at 11%.[233] But that sector is not alone in the drop in employment opportunities. *The Herald* has editorialized on the global unemployment picture. From some sources, the Editor notes, it is known that when Biya took office in 1982 there were some 750,000 paid jobs in Cameroon. But some estimates, the Editor states, "put the total [number] of paid jobs in Cameroon in 1998 at 300,000 or less. The public service which is by far the biggest employer counts no more than 150,000 workers by a generous estimate." Based on the 1982 labour force, the Editor concludes, one could say that unemployment in 1998 stood at 60% or more.[234] In this calculated strategy of stifling industrialization there is the use of (1) unknown rules and laws and (2) agriculture and poverty.

Developing with Confusing and Incomplete Rules and Laws

This economic decline can also be plainly seen in the administration's ill-conceived Objectives. Of the nine (out of the 'Thirty Objectives for Cameroon') that are devoted to the Economy (Objectives 10-18), only two merely refer to 'power production' 'aimed at achieving [economic] autonomy'; one mentions the credit and banking system (Objective 12);[235] and another one (Objective

---

[233] SDF (1996: 13). See also Aaron A. Nyangkwe, "Cameroon's Oil Production Suffers 3.7% Drop" *The Herald* (10-11 September 1997), 7.

[234] Boniface Forbin, "Unemployment: Action, Not Escapist Rhetoric" *The Herald* N° 572 (16-17 February 1998), 4.

[235] For an estimation of the frightful situation of the banking sector in Cameroon, see Tiani Kéou's three articles: "La crise des banques au Cameroun: une crise profonde" 4 *Juridis Info (Revue de Législation et de Jurisprudence Camerounaises)* (1990), 51; "La crise des banques au Cameroun" 1 *Juridis Info (Revue de Législation et de Jurisprudence Camerounaises)* (1990), 53; & "Les entreprises face aux banques dans le contexte actuel au Cameroun" 6 *Juridis Info (Revue de Législation et de Jurisprudence Camerounaises)* (1991), 71 (this last one being the integral text of a 'séminaire sur le droit et le redressement des entreprises en difficulté'); and J.M. Nyama, "Reflexion sur la responsabilité du banquier" 9 *Juridis Info (Revue de Législation et de Jurisprudence Camerounaises)* (1992), 33.

11) sparingly talks of the tertiary sector ('distribution'). Meanwhile, the remaining FIVE Objectives do harp on agriculture in order to make sure "that no effort is spared in bringing agriculture... to remain the mainstay of Cameroon's economy" (Biya, 1986: 129 – Objective 13). Indeed, as Protais Ayangma Amang (President of Association of Cameroon Insurance Companies, ASAC), declared in 1997 in an interview with Michel Eclador Pokoua, there is every indication that the Cameroon administration is doing everything to prevent the existence of strong private initiatives in boosting an industrial economy in this country ("I am of the opinion that the Cameroon government does not want to see the emergence of a strong private sector in this country"[236]). Confusion facilitates oppression; and it is promoted through the policy book and laws, as well as poverty and agriculture.

The whole philosophy in Cameroon that is geared toward confusing and compounding (so as to prevent industrialization that is required for authentic democracy) can also be seen in the policy book as well as in some pieces of legislation. Cameroon's policy book has gone on, for instance, to indicate that, in "order to be relatively independent Cameroon's economy will have to rely more on the private dynamism of Cameroonians than on foreign capital and undertakings" (Biya, 1986: 129 – Objective 12). But this seems to remain the contrary policy and on paper because, according to informed and prospective national business circles,

> [laws by way of presidential decrees] to *arbitrarily* increase and fix the minimum level of the capital of banks from CFA 300 million to CFA 1 billion will have the effect of discouraging, stifling and blocking the entry or establishment of new[] banks by nationals....In the spirit of liberalizing the economy, if a citizen wants to start a bank and limit his activities just to one province or just his village, he should not be saddled by a law which

---

[236] *"J'ai le sentiment que le gouvernement [Camerounais] ne veut pas d'un secteur privé fort."* See *Le Messager* (3 mars 1997), 6.

requires him to come up with a minimum capital of CFA 1 billion which he does not need.[237]

In view of the confusion here one might want to know who the Cameroonians in Objective 10 are: "Cameroonians have to preserve the prerogative of initiative in the running of Cameroon's economy by determining priorities and expressing the real needs of the nation. In this regard, it is important to ensure that our planning is democratized and not subordinated to foreign interests, with our sole motivation being the general interest of Cameroonians" (Biya, 1986: 128). If this is not confusion, what is it?

Qu'est-ce qu'il faut alors faire? Put differently, how do we reverse the trend in order to regain lost national pride? As a solution some critics have suggested the restructuring of certain sectors of the economy, marked by a drastic cut in the size of government. Some of these critics like Protais Amang think, for example, that 'the restructuring of the insurance sector would not cost even a tenth of the amount required for restructuring the banking sector'.[238] In the eyes of other analysts, this is no solution because it is not so much the sector-by-sector *restructuration* that should matter; it is that of the ground-rules of the entire legal and political system or edifice that is required. To support their stance, these critics have poignantly pointed out, for example, that the government (through then Minister of Economy and Finance, Justin Ndioro) made known its policy of the restructuring of the financial sector on September 12, 1986. But six years after its first dose of restructuring in 1989, it was like everything

---

[237] Lawrence L. Tasha, "Re: Capital of Banks" 0 *Juridis Info (Revue de Legislation et de Jurisprudence Camerounaises)* (1989), 38 at 39 (emphasis added). As Arthur N. Nwankwo doubted in his *Can Nigeria Survive?*, "Can a country be truly independent while its banking and insurance systems, distribution networks, manufacturing sectors, indeed nearly every facet of its commercial life, are controlled by foreign nationals?" A.B. Asenoh, "Who Chooses the Leader?" *West Africa* (6-26 April 1998), 400.

[238] "*La restructuration du secteur des assurances ne coûtera pas le dixième des dépenses de la restructuration du secteur bancaire.*" See *Le Messager* (3 mars 1997), 6.

needed to be done all over again (*"tout semblait encore à refaire"*²³⁹). These critics want to know when and how then there could be an end to this futile exercise. As they have already indicated, it is truly a question of refashioning the ground-rules of the entire legal and political system.

They could be quite right. No one in the right senses can argue that an economy like the one being propagated in Cameroon could never produce anything for advancement, except advancement in regression as can also be seen in the following pieces of confusing, incomplete and weird 'restructuring' legislation on both insurance and banking: *Loi N° 90/019 du 11 août 1990 modifiant certaines dispositions de l'ordonnance N° 85/002 du 31 août 1985 relative à l'exercice de l'activité des établissements de crédit*; *Loi N° 90/025 du 10 août 1990 modifiant certaines dispositions de l'ordonnance N° 85/003 du 31 août 1985 relative à l'exercice de l'activité d'assurance; Ordonnance N° 90/005 du 19 septembre 1990 modifiant et <u>complétant</u> les dispositions de l'ordonnance N° 003 du 27 avril 1990 fixant les conditions de liquidation de banques*;²⁴⁰ *Ordonnance N° 003 du 27 avril 1990 modifiant et <u>complétant</u> les dispositions de l'ordonnance N° 85/002 du 31 août 1985 relative à l'exercice de l'activité de crédit* (same underlining and comment as in last footnote); *Décret N° 89/1283 du 18 août 1989 portant création de la Société de Recouvrement de Créance du Cameroun;* and *Loi N° 89/021 du 29 décembre 1989 fixant une procédure <u>simplifiée</u> de recouvrement de créances.* The underlining has been added to this last law: What was the need to first complicate things for four months before now simplifying? What was also the use for promoting agriculture before but now abandoning it completely?

---

²³⁹ F. Bambou, "Sous le renouveau: échec de la restructuration" *L'Expression* (22 septembre 1997), 2. *"D'une restructuration à l'autre, le système bancaire a connu toutes sortes d'intervention supposées le remetre à flot. Si la mise en oeuvre respective de mesures de toilettage est étonnante du fait que l'héritage de Paul Biya était sain et prospère, force est de reconnaitre que les résultats laissent à desirer. Les assurances ont connu le même marasme."* Id.

²⁴⁰ Underlining has been added to draw attention to the fact that this government had been applying incomplete legislation for six months. There is commentary on this law by Paul-Gerard Pougoué in 4 *Juridis Info (Revue de Législation et de Jurisprudence Camerounaises)* (1990) 35-36.

The Role of Agriculture and Poverty

It is hardly surprising then that this administration is being blamed for little or no industrialization of Cameroon.[241] The blame has a solid base because, first, "Of what real use" then, Forbin (1997) wants to specifically know, "has the Biya regime been to the youth of Cameroon? Since the 1960's, unemployment has only grown worse by the year. No budget has ever as a matter of policy addressed the issue of unemployment. Almost every year the president's youth day speech is predictable – promise to 'the future rulers of tomorrow', what future?" Loweh and others make the same points.[242] Second, the goal of the relentless effort of Objective 13 is "to stimulate the interest of the people [only] in agricultural development and to... [prevent young people from going] in search of adventure [or Western-type democracy] in the towns" (Biya, 1986: 129 – Objective 14) because "Agriculture and the lives of the farmers form a whole, which implies a way of life, a culture and a philosophy. That is why the attention paid to agriculture cannot serve its purpose if it doesn't facilitate... that they [farmers] can enjoy relative[ly no] autonomy and [have] a minimum of industrialisation" (Biya, 1986: 130 – Objective 15). As Fonjong (2004: 14) has indicated, the principle idea is to "to discourage industrialisation and encourage an agricultural sector based on mono-cultural plantation economy."

Yet, it is this same administration that will genuinely be fighting to reduce (if not eliminate) poverty in Cameroon? On June 2, 1998, according to reports, Cameroon and United Nations International Children Emergency Fund (UNICEF) signed a five-year cooperation

---

[241] See Peterkins Manyong, "Gov't Blamed for Low Industrialization of North West Province" *The Herald* N° 513 (22-23 September 1997), 7. See also "Banks Don't Finance Businesses in North West – Ndifor Raphael, Delegate of Commerce and Industry" *The Herald* (17-19 July 1998), 9 [interviewed by Randy Joe Sa'ah]; and Fonjong (2004).

[242] See P. Loweh, "Biya Continues to Feed the Youth with Hope" *The Herald* N° 421 (17-18 February 1997), 4; and Clovis Atatah, "The Economy in 1997: Dashed Hopes" *The Post* (14 January 1998), 5.

agreement toward reducing poverty in some parts of the country.[243] Just sign all the agreements on planet Earth to camouflage since the strategy of deliberately preventing industrialization must be persisted in without even in the least "highlight[ing] the case of those who till the soil, namely farmers, who do not receive the benefits they deserve for their hard work" (Biya, 1986: 10). In spite of all this Zuhboshi (1997) tells us how the diligence of the Cameroon people (when it comes to farming) is not doubted:

> Notwithstanding the fact that my origin [Cameroon] is a land whose people are victims of unfair and inhuman treatment I, beyond all doubts, have an admiration for it as it is a magnet for tourists...[who] flow into the land like butterflies visiting a hibiscus to enjoy the beautiful Savannah scenery. Furthermore, it is a cemetery for Heroes. These corpses endowed with veneration, wisdom and probity manure the earth (of my origin) and act as undying inspiration for upcoming Heroes. The diligence of the people (when it comes to farming) is unde[ni]able.

What (other than their having been conditioned by some of the 'political myths' to just be contented in staying forever on the farms) can exactly satisfactorily explain this curious pride of Cameroonians?[244] The modus operandi of this country's administrators would seem to furnish the real inner meaning of the motto of 'Peace-Work-Fatherland' (1996 Constitution, article 1(4); and Federal Constitution, article 1). In other words, doesn't 'Peace-

---

[243] See Peter Ngea Beng, "Cameroon-UNICEF Agree on Poverty Reduction" *The Herald* (24-25 June 1998), 8. See also Alain Bengono, "Des avocats plaident contre la pauvreté" *L'Expression* (17 avril 1997), 3.

[244] Cameroonians "pride themselves of many things which, on the basis of existing evidence, are genuine for the most part; but if, by some remote coincidence, rationality is one of them, it raises an eyebrow for a people who easily consume myths." J.T. Ayeh, "The Political Origin of Hate Myths in Cameroon" *Cameroon Post* (2-9 May 1991), 6

Work-Fatherland' in Cameroon actually mean "Remain forever on the Farms"?

The role that agriculture, poverty and confusion have to play in the calculated process of frightening Cameroonians away from the normal type of democracy is thus evident. This is the more especially so for two reasons. The first has to do with the lectures of some Canadian experts called Rob McKenzie and Yvon Gasse. According to the time-tested thesis of these experts, "When you're a farmer... you develop a good tolerance for uncertainty." And this seemingly endless tolerance of a people, Director Gasse further explains, is true especially if you're one of the dozen or so children of families of double-digit broods.[245] Here then is apparently the haven wherein Cameroonian irrational pride and ridiculous democracy are relaxing in Perfect Peace rather than in irredeemable pieces.

The second factor concerns the glories surrounding agriculture that suddenly disappeared from the scene in the early 90s when the moves toward Western democracy began. A University of Buea lecturer (Fonjong, 2004: 14, note omitted) would tell this story exceedingly well:

> Government's commitment to ensure the future of agricultural development until the 1990s has been consistent. The agricultural show schemes and best farm competitions served as additional incentives to farmers. The creation of zones *d'action communautaire et culturelle* and community development in the former East and West Cameroons respectively were all signs of government interests in agricultural development. These realizations were further extended to the development of agro-pastoral infrastructure. One can cite the examples of schools, agricultural research centres (e.g. IRZ and IRAD in Ekona, Bambui, Mankon), agricultural training institutions and credit

---

[245] Rob McKenzie, "Vivre la différence" *Canadian Business* (December 1996), 44 at 47, quoting Director Yvon Gasse of the Entrepreneurship Center at Université Laval.

schemes that serve both regional and national interests. All these investments in agriculture and the rural economy produced far-reaching results in the domain of population and political stability, as well as economic growth.

However, this has not lasted for ever as the situation has changed in recent times [with the unexpected arrival of the quest for Western-type multi-party democracy]. There has been a systematic neglect of the agricultural sector and its infrastructure while, at the same time, a lot of lip-service is paid to its importance. Such abandonment of the nerve centre on which the Cameroonian economy revolves has opened the way for poverty, rural exodus, hunger, crimes, etc, to gradually but steadily infest a country of great economic potentials. Economic development has generally slowed down and the living standards of the population in most localities are deplorable. Although many are quick to attribute this situation to the economic crisis of the mid-80s and the harsh structural adjustment measures that followed in the 90s, the central issue remains that the deteriorating state of agro-pastoral infrastructure in Cameroon is a call for concern.

As Fonjong explains in the missing footnote, IRZ is the Institute of Zoo-technical Research and IRAD the Institute for Agricultural Research and Development.

To properly address that concern, local government (I must keep repeating) is the way to go for developing states since it is in a sense the science of the second best because Kneier (1939: preface) points out that it is not always the question of what is the most desirable way of meeting a problem, but what is the best of the practices which will secure court approval and not be held unconstitutional. In putting development into perspective, Magstadt (1991: 60) has also indicated that it is "a key concept in nearly all the natural and social sciences." One of such sciences is local government which is furthered by what Stevenson (1989: 3) describes as "federalism as a form of *decentralized* government." What Third World states generally need therefore as the right path to national integration would be decent education, rigorous training and clear-cut recruitment procedures for/of the citizenry and the national bureaucracy. Since only authentic education is the key for awakening the people, the need for effective civic education is simply axiomatic. Just as the only real solution to social problems is moral education,[246] the only real solution to political problems is sound civic and legal education – a type of education that cannot be divorced from the people's authentic history or culture. Genuine multiculturalism thus becomes inevitable. The centralized unitary state is incompatible with this.

Closing Observation

This survey of the hopeless econometrics of the Cameroonian authorities (coupled with their own uncensored recognition of the dynamism and strong conviction of Cameroonians in peaceful and orderly development) has led some Canadian experts such as Newman to conclude that "the country [is] being governed by fools [and not that] it [is] ungovernable."[247] Who will genuinely argue with these experts who describe the Cameroonian administration as a bunch of fools? These administrators are the actual problem, not the country's impressive diversity. It is rather their regressive attitude of antagonizing the people, spiced with the deliberately generated legal, constitutional and political confusion that should be blamed for the ills in Africa. The prevailing opinion almost everywhere is that the only real problems in Africa, according to Franck (1968: 187), are those in leadership non-charisma and in non-challenge of historic trivia.

---

[246] See Earl Rubington and Martin S. Weinberg, "Social Pathology" in Earl Rubington and Martin S. Weinberg eds., *The Study of Social Problems: Five Perspectives* 3rd ed. (New York: Oxford University Press), 15 at 21, referring to Charles A. Ellenwood, *The Social Problem: A Reconstructive Analysis* (New York: Macmillan, 1919). See also Richard L. Henshel and Anne-Marie Henshel, *Perspectives on Social Problems* 2nd ed. (Don Mills, Ontario: Academic Press Canada, 1973) chapter 3.

[247] Peter C. Newman, *The Distemper of our Times – Canadian Politics in Transition: 1963-1968* (Toronto: McClelland and Stewart Limited, 1968) at xii.

Africa is thus only being mismanaged and not that it is ungovernable. Its apparent "un-governability" is the result of the deliberately engendered confusion, not of its diversity or any mysterious forces. "To conclude, Your Excellency," Taku (1995: 3) writes, "I have always held the view that what is perceived as a stalemate in the Cameroons is a deliberate choice by the regime of personal powers and not a result of some mysterious forces." The country's impressive diversity per se cannot be such "mysterious forces," as claimed by the Unity Palace occupants. Taku is not alone in making the point because some other experts, after meticulously going through the 1996 Constitution that is camouflaging biculturalism, have simply concluded that "It is now clear that Biya tends to see power only in absolute categories. Power, to self-professed animal man (Lion man) is real when it is undiluted; when it is a handy tool for liquidating all opposition; when it is the one simple but potent formula for playing God without being encumbered by God's infinite humanness – love and goodness; by simply spelling God the other way round."[248]

In view of rectifying and retracing its steps forward (through the institution of good governance) one of the leading opposition parties in Cameroon, SDF (1996: 2), has invited Cameroonians "regardless of your political affiliation" to understand that "the [on-going] battle for that [NESPROG] alternative is not an SDF battle but a battle for national salvation, the restoration of our lost national pride and dignity and an end to the international humiliation which the present regime has brought on this nation." To successfully salvage that lost pride, a proper federal devolution, inter alia, is very much required. The institution of a responsible federal democracy in Cameroon now poses no threat to the country's integrity as might have been claimed during the 1961 Foumban Conference. Circumstances have since changed and it is time to alter the principles accordingly.

It is undeniable that the conditions at the time of the UPC

---

[248] "Front Page Comment: Trashcan Stuff" *Cameroon Post* N° 0274 (11-18 December 1995), 1.

rebellion no longer prevail and the rules have to change accordingly. The fact that the risk of the disintegration of Cameroon has long gone is seen clearly in the statements of the current POR that would be praising the dynamism of Cameroonians to cooperate in spite of their marked differences. In Biya's (1986: 31-32) words, "These [ethnic, cultural and regional peculiarities], in some respects, are national socio-cultural resources, given their unquestionable contribution to the dynamism and co-operation for which our country is well known." I therefore think it is about time for African states to rethink their way of doing the business of governing their diverse populations. Time and dialogue are certainly on their side. Like several experts,[249] Maneli (1994: 3 & 9, 104-105, 11 & passim) tells us that Perelman, for instance, considers dialogue not only as a simple exchange of ideas but also as a social category that promotes an endless competition of arguments in order to establish the best possible solution in a given situation and at a given time.

Maneli (1994: 3) further emphasizes that when even one of the factors of reality changes, even through a mere lapse of time, a valid cause arises to reopen dialogue and assess the situation *ab initio*, from the very roots; concluding that during this reassessment, nothing should be regarded as sacred or established once and for all. The conditions in Cameroon in the sixties and seventies *might* have justified the harshness of the laws but Galega has "strongly urged that this should not be an excuse to refrain from confronting change when change is imperative."[250] That is the undemanding truth. The question remains though: Can and will the SDF really be able to

---

[249] See Annette T. Rottenberg, *Elements of Argument* (New York: St. Martin's Press, 1985); Ikeda (1987: 248-269) ('Dialogue for Lasting Peace'); J. Stone, *Visions of World Order: Between State Power and Human Justice* (Baltimore: The John Hopkins University Press, 1984) at 72; and Earl Rubington and Martin S. Weinberg, "Social Problems and Sociology" in Earl Rubington and Martin S. Weinberg, eds., *The Study of Social Problems: Five Perspectives* 3rd ed. (New York: Oxford University Press, 1981), 3 at 7.

[250] Samgena D. Galega, "Strict Liability for Defective Products in Cameroon? Some Illuminating Lessons from Abroad" 48 *Journal of African Law* (2004), 239 at 267.

deliver the cherished goods (as some like Gros say[251]) with what I would want to characterize as their sour, out-of-touch and disguised mono-cultural Four-State Federation? Doesn't Africa deserve better from Cameroon?

---

[251] See Jean-Germain Gros, "The Role of the Military and France in Cameroon Politics" *The Herald* N° 288 (26-28 February 1996), 6.

Conclusion

The politics of history and of education has been studied here to make the point on pointless multiculturalism and camouflaged national unity and integration in multicultural Africa. Genuine multiculturalism requires the constitution capturing what Cameroonians, for instance, represent as a country and what they desire to become as a people. This is however not what is in place in the 'Microcosm of Africa'. 'Advanced multiculturalism' in Cameroon is not cultural equality and diversity. Anyone interested in studying issues tied to multiculturalism must therefore forget about Cameroon and go elsewhere, preferably to Canada or Belgium. Multiculturalism has only one area in which to be comprehended in Cameroon – the advanced study of confusion. In other words, the only thing that any expert can validly go to Cameroon to study is advanced multiculturalism whose plain name is assimilation. With the curtain now pulled apart, gone therefore may be the days when people with dubious "special duties" at the country's embassies or high commissions could have very easily sold 'advanced' multiculturalism to their targeted importers. These targeted people may now know that, until new and acceptable ground rules that duly emphasize separation of powers are firmly laid down and upheld by independent courts, doing business or living in Cameroon will continue to remain a very dangerous gamble.

Federalism (combining with genuine multipartism) is obviously one of the effective modes of separating powers and dividing competence, both institutionally and territorially, so as to save the people and federating entities from autocracy. This is the state form that African states so badly need to be able to effectively tackle their ethnic and other conflict-management problems. An important human rights protecting instrument, federalism could be the real solution to most of the conflict-management problems and other threats of break ups (secession) that most of Africa's new states are confronted with. Lack of vision and commitment to popular rule apart, it is evident that this federal undertaking is something that will not be impossible in African and other developing states: absent confusion and manipulation. This sane solution to nation-building in diverse Africa has consequently often been regarded with suspicion by most of the official who pretend at the same time to be after the good and well-being of Africans. I am currently working on elaborating this important issue in another contribution on 'federalism, separation of powers and constitutionalism in Africa'. This attitude of African leaders has not meant well, the disheartening human rights abuses that the continent is noted for being the proof; with most of them instead arguing that federalism poses a threat to their nation-building efforts and can only be considered after the attainment of what they call 'national unity'.

It has been shown in this particular study that the schizophrenic craving by nation-builders in Africa to assimilate national minorities does not augur well for human rights – the driving force behind development or nation-building. Such assimilation-driven 'nation-builders' (and those industrialized or First World nations assuring their brutalization of Third World peoples) have to be told certain basic facts. The first is that human rights are the catalysts for development or nation-building, not its end product; that respect for human rights cannot and should not be restricted to certain people, places or parts of the world. Human rights are human rights, irrespective of where on the globe one happens to be situated – a thesis that is buttressed by the plain fact that there is the well-known *Universal Declaration of Human Rights* (signed on 10 December 1948) and not a 'First and Second World' Declaration of Human Rights. Most, if not all, independent African States that are Members of the United Nations, have affirmed their attachment to that *Universal Declaration*. Second, the attainment of national unity (assuming that this is actually what is desired in Africa and the Third World generally) has to pass through democracy and not democracy passing through national unity. Making it otherwise would only be confusion and manipulation, just as a copycat democracy that is wholly cut off from the people's cultures/traditions and realities.

The necessity for governing with due regard for human rights can hardly escape the attention of genuine intellectuals in political science in particular and intellectuals generally. Good governance, I suppose, presupposes (for example) that the decision as to what system of government and/or form of state, and as to whether Pauline continues governing or Paul steps in to replace her, must remain with the people and with the people alone for any talk of democracy to be meaningful. It is not democracy if once "elected" or appointed, a government cannot be dethroned by the people except through bloodshed. It is no democracy simply by saying it is democracy in the One-Party. Not even by merely affixed 'Advanced' to it will it become one. I believe democracy is more in the being and doing than in saying and talking. That is also precisely why lawyers and media practitioners who can talk the talk but very easily shrink or only mimic when tested, have been seriously censored and told by the experts to reconsider if they had chosen the right profession.

As some political pundits have pointed out, one of the indispensable prerogatives of good leadership is the simple ability of identifying a crisis from a distance and seeing how best it can be averted in the general interest. Therefore, they have concluded, to pretend "not to perceive the approach of an ill-wind is itself a negative dispensation of judgement in the fine art of collective bargaining."[252] Politics certainly involves this kind of bargaining and any "politician" who does not recognize this plain fact, it is believed, must evoke the same thought as lawyers who do not know that their job is to fearlessly defend human rights without discrimination. Good governance can clearly not exist without these basic rules being realized.

Some distinguished Harvard University professors of government (Banfield and Wilson, 1963: 18-19) posited as far back as 1963 that a

---

[252] A.M. Dipoko, "Was Biya's Speech Necessary?" *Le Messager* N° 029 (18 July 1991), 7.

government normally should perform two principal functions – the service and political functions. The first (administrative) involves the provision of goods and services, such as police protection, that are not usual to be supplied under private auspices. The second (governing) involves the management of conflicts in matters of public importance. These two functions are often concretely indistinguishable although the tendency in undemocratic states will be to prefer the entire absence of politics since no conflict and struggle for power are tolerated – with all important and unimportant matters being decided by one person or idea; all this solely predicated on purely technical and efficiency grounds. Meanwhile media professionals and university students (for example) who do see why and how they could be reduced to simple automatons, are systematically singled out and cowed into silence or death. It is my belief that all this must no longer happen while the bulk of Africans are looking on helplessly because it is really time "this co[ntinent] grew up constitutionally and stop mumbling feebly that nothing can be done."[253] Research *about* Africa's law (like this book) is obviously an appropriate step in the growing-up direction.

It is doubtful how anyone can expect to sell their goods unless potential buyers are able to trust and believe in the goods' merchantability and fitness (risk-free) for the purpose.[254] Aware of the distrustful and designing nature of the unknown "missions" of most of the appointed officials in the Hinge of Africa, a powerful *Jeune Afrique Economie* editorial (incidentally from a Cameroonian) has indicated that if Africans fail to respect themselves, they cannot be respected by others, let alone be given the places that are supposed to

---

[253] H.W.R. Wade, *Constitutional Fundamental* (London: Stevenson and Sons, 1980) at 34.

[254] For further discussion of these aspects, *see*, e.g., J.A. Henderson and A.D. Twerski, "A Proposed Revision of Section 402A of the Restatement (Second) of Torts" 77 *Cornell Law Review* (1992), 1512-1557; and the May 9, 1963 New York Court of Appeal case of *Goldberg v. Kollsman Insurance Corporation* [Aviation Cases N° 320-115], 17629.

be theirs.[255] It is about time therefore that personification of public affairs be erased from this continent because Africa rightly deserves and must get civilized governments and lots of apparatchiks. *Apparatchiks* might so far have been wanting particularly in the Hinge of Africa because of the unnecessary darkness created by the myriad of "intellectuals in politics". Now that some light has been lit and is shining on the darkness the *apparatchiks* must surely begin to see the issues differently and, hopefully, come out openly. The concerned Africans thus have the choice: they must have to analyse their situation from top to bottom and either keep on doing what they have been doing, or discard even widely held premises whose time has passed. To avoid bloodshed by solving problems as and when necessary, they can now, like Vanderlinden (1993: 573), genuinely and firmly say 'Enough is enough' and, consequently, 'I am going to effectively burn in your presence all this thrash that I have adored and worshipped for so many years now' (*"Je vais en effet brûler aujourd'hui devant vous ce que j'ai adoré pendant plus de vingt ans"*). And they would not be breaking any completely new grounds by doing so, because recent history would amply provide members of the former ruling institutions and privileged administrations who have done this by actively supporting democracy and renewal. These are those that Maneli (1994: 12 & 11) has called the *apparatchiks*, and would include Russia's Gorbachev, Yelsin, Shevardnaze and South Africa's F.D. DeKlerk, all of whom raised their hands against the Party and bureaucracy. Isn't it about time (Black) Africa had its own *apparatchiks*?

It is thought that decentralization, if proper and effective, might also ameliorate things in Africa. But federalism and/or decentralization cannot be effective in the absence of liberalism. Liberalism, Corbett (1995: 625-26) has stated, presupposes the

---

255 *"Si nous ne savons pas nous 'vendre', au sens le plus noble du terme, les autres n'accepteront pas de nous donner la place que nous méritons réellement sur cette planète. Cela est valable dans tous les domains."* Blaise-Pascal Talla, "Le poids de nos États" 173 *Jeune Afrique Economie* (novembre 1993), 3.

presence of disagreement on important questions and recognizes that while religious and ethnic differences require political solutions, no particular ethnic or religious tradition can be the single source of those solutions. Like classical politics, and unlike the ethos of consumer capitalism, liberalism is a political theory grounded in the idea of self-control. Cameroon's 1996 Constitution (or its offspring: 1998 Education Law) is however not the beginning of this lack of self-control in Cameroon. Everything that is now happening in the country would find roots in the 1961 Federal Constitution; a constitution which grossly betrayed the aspirations of the English-speaking because its architects exhibited a gross lack of self-control and of a sense of duty to the public they were purportedly representing. It is this self-control that makes the struggle for power civilized; with this politically civilizing process being what Riemer (1983: 122) says, at the highest level, "makes fuller individual realization possible." Making this fuller individual realization possible in Cameroon would necessitate the provision of honestly decent answers to the questions on authentic education and multiculturalism.

There is indeed no reason for useless excuses in Africa; and none for advancing pointless biculturalism, whose real name is assimilation. Assimilation promotes only regression in human rights and that is surely not what Africa deserves from its leader (Cameroon). Africa is not especially interested in having a leader who, moreover, does not genuinely seek to know what holds a society together, where the society is going, nor how it is getting there. Until all these vital issues are properly addressed in Africa, there is just no point in employing terms like democracy and biculturalism in this continent, a continent that would then, according to Frye (1986: 33), simply continue to remain "a blank area of natural resources to be exploited by countries that are more advanced and better organized than we [Africans] are because they've spent more on their education."

References

Adams, Melinda. "Colonial Policies and Women's Participation in Public Life: The Case of British Southern Cameroons" 8:3 *African Studies Quarterly* (2006): 1-22.

Ahidjo, Germaine: "Confidences: Germaine Ahidjo à coeur ouvert à Honoré De Sumo" *La Nouvelle Expression* N° 319 (28 juin 1996), 1 & 12.

Ajulo, Sunday B. "Myth and Reality of Law, Language and international Organization in Africa: The Case of African Economic Community" 41:1 *Journal of African Law* (1997) 27-42.

Anyangwe, Carlson "Administrative Litigation in Francophone Africa: The Rule of Prior Exhaustion of Internal Remedies" 8 *Revue Africaine de Droit International et Comparé* (1996), 808-826.

Anyangwe, Carlson, *The Cameroonian Judicial System* (Yaoundé: CEPER, 1987).

Anyangwe, Carlson, *The Magistracy and the Bar in Cameroon*. Yaounde: PANAG-CEPER, 1989.

Appiagyei-Atua, Kwadwo, *An Akan Perspective on Human Rights in the Context of African Development* (Unpublished Doctor of Civil Law Dissertation, McGill University, 1999).

Azeng, Randy Joe Sa'ah, "Federalism is Best Option for Cameroon – Garga Haman Adji" *The Herald* N° 468 (6-8 June 1997), 6.

Banfield, Edward C. and James Q. Wilson, *City Politics* (Cambridge, Mass.: Harvard University Press and The M.I.T. Press, 1963).

Bangsi, K.A. "Ambassador, University Don Decry Gap between Policy and Practice of Bilingualism," *The Herald* N° 446 (16-17 April 1997), 2.

Baumol, William J., Alan S. Blinder and William M. Scarth, *Economics: Principles and Policy* 2nd Canadian ed. (Toronto: Harcourt Brace Javanovich, 1988).

Bayefsky, Anne F., *Canada's Constitution Act 1982 and Amendments* Vol. 1 (1989, McGraw-Hill Ryerson).

Benjamin, Jacques, *Les camerounais occidentaux: la minorité dans un état bicommunautaire* (Montréal: Université de Montréal, 1972).

Biya, Paul, *Communal Liberalism* (London: Macmillan, 1986).

Bjornson, Richard, *The African Quest for Freedom and Identity: Cameroonian Writing and the National Experience* (Bloomington & Indianapolis: Indiana University Press, 1991).

Bladen, V.W., *An Introduction to Political Economy* rev. ed. (Toronto: University of Toronto Press, 1956).

Blondel, Jean, "The Government of France" in Michael Curtis, Gen. ed., *Introduction to Comparative Government* (New York: Harper and Row, Publishers, 1985), 115-190.

Boyle, Patrick M., "Parents, Private Schools, and the Politics of an Emerging Civil Society in Cameroon" 34:4 *Journal of Modern African Studies* (1996): 609-622.

Bringer, Peter, "The Abiding Influence of English and French Criminal Law in One African Country: Some Remarks Regarding the Machinery of Criminal Justice in Cameroon" 25:1 *Journal of African Law* (1981), 1-13.

Brunnell, Matthew A., "What *Lawrence* brought for 'Show and Tell': The Non-Fundamental Liberty Interest in Minimally Adequate Education" 25:2 *Boston College Third World Law Journal* (2005): 342-382.

Chinje B., "Promises... Promises..." *The Herald* N° 521 (10-12 October 1997), 7.

Clément, Jean A.P. with Johannes Mueller, Stéphane Cossé, and Jean Le Dem, *Aftermath of the CFA Franc Devaluation*. Washington, D.C.: IMF, 1996.

Commager, H.S. *Majority Rule and Minority Rights* (Gloucester, Mass.: Peter Smith, 1958).

Corbett, S.M., "Book Review of George Grant: A Bibliography (Toronto: University of Toronto Press, 1993) by William Christian" 20:2 *Queen's Law Journal* (1995), 611-27.

Couloumbis, Theodore A. and James H. Wolfe. *Introduction to International Relations: Power and Justice*, 3rd ed. (Englewood Cliffs, N.J.: Prentice-Hall, Inc., 1986).

Das, Satya, "Playing by the Rules in Indonesia: A Little Homework Goes a Long Way for Investors" *The Edmonton Journal* (26 December 1996), E1.

Dawson, R. MacGregor, *The Government of Canada* [5th ed. revised by Norman Ward] (Toronto: University of Toronto Press, 1970).

de Jorge, Hans "Democracy and Economic Development in the Asia-Pacific Regions: The Role of Parliamentary Institutions" 14:9-10 *Human Rights Law Journal* (1993), 301.

Delancey, Mark W., *Cameroon: Dependence and Independence* (Boulder: Westview Press, 1989).

Driedger, Leo, *The Ethnic Factor: Identity in Diversity* (Toronto: McGraw-Hill, 1989).

Dzidzornu, D.M., "Marine Pollution Control in the West and Central African Region" 20:2 *Queen's Law Journal* (1995) 439-86.

El Obaid, Ahmed El Obaid, *Human Rights and Cultural Diversity in Islamic Africa* (Unpublished Doctor of Civil Law Thesis, Institute of Comparative Law, McGill University, 1996).

Enonchong, H.N.A. *Cameroon Constitutional Law – Federalism in a Mixed Common-Law and Civil-Law System* (Yaoundé: Centre d'Édition et de Production de Manuel et d'Auxiliares de l'Enseignement, 1967).

Etinge, C.N., "Proposition for the Agenda of a National Conference" *Le Messager*, Special Political Issue (6 June 1991), 6-7.

Eyinga, Abel "Le régime néo-colonial actuel a atteint un autre niveau dans la lutte contre la conscience nationale" *La Nouvelle Expression* N° 338 (30 août 1996), 6-7.

Eyoum'a Ntoh, Patrick-Thomas "13 millions de voyous!" *Le Messager* (12 septembre 1996), 2.

Fohtung, Barry B. "The Gambler" *Cameroon Post* (11-18 December 1995) 11.

Fohtung, Barry B. "Yaounde or the ACME of Anglophone Masturbation-I" *Cameroon Post* N° 0028 (8-14 October 1996), 8.

Fombad, Charles Manga, "Protecting Constitutional Values in Africa: A Comparison of Botswana and Cameroon" 36:1 *Comparative and International Law of Southern Africa* (2003), 83-105.

Fonjong, Lotsmart N. "Changing Fortunes of Government Policies and its Implications on the Application of Agricultural Innovations in Cameroon" 13:1 *Nordic Journal of African Studies* (2004), 13-29.

Fonkeng, E.F. *The Captive* (Ottawa: Bhakti Press, 1990).

Forbin, Boniface. "Youth Day: A Denial of History" *The Herald* N° 419 (12-13 February 1997), 4.

Fossungu, Peter Ateh-Afac, "Separation of Powers in Public International Law: Is the International Civil Aviation Organization (ICAO) Out of or Within the United Nations System? A Critique of ICAO Assembly Elections" 35 *Annals of Air & Space Law* (2010), 267-96.

Fossungu, Peter Ateh-Afac "Mocking the Bijuralism and Bilingualism Birds" *The Herald* N° 657 (7-8 September 1998a), 10.

Fossungu, Peter Ateh-Afac, "Language Confusion in Ngoa-Ekelle" *The Herald* N° 657 (7-8 September 1998b), 4.

Franck, Thomas M. "Why Federations Fail" in T.M. Franck, ed., *Why Federations Fail: An Inquiry into the Requisites for Successful Federalism* (New York: New York University Press, 1968), 167-199.

French, Howard W. "President Re-Elected in Cameroon: Biya Returned in Lacklustre Vote that Augurs Poorly for the Country's Future" *The Edmonton Journal* (14 October 1997), F12.

Frye, Northop, "Language as the Home of Human Life" in Michael

Owen, ed., *Salute to Scholarship: Essays Presented at the Official Opening of Athabasca University* (Athabasca, Alberta: Athabasca University, 1986), 20-33.

Hogg, Peter W. *Constitutional Law of Canada* 4th Student ed. (Toronto: Thomson Canada Limited, 1996).

Ikeda, Daisaku, *A Lasting Peace* Vol. II (New York & Tokyo: Weatherhill, 1987).

Johnson, Willard R. *The Cameroon Federation: Political Integration in a Fragmentary Society* (Princeton, N.J.: Princeton University Press, 1970).

Johnson-Hanks, Jennifer *Uncertain Honor: Modern Motherhood in An African Crisis* (Chicago: The University of Chicago Press, 2006).

Kanyongo, Gibbs Y. "Zimbabwe's Public Education System Reform: Successes and Challenges" 6(1) *International Education Journal* (2005), 65-74.

Kneier, Charles M. *Illustrative Materials in Municipal Government and Administration* (New York: Harper & Brothers, 1939).

Konings, Piet and Francis B. Nyamnjoh, "The Anglophone Problem in Cameroon" 35:2 *The Journal of Modern African Studies* (1997), 207-29.

Lantum, Dan N. "Dr. Bernard Nsokika Fonlon: An Intellectual in Politics" *Le Messager* Special Political Issue (Thursday 6 June 1991), 20-22, continued in *Le Messager* N° 028 (20 June 1991), 11-13.

Le Vine, Victor T. *The Cameroon Federal Republic* (Ithaca and London: Cornell University Press, 1971).

Le Vine, Victor T. "Political-Cultural Schizophrenia in Francophone Africa" in I.J. Mowoe and Richard Bjornson, eds., *Africa and the West: The Legacies of Empires* (New York: Greenwood Press, 1986), 159-173.

Le Vine, Victor T. and R.P. Nye, *Historical Dictionary of Cameroun* (Metuchen, N.J: The Scarecrow Press, 1964).

Liebich, André. "Federalism Swiss Style" *McGill News* (Alumni Quarterly, Spring 1996), 11.

Magstadt, Thomas M. *Nations and Governments: Comparative Politics in Regional Perspective* (New York: St Martin's Press, Inc., 1991).

Maneli, Mieczyslaw *Perelman's New Rhetoric as Philosophy and Methodology for the Next Century* (Dordrecht: kluwer Academic Publishers, 1994).

Mback, Charles Nach. "One Century of Municipalization in Cameroon: The Miseries of Urban Democracy" in Dickson Eyoh and Richard Stren, eds. *Decentralization and the Politics of Urban Development in West Africa* (Washington D.C.: Woodrow Wilson International Centre for Scholars, 2007).

Mbuy, Tatah H. "Post Synodal Reflections: Why Africa Falters (The Weevils in Our Beans)," *Cameroon Post* N° 0021 (20-26 August 1996), 11.

Mensah-Gbadago, M.M. "9 Years of Political Transition: From Ahidjo to Biya and the Hayatou Connection – How Far Have We Moved?" *Le Messager* Special Political Issue (6 June 1991) 1.

Mewett, Alan W. "Editorial: Statements Admissible in Narrative" 38 *The Criminal Law Quarterly* (1996), 385-86.

Moorhouse, Geoffrey, *The Diplomats: The Foreign Office Today* (London: Jonathan Cape Ltd., 1977).

Moosnitec, Th. "La montée de l'intégrisme hindou" *Jeune Afrique* (18-24 mars 1993), 60.

Muabe, Fidèle "Women Bemoun Their Decline in Politics. Say Representation Has Dropped From 23 to 10 in Parliament" *The Herald* N° 485 (16-17 July 1997), 3.

Ndamukong, Gilbert "Financial Subvention to the G.C.E. Board" *Cameroon Post* N° 0028 (8-14 October 1996), 2.

Ndi Chia, Charly "We May Not Be the World But We Are the People" *Cameroon Post* N° 0274 (11-18 December 1995), 4.

Nelson, Harold D., Margarita Dobert, Gordon C. McDonald, James McLaughlin, Barbara Marvin and Philip W. Moeller, *Area Handbook for the United Republic of Cameroon* (Washington, D.C., 1974).

Newman, Peter C. *The Canadian Establishment* Volume 1 (Toronto: McClelland and Stewart Limited, 1975).

Ngefac, Aloysius, "Linguistic Choices in Postcolonial Multilingual Cameroon" 19:3 *Nordic Journal of African Studies* (2010), 149-64.

Ofege, Ntemfac, "Constitutional Revision: Vistas of Anglophone Exclusion and Presidential Hypocrisy" *Cameroon Post* N° 0274 (11-18 December 1995a), 8.

Ofege, Ntemfac, "Autopsy of a Most Outrageous Document" *Cameroon Post* N° 0274 (11-18 December 1995b), 8.

Okafor, Obiora Chinedu, "Newness, Imperialism, and International Legal Reform in Our Times: A TWAIL Perspective" 43.1 & 2 *Osgoode Hall Law Journal* (2005), 171-191.

Pearson, F.S. and J.M. Rochester, *International Relations: The Global Condition in the Late Twentieth Century* 2nd edition (New York: Random House, 1984).

Peaslee, Amos J. *Constitutions of Nations* Vol. I – Africa (The Hague, Netherlands: Martinus Nijhoff, 1974).

Pirie, Andrew J. "Objectives in Legal Education: The Case for Systematic Instructional Design" 37 *Journal of Legal Education* (1987): 576-597.

Riemer, Neal, *Political Science: An Introduction to Politics* (New York: Harcourt Brace Jovanovich, Inc., 1983).

Robertson, Ian, *Sociology* 3rd ed., (New York: Worth Publishers, 1987).

Rubin, Neville, *Cameroon: An African Federation* (New York: Praeger Publishers, 1971).

SCFAQ: "Southern Cameroons Frequently Asked Questions", available @ http://www.southerncameroons.org/index3.htm (last visited in March 2011).

SDF, 'SDF Launches National Economic Salvation Programme (NESPROG)" *Cameroon Post* Special Edition (December 1996), 1.

Shapiro, Evan Joel, *The Supranational Challenge: Federal and Decentralized Unitary States Within the European Union* (Unpublished LL.M. Thesis, McGill University, 1995).

Shenoy, R.B. "Introduction" in Gilbert Tixier, *A Comparative Study of the Economic Policies of the Cameroons and Ivory Coast* (Paris:

International Institute for Economic Research & LGDJ, 1974), 7.

Sim, R. Alexander "The Innocence of Community Development" in James A. Draper, ed., *Citizen Participation: Canada* (Toronto: New Press, 1971), 171-186.

Southall, Roger, *Federalism and Higher Education in East Africa* (Nairobi: East African Publishing House, 1974).

St. John-Stevas, Norman "Foreword" in Humphry Berkeley, *The Power of the Prime Minister* (London: George Allen and Unwin, 1968) 7-11.

Stark, Frank M. "Federalism in Cameroon: The Shadow and the Reality" 10:3 *Canadian Journal of African Studies* (1976), 423-442.

Stevenson, Garth *Unfulfilled Union: Canadian Federalism and National Unity* 3rd ed. (St. Catherines, Ontario: Gage Educational Publishing Company, 1989).

Students' Letter of 20th August 1985: "Letter From the English-speaking Students of the North West and South West Provinces to their Parents", available at "Southern Cameroons Landmark Documents": http://www.southerncameroons.org/index3.htm (last accessed in August 2010).

Suifon, Takwa, "University of Buea: The Place to Be..." *The Herald* N° 523 (20-21 October 1997), 6.

Taku, Charles Achaleke, "Lawyer Alerts British Gov't: C'wealth Systems Are Being Destroyed in Cameroon" *Cameroon Post* N° 0274 (11-18 December 1995), 1.

Tamanaha, Brian Z. "The Folly of the 'Social Scientific' Concept of Legal Pluralism" 20:2 *Journal of Law & Society* (1993) 192-217.

Tangwa, Canute C.N. "Our Patrick Akoh Mbawa: Casualty of Daredevilling," *Cameroon Post* N° 0021 (20-26 August 1996), 8.

Teubner, Gunther "The Two Faces of Janus: Rethinking Legal Pluralism" 13:5 *Cardozo Law Review* (1992), 1443.

Tixier, Gilbert *A Comparative Study of the Economic Policies of the Cameroons and Ivory Coast* (Paris: International Institute for Economic Research & LGDJ, 1974).

Toope, Stephen J. "Cultural Diversity and Human Rights" 42 *McGill Law Journal* (1997), 169-185.

Turpel, Mary Ellen "Aboriginal Peoples and the Canadian Charter: Interpretive Monopolies, Cultural Differences" in R.F. Devlin, ed., *Canadian Perspectives on Legal Theory* (Toronto: Emond Montgomery Publications Limited, 1991), 503-538.

Vanderlinden, Jacques, "Vers une nouvelle conception du pluralism juridique" dans *Revue de la recherché juridique droit positif* 1993-2, N° XVIII-53, 573.

Zama, Isaac Fru "Legal Guarantee of Environmental Protection within the Industrial Free Trade Zone in Cameroon" 9 *Juridis Info (Revue de Legislation et de Jurisprudence Camerounaises)* (1992), 43–45.

Zuhmboshi, Eric Nsuh, "Pride in Dying for a Just Cause" *The Herald* N° 446 (16-17 April 1997), 4.

Legislation

1996 Constitution : *Loi N° 96-06 du 18 janvier 1996 portant révision de la Constitution du 02 juin 1972.*
1984 Constitution : *Loi N° 84-1 du 4 février 1984.*

1972 Constitution: *2 June 1972 Constitution of the United Republic of Cameroon*

Federal Constitution: *Loi N° 61-24 du 1er septembre 1961 portant révision constitutionnelle et tendant à adapter la constitution actuelle aux nécessités du Cameroun réunifié.*

Education Law: *Law N° 98/004 of 14 April 1998 to Lay Down Guidelines for Education in Cameroon.*

www.ingramcontent.com/pod-product-compliance
Lightning Source LLC
Chambersburg PA
CBHW021940290426
44108CB00012B/903